Navigating Your Later Years

A Wiley Brand

Navigating Your Later Years

by Carol Levine

Navigating Your Later Years For Dummies®

Published by: **John Wiley & Sons, Inc.,** 111 River Street, Hoboken, NJ 07030-5774, www.wiley.com

Copyright © 2018 by AARP. All rights reserved. AARP is a registered trademark.

Published simultaneously in Canada

No part of this publication may be reproduced, stored in a retrieval system or transmitted in any form or by any means, electronic, mechanical, photocopying, recording, scanning or otherwise, except as permitted under Sections 107 or 108 of the 1976 United States Copyright Act, without the prior written permission of the Publisher. Requests to the Publisher for permission should be addressed to the Permissions Department, John Wiley & Sons, Inc., 111 River Street, Hoboken, NJ 07030, (201) 748-6011, fax (201) 748-6008, or online at http://www.wiley.com/go/permissions.

Trademarks: Wiley, For Dummies, the Dummies Man logo, Dummies.com, Making Everything Easier, and related trade dress are trademarks or registered trademarks of John Wiley & Sons, Inc., and may not be used without written permission. AARP is a registered trademark of AARP, Inc. All other trademarks are the property of their respective owners. John Wiley & Sons, Inc., is not associated with any product or vendor mentioned in this book.

For general information on our other products and services, please contact our Customer Care Department within the U.S. at 877-762-2974, outside the U.S. at 317-572-3993, or fax 317-572-4002. For technical support, please visit https://hub.wiley.com/community/support/dummies.

Wiley publishes in a variety of print and electronic formats and by print-on-demand. Some material included with standard print versions of this book may not be included in e-books or in print-on-demand. If this book refers to media such as a CD or DVD that is not included in the version you purchased, you may download this material at http://booksupport.wiley.com. For more information about Wiley products, visit www.wiley.com.

This and other AARP books are available in print and e-formats at AARP's online bookstore, www.aarp.org/bookstore, and through local and online bookstores.

Library of Congress Control Number: 2018950670

ISBN 978-1-119-48158-4 (pbk); ISBN 978-1-119-48160-7 (ebk); ISBN 978-1-119-48162-1 (ebk)

Manufactured in the United States of America

C10002853_072718

Contents at a Glance

Table of Contents

Introduction

I f you've opened this book, then you're thinking about how best to navigate this next stage of life, whether for yourself or for a relative. (For simplicity, I'll refer to "you.") Here, you find a road map to move forward, step by step.

Turn back, for a moment, to the cover of this book. What I want you to notice is the illustration: a person at the middle of a constellation of people, activities, and services. The icons suggest a full and satisfying life — family, of course, as well as social connections, healthcare and healthy living, community involvement, and resources. The goal of this book is to help you put everything in place now for the best possible future, both for the person at the center and those who care about, and may care for, that person.

Because you've picked up or downloaded this book, you probably already know that you have questions. What you may not know is the broad scope of decisions, services, and choices that may arise. In my many years in the fields of health policy, aging, and family caregiving, I have seen that people often start with a specific question about topics such as buying long-term care insurance or choosing an independent- or assisted-living facility and soon find that they need to explore many other avenues as they pursue their goals of good health, independence, choice, and quality of life.

Times have changed, and there are many more options than there were decades ago, so keep an open mind. Learning about these options can be challenging, but finding the answers you need and creating a comprehensive and workable plan that fits your needs are well worth the effort. Like any other major decision in life, planning requires weighing risks and benefits, being flexible, and staying open to change. It can be unsettling. Some of your assumptions and preconceptions may be challenged. Even though I have many years of experience in this field, writing this book has given me new insights into the difficulties that individuals and families face in planning. I have new respect for their diligence and devotion.

About This Book

I wrote this book to offer the broadest possible view as well as to provide information about specific topics. You'll find out about

- >> Modifications you can make to your home so you can stay independent and live at home as you age
- >> Downsizing your current home or planned move
- >> Options for housing such as independent and assisted living or specially created communities
- >> Multigenerational living
- >> Personal care and homemaker services
- >> Transportation and other community services
- >> Medical care, which may be primary care, preventive care, hospitalization, or rehabilitation services
- >> Financial issues and tips for managing money
- >> Advance directives so your wishes concerning healthcare are known
- >> Wills and estates

Throughout this book, I present you with a range of options to consider, always with the caveat that no one solution works for everyone. You may, for instance, need to make modest adjustments to your home, or you may need to move to an assisted-living community. I also include your family, partner, neighbors, and friends — and the community in which you live — as crucial factors in decision making. Remember too that the emotional aspects of a plan are often underestimated but can determine its success or failure.

I've read and contributed to many books that tackle one subject at a time. They are valuable resources but don't cover the wide landscape. This book is a blend of what I've learned from all these approaches, but it presents the big picture and then zeroes in on the practical, hands-on information that is often difficult to find in one place.

You, the reader, decide how to use this book. It is organized so that you can easily find the topics you want to know more about and skip the ones that don't apply to your situation. There are many ways to get to various chapters and parts of chapters. You don't need to read the chapters in order, although I would recommend at least skimming the chapters in Part 1 for an orientation to the book's broad perspective. Of course, you can always come back to these chapters after you have reviewed the areas you want to concentrate on.

Many chapters have separate sections called *sidebars*, which are brief digressions into history, public policy, little-known facts, or other kinds of information that are not essential to the text but add to its depth. You can safely ignore them, but I hope you at least dip into a few.

Every chapter has web links to other resources to help you get more specific information about a particular topic, find information about your state's regulations, or delve deeper. You may note that some web addresses break across two lines of text. If you're reading this book in print and want to visit one of these web pages, simply key in the web address exactly as it's noted in the text, pretending that the line break doesn't exist. If you're reading this as an e-book, just click the web address to be taken directly to the web page.

This book is meant to serve as a reference, so you don't have to commit any information to memory. It's all there, waiting to be read and re-read.

Additionally, two other *For Dummies* books from AARP — *Social Security For Dummies* (by Jonathan Peterson, published by Wiley) and *Medicare For Dummies* (by Patricia Barry, published by Wiley) — are helpful adjuncts to this book and offer more detail about those two important public programs.

Foolish Assumptions

This book makes a few assumptions about you, the reader:

» You probably don't know a whole lot about various aspects of housing, finances, legal directives, and medical coverage you'll want or need to consider as you age. And even if you have some professional or personal background in the field, you can benefit from new information and different perspectives.

» You may be starting to plan, or already planning, for yourself or your spouse or partner. You probably have some time to plan before the need arises — but don't underestimate how long it may take.

» You may be starting to plan, or already planning, for an older person such as a parent. The time for planning in this situation may be short; it may follow a health crisis. You need help now. But don't make quick decisions that will be hard to reverse.

» You may be comfortable using the Internet to find additional resources.

» You are worried about making the best choices and how to pay for them. Rest easy: You are not alone.

Icons Used in This Book

Throughout the book, you will see several icons that draw your attention to certain kinds of information.

TIP

The Tip icon links to an additional resource or offers advice about the topic discussed in the preceding text.

REMEMBER

The Remember icon is not a literal order to memorize the information but a word to the wise, a reminder of what you should be considering.

WARNING

The Warning icon signals important information that alerts you to a potential problem — for example, a fraudulent practice or a scam aimed at older adults.

TECHNICAL STUFF

Technical stuff is just what it sounds like — more detailed information than you don't absolutely need but that you may find helpful just the same.

Beyond the Book

As they say, "But wait! There's more!" Online you'll find extras that come with the book. *For Dummies* Cheat Sheets are handy online reference tools that you can use over and over — for example, a list of questions to ask when you visit an assisted-living facility or some easy fixes you can make to your home to prevent falls. To get the Cheat Sheet for this book, simply go to www.dummies.com and search for "Navigating Your Later Years For Dummies Cheat Sheet" in the Search box.

Where to Go from Here

With all the flexibility inherent in the *For Dummies* format, where should you start? If you know that you want information about a specific topic (for example, reverse mortgages or advance directives), by all means use the table of contents and index to find those sections. If you're still getting your head around the idea of making long-range plans, pick a chapter that interests you and dig in. You don't even have to start at the beginning of that chapter. But remember what Maria in *The Sound of Music* told her young pupils: The beginning is a very good place to start.

1
Getting Started with Navigating Your Later Years

Find out how planning for your future yet staying flexible can help you stay in control and avoid crises.

Start assessing your current and future needs by creating a personal inventory of your health status, family and friends, personality characteristics, and attitudes about money. All these factors affect your plans, and some may make you think more deeply about your own preferences and values. You can also draw a CareMap, as shown in Chapter 2.

Start researching your options through federal resources, state and local resources, and private groups. Being inquisitive but skeptical is a good approach.

Make decisions a family affair. I suggest when a family meeting may be advisable, whether you need to invite an outside mediator, and how to avoid or deal with conflict.

Chapter **1**

Looking Ahead: The Big Picture

Just by opening this book, you have become a member of a select group of people who are taking a big step toward a better future for yourself and your family. Most studies show that only a third of Americans have made even the most basic plans to prepare or pay for their future needs. Studies show that few older Americans have done substantial planning or saving for their future needs.

Thinking about the many aspects to consider — from finances to housing to healthcare and more — may be challenging because the choices available are often complex. They may involve myriad financial calculations as well as personal and family preferences. But planning today lets you envision the tomorrow of your choice and make it happen. In this chapter, I help you start to think about future needs in a proactive, calm, and positive way.

Planning for the Future Starts with You

REMEMBER

Future care is different for each individual, tailored to a person's needs and preferences. I want to reinforce this notion: Your plans today do not start with a place or a payment mechanism or a set of services; they start with a person.

Throughout this book, I reinforce the idea that a future plan is not just about where you live or what services you get but also about how you want to live and how to achieve your goals.

In addition to being person-centered, planning should start early. You'll want to start to think about housing, for instance, at a point when you have various options — whether at home or in a community — that prolong independence and make it less likely that institutional care will later be needed. From that perspective, modifying, and downsizing your home to make it safer and more accessible may be part of your plan. So is considering the possibility of multigenerational living and various forms of group residence in the community. Transportation options are critical to the success of your plan. These options are discussed in Part 2.

The chapters in Part 3 take up the important issues of financial and legal planning. What will Medicare pay for? What are the eligibility criteria for Medicaid? Should you consider buying long-term care insurance? What new products are available to meet financial needs? What steps can you take to draw up a will and other legal documents when you are healthy and able to make your preferences known?

Part 4 addresses managing your healthcare, from choosing a doctor to understanding different types of home care to the changes in skilled nursing facilities that are making these facilities more home-like and person-centered.

Part 5 looks at the special issues you may face if you are LGBT, a family caregiver, or a veteran of military service.

Finally, Part 6 has a chapter on common myths about aging and care. Here you'll also find a list of websites with state-by-state information, valuable because so much of future care is determined by state, not federal policies. Appendix A is a glossary of terms you may encounter, and Appendix B is a list of resources.

Navigating the Roadblocks of Planning

Aging is a reality. And an undeniable part of that reality is that most people, especially those who live to an advanced age, will need assistance in some aspects of their lives. If you are 65, you have nearly a 70 percent chance of needing some type of extended care and support at some future point, according to the U.S. Department of Health and Human Services. One-third of 65-year-olds may never need it, but 20 percent will need it for more than 5 years.

Yet what is undeniable in terms of demographics is easily deniable when it comes to anticipating our own lives and those of our older family members. About half of Americans over the age of 40 believe that "almost everyone" is likely to require long-term care at some point, but only a quarter think they themselves will need it, according to a 2016 survey conducted by the Associated Press-NORC Center for Public Affairs Research.

I can check off quite a few reasons for delaying the planning process, but there are just as many benefits to starting now.

Reasons for resistance

It isn't hard to understand why we resist planning for our future needs. The usual suspects are societal attitudes that glamorize youth, attempts to erase signs of aging, denial of mortality, and fear of dependence.

Another reason for resistance to planning is the high financial cost, which is usually described in terms of skilled nursing facilities or extensive home care services. Search the Internet for "long-term care" and you will be directed primarily to articles on its financial aspects, offering suggestions about financial planning or advertising facilities and services. Paying for long-term care is a major topic (and it comes up repeatedly in this book; check out Part 3), but it is by no means the only topic to consider. Sometimes the focus on the high cost is itself a deterrent to planning. It may seem impossible to save or obtain that much money, so why try? Again, costs are a reality but should not deter planning.

WARNING

Only about a third (35 percent) of the respondents in the AP-NORC survey I cite earlier had saved money to pay for their long-term needs. Moreover, their understanding of costs was wide of the mark, both in underestimates and overestimates. Under a third can correctly identify the range of costs for nursing homes, assisted living, and home care aides. And they didn't expect to pay the bill themselves. They expected Medicare to pay for a home health aide or a nursing-home stay, which is covered only for short-term care, not long-term care, and then only under certain circumstances. (For more on what Medicare covers, see Chapter 11.)

The benefits of planning

Decisions made in a crisis are often hasty and ill-considered. This is true in many aspects of life but is particularly problematic when a person's health and well-being are at stake. Not all crises can be avoided, but when they do occur, having a plan in place reduces the likelihood of the most severe unintended consequences.

For example, an important part of a plan is having an advance directive and identifying a healthcare proxy (a person legally authorized to speak for you; see Chapter 17 for more information). In a medical emergency where you can't speak for yourself, an advance directive and a healthcare proxy can make it more likely that you get the types of treatment you want and — even more difficult to achieve — don't get what you don't want. Certainly, it can be hard to think about this kind of situation, but the alternative is worse. Without some form of advance directive, no one will know what you want or don't want, and it will be unclear who has the authority to speak for you. If your family members can't agree, the decision will be made by strangers, and in the worst-case scenario, there will be litigation. The effort involved in planning ahead is minimal compared to the consequences of not doing so.

This example also underscores another benefit of planning: making decisions for yourself instead of leaving them to others or to chance. Having absolute control is unrealistic and possibly even undesirable, but letting family and other intimates know your values and preferences about treatment goals leaves more in your hands.

Some families are used to discussing and even arguing about all sorts of things, from trivial to significant. Others avoid conversations about serious matters. You can't change family dynamics that developed over years, but you can work within that framework to make your wishes known and to anticipate objections. Sometimes you may have to make some compromises, such as limiting when and where you drive or accepting some help at home. In other situations, your family may have to accept a less-than-perfect living situation out of respect for your wishes, such as staying in your own home. If you and your family can negotiate these bumps, you are all less likely to find yourselves in opposite camps when it comes to making major decisions.

REMEMBER

Planning ahead also allows you to investigate more choices more thoroughly. You will still have hard decisions to make, but you will have the benefit of information, discussion, and time. Still, your planning should be flexible. Try to build in as many alternatives as possible to allow for changes in health, finances, family situations, and all the other elements that can make a difference.

Unraveling the Meaning of Long-Term Care

Although I use it sparingly in this book, you've probably heard the phrase *long-term care*. This phrase, still used throughout much of the field of aging and healthcare, is not straightforward. Many people in the field of aging consider long-term care to be services that are nonmedical, such as personal care (bathing, dressing, feeding) or household tasks (shopping, cooking, transportation). Although these aspects of assistance are essential, in this book I take a broader view to include factors like medical care, housing options, financial considerations, advance care planning, and the community environment. I believe that when considering future care, most people should look at the whole spectrum of need rather than only specific segments.

TIP

A good introduction to the basics of long-term care is this government publication: longtermcare.acl.gov/the-basics/.

TECHNICAL STUFF

The National Center for Health Statistics found that about 67,000 long-term care providers served about 9 million people in the United States in 2013–2014. These included 30,200 assisted-living and other residential care communities, 15,600 nursing homes, 12,400 home health agencies, 4,800 adult day services, and 4,000 hospices. The majority of home healthcare agencies, hospices, nursing homes, and assisted-living and other residential care communities were run by for-profit companies, often affiliated with chains. Only adult day services were mostly non-profit. It's a myth that most older adults are in nursing facilities: the actual number is about 1.4 million out of a total population of 47.8 million over the age of 65. The full report is available at www.cdc.gov/nchs/data/series/sr_03/sr03_038.pdf.

REMEMBER

As I frame it, long-term or future care includes the various kinds of assistance a person needs to maintain the highest possible level of health and quality of life over time. As the population ages and increasingly more people face chronic illnesses, which often diminish the ability to function independently, future care needs to encompass and integrate a broader range of services to meet complex needs. Some aspects of planning concern immediate or foreseeable needs — for example, for a person with chronic illnesses or disabilities. Other aspects may fall under the heading of long-range planning — for example, considering long-term care insurance or establishing a regular savings plan. Some aspects of planning, such as preparing a will and an advance directive, should be done by every adult, even those in excellent health.

Defining long-term services and supports

One term you may run across as you plan for the future is *long-term services and supports,* or LTSS. This term typically refers to nonmedical services paid for privately or by Medicaid, although it can also apply to services such as transportation and homemaker visits provided by community agencies. By replacing the *care* in *long-term care* — which some people with disabilities see as a negative term — with the more impersonal *supports and services,* the new terminology is intended to stress an individual's independence and control over who helps and how that assistance is organized. Whichever term is used, a person- and family-centered approach is key, and this is something I stress throughout this book.

Noting that "LTSS has traditionally been provided in a fragmented, uncoordinated system of care provided by disparate agencies, each with its own funding, rules, and processes, and which are separate from the healthcare system," the federal Commission on Long-Term Care in its 2013 report to Congress recommended that individuals and service providers "align incentives to improve the integration of LTSS with healthcare services in a person- and family-centered approach." The Commission's final report is available at www.gpo.gov/fdsys/pkg/ GPO-LTCCOMMISSION/pdf/GPO-LTCCOMMISSION.pdf. While some states and localities have taken steps to achieve this goal, it remains unfulfilled for many people.

Understanding what Medicare covers

"Medicare does not cover long-term care." You'll probably come across this mantra again and again in your research. Yet in this book I devote considerable attention to Medicare, precisely because many beneficiaries consider it their starting point in thinking about their future care needs. So, what will Medicare cover? Understanding its limits is a first step in your reality check. What Medicare covers (after deductibles, coinsurance, and copays), you do not have to pay for; what Medicare does not cover requires additional resources.

To help you understand what Medicare covers, here is its definition of long-term care, as stated in its 2018 handbook "Medicare and You":

> Long-term care includes nonmedical care for people who have a chronic illness or disability. This includes nonskilled personal care assistance, like help with everyday activities, including dress, bathing, and using the bathroom. **Medicare and most health insurance plans, including the Medicare Supplement Insurance Plans (Medigap) policies, don't pay for this type of care, sometimes called "custodial care."** Long-term care can be provided at home, in the community, or in various other types of facilities, including nursing homes and assisted-living facilities.

And here's Medicare's definition of custodial care:

> Nonskilled personal care, such as help with activities of daily living like bathing, dressing, eating, getting in or out of a bed or chair, moving around, and using the bathroom. It may also include the kind of health-related care that most people do themselves, like using eye drops. In most cases, Medicare doesn't pay for custodial care.

Custodial care, a term many people find demeaning, is often called *personal care*. Whatever term you use, personal care does require considerable skill, as anyone who has performed these tasks knows.

Discovering How Your Options Are Changing

Your options for the future are expanding — and that's a good thing. There are many more alternatives for living at home or in the community, where the clear majority of people want to be. Technology is making it possible to have your healthcare monitored at home and to keep you in touch with family and friends. There is a greater awareness of the importance of a stimulating environment and social connections for mental and physical health.

Skilled nursing facilities are changing too, as they move toward a more person-centered focus and introduce elements of stimulating activity and participation for their long-stay residents.

Looking at why changes are being made

There are several reasons for these changes in the landscape.

Money is a factor

One reason is economic: Medicaid — the federal-state program for low-income people — is the major payer of nursing homes and community-based services, and policymakers want to keep those costs in check. According to a 2013 report from the Scan Foundation, in fiscal year 2010 Medicaid paid 62.2 percent of long-term care expenditures. Only 21.9 percent was paid for out-of-pocket; 11.6 percent by other private sources, including long-term care insurance; and 4.4 percent by other public sources, such as the U.S. Department of Veteran Affairs (VA). Medicaid's long-term care expenditures are expected to increase from $207.9 billion in 2010 to $346 billion in 2040.

To keep this spending in check, Medicaid has tried to move away from what has been called an "institutional bias," which means that the bulk of funding goes toward skilled nursing facilities, putting it instead toward more community-based care. In 1995, for example, 80 percent of Medicaid spending on long-term care was for institutional care; by 2011 that percentage had dropped to 55 percent. Community-based care is typically cheaper than skilled nursing facility care, which makes it attractive to Medicaid programs faced with escalating costs, and it is also preferred by individuals.

WARNING

While this should be a win-win situation, it has proven difficult to implement fully, partly because of the need for more housing options and direct-care workers to provide community care. Another reason is that federal rules require state Medicaid programs to provide institutional care and home health services, while coverage of home- and community-based services is optional. States differ in what they cover under this optional category.

Legal reasons

The federal Americans with Disabilities Act (ADA) is another reason for changes. In 1999, the U.S. Supreme Court held in *Olmstead v. L.C.* that unjustified segregation of persons with disabilities in nursing homes constitutes discrimination in violation of Title II of the ADA. The Court held that public programs such as Medicaid must offer community-based services to people with disabilities when such services are appropriate, the affected person doesn't oppose community-based treatment, and community-based services can be reasonably accommodated, considering the resources available and the needs of others who are receiving disability services from the entity.

In its ruling, the Supreme Court explained that "institutional placement of persons who can handle and benefit from community settings perpetuates unwarranted assumptions that persons so isolated are incapable of or unworthy of participating in community life." Furthermore, "confinement in an institution severely diminishes the everyday life activities of individuals, including family relations, social contacts, work options, economic independence, educational advancement, and cultural enrichment." Although the case that reached the Supreme Court was about two young people with mental disabilities, the *Olmstead* decision applies to people of all ages and all different kinds of disabilities. (Many states have yet to implement fully a plan for moving eligible people from institutions to the community.)

While the *Olmstead* ruling is limited to a defined group of nursing-home residents, it acts as an incentive for federal and state programs to develop appropriate community-based alternatives to institutions, which may benefit a larger group of people. It also reaffirms the importance of consumer choice in long-term care.

People want change

In addition to economic incentives and legal rulings, consumer demand has also played a part in moving away from old forms of long-term care — think traditional skilled nursing homes — to more home-like and person-centered settings. As people live longer — often into their 90s and beyond — the length of time a person needs various forms of care has increased and has required accommodation to various levels of need.

Although the trends of home-like and person-centered settings are positive, implementation across the country is inconsistent and variable. At best, the system is a patchwork quilt of settings and services, some strong and some weak, with different eligibility requirements and payment sources. But compared to a few decades ago, the quilt itself is bigger because people have demanded better options. In later chapters (especially in Part 2), I describe several of these newer options, with some suggestions about how to find out more about what is available in your community.

Keeping up with insider language

Every industry and service enterprise has its own language. As with long-term care and long-term services and supports, the terms are constantly evolving. Those who are fluent in this language sometimes forget that newcomers to the field don't understand their acronyms, shorthand, and jargon. Throughout this book I explain terms as they come up, and I include a glossary in Appendix A. Just to get started, however, here are a few of the terms that you may encounter. As you move forward, don't hesitate to ask when someone uses a term you don't understand or seems to be using a term in a way that is unfamiliar:

>> **Activities of daily living (ADLs):** These activities are ordinary tasks like bathing, eating, getting dressed, and going to the bathroom that most people don't think twice about but that become difficult for a person who is ill or frail or has a disability. Assistance with ADLs can range from lending a hand, literally or figuratively, to heavy lifting and taking total responsibility for carrying out the task. (Also see IADLs later in this list.) The number of ADLs is often used as a benchmark for eligibility for long-term care insurance benefits or nursing-home or home-based services.

>> **Acute care:** This type of care is provided in hospitals to treat an illness or accident that needs immediate attention. Acute care is distinguished from *chronic care,* which treats illness that lasts for a long time; *post-acute care,* which includes care at home or in a skilled nursing facility after a hospitalization; and *long-term care,* which may involve episodes of both acute care and chronic care. Coordinating care among acute care and chronic and long-term care is often a job that falls to family members or to the person needing the care.

>> **Assisted-living facilities:** Even though most people have heard of assisted living, there is no standard definition. States vary in what they call these facilities and how they regulate them, if they do at all. Generally, however, assisted-living facilities are group settings for people who need assistance in ADLs or IADLs but do not require the medical care typically provided in skilled nursing facilities. (See Chapter 8.)

>> **Instrumental activities of daily living (IADLs):** These activities are the common household or management tasks such as paying bills, organizing transportation, shopping, and doing laundry. They often go hand in hand with ADLs because the person who needs assistance with physical care may not be able to drive or shop alone. Even using the phone with all the complicated prompts that you encounter today may be difficult for someone with, for example, severe arthritis. But needing assistance with ADLs or IADLs is not necessarily associated with cognitive decline.

>> **Skilled nursing facility (SNF):** These facilities provide skilled care that can only be provided by a nurse, such as injections, and rehabilitation services, such as physical therapy, and are certified to meet federal and state standards.

>> **Transfer:** Here's a term that has several meanings. In long-term care jargon, it usually means moving a person from bed to chair or the reverse. Someone who is a *two-person transfer* requires two aides to do the job. This may be because the person is obese or paralyzed, or has another condition that makes it unsafe for both the person and the helper to manage alone. The second meaning of transfer refers to moving a person from one setting to another, such as from an assisted-living facility to a hospital emergency department. This is often called a *transition.*

TIP

A good place to look up terms that relate to Medicaid and financial issues is the glossary at `longtermcare.acl.gov/the-basics/glossary.html`. Another resource is the United Hospital Fund's Next Step in Care "Terms and Definitions" at `www.nextstepincare.org/Terms_and_Definitions/`. For medical terms, consult a medical dictionary or the resources, including videos, from the National Institutes of Health Medline Plus at `www.nlm.nih.gov/medlineplus/`.

TIP

You will find that different people interpret terms differently and that agencies and insurance companies often have their own interpretations of what counts as, for example, *medically necessary,* which is often the trigger for benefits. To keep everything straight, I suggest writing down the information you're given when it relates to eligibility or another aspect of services, along with the name, title, and contact information of the person who gave you the information. And if you don't like the definition you're given by someone, you may be able to get a more favorable interpretation from a supervisor after you've explained the situation.

Meeting Your Changing Needs

Planning should be a dynamic process. Where you want to live in your 60s may look very different from where you'll want to be in your 80s. Your needs change based on your finances, family circumstances, health, and more. Someone considering moving from a single-family house to an apartment or assisted-living facility should think about whether this is a move that can satisfy future needs as well as immediate ones. Not everyone moves though the spectrum of needs at the same pace, or even goes through all the same stages. The needs of a person with mild cognitive impairment, for instance, are very different from the needs of a person with advanced dementia. As another example, someone diagnosed with diabetes needs chronic care — that is, doctor or nurse visits; ongoing monitoring, including blood tests; medications; and foot and vision exams. If the diabetic condition deteriorates to the point where the person is unable to walk or perform daily activities independently, then significant changes need to be made.

Some future needs can be anticipated, and others cannot. The goal is not to have a detailed plan for every possible contingency but a general idea of what can reasonably be anticipated and planned for.

Location, location, location

The well-worn real estate adage of choosing a home based on location applies to this stage of your life as well. In this case, location is not so much an economic asset (although in some cases it can be) as a symbol of personal comfort and satisfaction and, often, being near family and close friends. Consider how you will meet all your needs — including the social and emotional aspects.

Many people just say, "I want to stay in my own home!" And indeed, that's a reasonable short-term goal, but it may not be feasible in the long run. Beyond their initial statement, many people just stop thinking about it or assume that their children (or more likely, a particular child) will say, "I'll move in with you so you can stay at home." Maybe that will happen, and maybe it won't. But it certainly requires an explicit understanding, not just an assumption.

In thinking about location, you want to consider:

>> **Family:** Moving to another community to be nearer children, often at their urging, may be an option. You should consider what you may lose and what you may gain. Someone with strong ties to a particular community — for example, a faith community or club or other group — may miss that connection. On the other hand, you may be able to re-create those ties in another setting. A lot depends on the type of community you would move to, whether you have spent enough time there to be confident you would like it, and whether you will have to depend on your children for transportation and other needs. Visiting your children as a guest and participating in their activities is different from being a permanent resident. Some social groups welcome newcomers, but others closed their ranks a long time ago.

>> **Climate:** It's almost a stereotype that older people want to move to warmer places, but in fact that is one main reason people do relocate. There may be health reasons to move to a different climate, or the upkeep on a house and car in a winter zone may be too onerous to sustain. But not everyone adjusts easily to a more or less constant temperature, especially if it's very hot. And although blizzards can create dangerous situations for someone living alone, so can hurricanes and tornados, which generally occur in warmer areas.

>> **Cost of living:** Different regions of the country are more or less expensive places to live. This applies to costs of housing, medical care, food, personal care services, transportation, and other items that will figure into your plan as well as independent or assisted living.

TIP

An extended visit to a community you're considering is a good way to find out whether you like it or not. Before or after your visit, you can look online to get an idea of prices for everything from groceries to rentals. You'll also see what social, sporting, and cultural events are featured. Think about what you most like to do now and what you would like to be able to do in a new location.

Timing and flexibility

If you're going to make a change, when is the best time to do it? I can't give you the perfect answer. Still, if you're planning to stay where you are for the immediate future, you should start now to reassess your home for safety and accessibility. The mostly minor modifications you can make now (see Chapter 5) will help prevent falls, which are the most common reason for a need for more intense long-term care services. Even if you don't expect to stay in this location permanently, the modifications will add value to your home because they will also make it safer for others, including families with young children.

At the same time, you should begin to investigate alternatives. Without the pressure of family members or doctors insisting that you make a change, you can think about what matters most to you and what you have become used to but can live without.

REMEMBER

If a change does fit into your plan, allow enough time to make all the arrangements and consider all the pieces that need to be reassembled in a new location, whether that is independent living, assisted living, or another option. Downsizing and moving is one of life's most stressful events, even if it is well-planned and desired. Take your time.

You may not have enough space in your new location for the lifetime of memorabilia and objects you have collected. You may have to donate or sell some possessions. If you're moving from a big house to a smaller house, apartment, or condo, you may have to decide what furniture to keep and what won't work in the new setting. This process — with the emotional impact of dealing with so many memories at once — stops many people from moving forward. But if you enlist help from family, friends, and, if need be, from professional organizers, it can be liberating. (See Chapter 7 for more information.)

REMEMBER

Be flexible. Even if you aren't moving to a different location or a different community, you're entering a new stage of life. Change can be stimulating but also disorienting.

Paradoxically, remaining independent often means asking for help. Asking for and accepting help is often a major hurdle in any future plan. Being willing to acknowledge that you can't do everything alone (and probably you never really did) is the first step toward a person-centered plan. Family and friends are your first sources of help, but they are not the only ones. Neighbors, volunteers from community groups, building contractors, home care aides, and transportation services can all play a part in helping you achieve your goals.

Getting Professional Advice

Among the people you may need to consult as you navigate this path are professionals such as doctors, lawyers, and accountants. These professionals can help you make realistic plans and avoid costly and potentially damaging errors.

Choosing these advisers can be tricky. Your niece who just graduated from law school may offer to help you write a will, but she lives in a different state and doesn't know the law in your state. You have some investments with a local broker, and you have done well with his recommendations. But he has a financial interest in guiding you toward certain choices, which may not serve you well as you contemplate the future. And even your doctor, who has taken care of you for years, sees you as you are, not necessarily as you may become. She may or may not be the best person to give you a completely honest appraisal of your health outlook for the future.

These people may be competent advisers. It makes sense, however, to consult with others so that you can be sure you're getting objective and accurate information.

For example, you may want to ask for a geriatric evaluation from a physician who is experienced in caring for older adults, whose course of illness and reactions to medications may differ significantly from younger people. An attorney who specializes in elder law has particular expertise and can guide you toward creating documents that contain the precise instructions you want. And a financial adviser who charges a fee but does not gain from your investment choices may be a good person to help work out the financial aspects of your plan.

When considering using the services of a specific professional, ask about the following issues before moving forward:

>> Experience with working with clients with similar needs

>> Length of time in practice

>> Recommendations

>> Fees for the service

REMEMBER

Even with good advisers, you need to be intimately involved in all decisions (or have a family member do this on your behalf). The investment of your time and money helps ensure that you get the kind of future care you want.

Chapter **2**

A Personal Inventory: Past, Present, and Future

Your vision of your future reflects you as you are now and what you have experienced in the past. A lot depends on your current health status and anticipated future needs, of course, and your preferences for assistance in managing day-to-day activities. Finances are an important part of the equation as well.

But two people with the same health and financial profile may want to live in different types of settings and receive help in different ways. In this chapter, I help you step back from short-term decisions and think about the kind of person you are and how you want to spend your time. If another person will be sharing this stage of life with you, you should both undertake this exercise. It may reveal some surprises as well as similarities in goals. If you're helping a parent or other older relative plan, you can encourage them to go through the process with your help. You'll get to know each other in new and possibly revealing ways. This chapter guides you through finding out what type of setting best suits your needs and lifestyle. It also helps you create a plan to steer you in the right direction for the future — including a tool called a CareMap.

Looking at the Present — and the Future

Imagining what you'll be like in 10, 15, or 20 years is hard. But your life so far gives you some clues. What were you like 10, 15, or 20 years ago? Have you changed a lot, or is there a consistent pattern? Have you changed jobs or careers? Have you moved around the country or internationally? Have you been married, divorced, or widowed — more than once? Have your spending or savings habits changed? Or has your life gone along in more or less planned and predictable ways?

These questions aren't intended to be value judgments about one lifestyle versus another but simply a way for you to consider your tolerance for risk (or, if you prefer, adventure), need for stability, and comfort with change. In the following sections, I organize the inventory around four categories: healthcare needs; family, friends, and professionals; personality characteristics; and attitudes about money. Each is an important element in creating your personal profile.

Healthcare needs

Your overall health and any special considerations are clearly important aspects to consider not only on their own but because they will affect many aspects of the nonmedical assistance you may need.

Here are some questions to ask yourself. Be ruthlessly honest. No one else has to see your list unless you want to share. It is intended to give you a template to think about your healthcare needs and how they would be incorporated into a future plan:

>> How would you describe your overall health — poor, fair, good, excellent? Has this status changed in the past few years?

>> Do you have any chronic conditions? (Examples are high blood pressure, diabetes, arthritis, and heart problems.) What are they? Are they under control?

>> Is the condition expected to get worse as you age?

>> How many doctors do you see regularly? Are your appointments regularly scheduled checkups or as-needed visits? Do these doctors share information with each other and with you?

>> Do you see any other healthcare professionals — home care nurse, physical therapist, or chiropractor, for example?

>> Do any of your health conditions limit your ability to function at home or in the community?

» Do you use mobility assistive devices of any kind — cane, walker, or wheelchair, for example?

» How many prescription medications do you take?

» How many over-the-counter (OTC) medications such as vitamins or aspirin do you take?

» Do you have an up-to-date list of all your prescribed and OTC medications?

» Does anyone help you with healthcare tasks such as giving injections, monitoring machines like oxygen tanks, or taking care of wounds? If so, who helps?

» Have you had your vision and hearing checked in the past year?

» Do you wear glasses or a hearing aid?

» Do you smoke?

» Do you drink alcohol or use recreational drugs? How often?

» Do you see a dentist regularly?

» Do you eat nutritious meals (most of the time)?

» Have you fallen in the past year? Were you injured?

» Do you have trouble sleeping?

» Do you exercise regularly? Or at all?

» Do you often feel sad or lonely?

» Are you concerned about memory loss?

» Do you have clear preferences about the kind of care you would want or not want if you were in a coma after extensive brain damage, or if you were not expected to recover from an illness?

» Have you told anyone about these preferences and documented them in an advance directive?

» Do you worry about your health? If you do, what worries you the most?

REMEMBER

Even this schematic outline should help you assess your current and potential future needs for healthcare. If you have generally good health and manage your healthcare needs with a minimum of professional involvement, then you should be able to maintain this level of healthcare wherever you are. There are also options for home–based care, which are discussed in Chapter 15. But if you already have serious chronic health conditions that require frequent doctor visits and multiple medications, moving away from your regular source of care may present problems.

For example, a move to assisted living may appeal to you because of the attractive setting, the availability of meals and housekeeping services, and the promised activities. But most assisted-living facilities don't have the capacity to serve the medical needs of someone with serious chronic conditions, and the location may not be convenient to your usual doctors' offices. On the other hand, you may be able to maintain your current healthcare arrangements in an assisted-living facility. It's important to find out.

TIP

If you're thinking of moving to a nearby assisted-living facility where your contact with your regular healthcare providers can be maintained, it is a good idea to let them know of your plans and to ask whether they have any reservations about the idea. If you're thinking of moving far away, then you can ask for referrals to providers in your new location. But remember that assisted-living facilities don't provide medical care, and you'll need to build that into your plan. Find out more about assisted living in Chapter 8.

Family, friends, and professionals

Healthcare may be a critical factor in your plans for the future, but it's not the only one. Just as important are your values and preferences about the kind of life you want to continue (or begin) to live.

This section asks for an inventory of the people in your life, what roles they play now, and how you would like them to be able to participate if your needs for assistance grow.

>> Who do you consider your family? The people you include can be your spouse, parents, children, grandparents, siblings, cousins, or other relatives. They can also be domestic partners, companions, and other people with whom you have a very close relationship.

- Which of these people do you rely on most for emotional support and comfort?

- Who would you call first if you needed help in making a medical decision? Settling a financial problem? Talking about your will?

- Who lives closest to you? Or with you? Does distance present a problem in getting together regularly or on short notice? You may be able to discuss a problem with someone far away, but that person isn't going to be able to help in an emergency.

- Do any of these people rely on you for the same sorts of assistance? For example, financial support? Advice and counseling? Day-to-day assistance?

- How do you currently communicate with your family? Frequent visits? Phone? Email? Texts? Or only at special events?

- Are there tensions within your family about money, relationships, obligations, or other factors?

- Are there family members with whom you have no relationships that you would like to involve in your life?

» Overall, how important is it to you to be close (geographically and emotionally) to your family?

» Beyond family, do you have close friends who in some ways substitute for family or add to family support?

- Can you call on them for the kinds of assistance that may be expected first from family?

- What limits would you anticipate friends may place on assistance?

» Do you have trusting relationships with professionals such as doctors, lawyers, accountants, clergy, and others who may be able to advise you on medical, financial, or personal matters? If not, can you identify people who may fill these roles?

Personality characteristics

Having looked at your health status and your available family resources in the previous sections, now take a clear look at your own preferences and values. This is where you can list what is important to you and what doesn't matter all that much. Again, be candid.

» Does religion play an important role in your life? If so, does this mean going to religious services regularly and observing religious practices? Or is it a less organized but still significant influence guiding how you live? Or do you consider yourself a spiritual but not religious person?

» If you're still employed, how important is your job to your sense of well-being? Would you miss that role? What in particular do you value?

» If you are retired, do you miss any part of your working life? Or are there aspects of working that you don't miss at all?

» Would you describe yourself as shy, outgoing, or somewhere in between?

» Do you make friends easily?

» Have you made any new friends in the past year?

>> Do you like everything to be neat and tidy? Does clutter bother you?

>> If you don't mind clutter, does it result in what some people may call a total mess or hoarding?

>> Do you like to be around animals? Have you always had pets? Do any particular kinds of animals frighten or annoy you?

>> Do you like to be part of a group and participate in activities with people you know? If so, what kinds of activities do you most like to share? Some examples are travel, community service, sports (watching or playing), avocations like music or gardening, cooking, or any other leisure-time pursuit.

>> Do you like the idea of being in a group of people you don't know? Would you enjoy meeting people from different backgrounds? Or do you prefer to be around people whose backgrounds are like yours?

>> Do you find the idea of group activities unappealing? If so, what aspects do you dislike?

>> Do you prefer to do things on your own or with one or two people?

>> If you are a loner rather than a group person, would you find it hard to adjust to group living, even if you had your own living space?

>> Do you like to do things on your own rather than rely on others for help?

>> Even if you ask for help, do you like to oversee the details?

>> Do you have a cooperative nature — that is, do you like to work out problems with other people, or would you prefer to take charge or have someone else take charge of the solution?

>> Do you value stability and security above the possibility of change, even if it improves your life?

Attitudes about money

Now I come to the most sensitive part of the inventory. (I haven't included sex, but you can add that to your list if you like.) It's money — not just how much you have but how you think about it. Here too the goal is not to make a judgment about your financial-management skills but to provide a way to think about how you'll approach your future. In nearly every case, future care does involve spending money, and much of it will be from your own or your family's resources.

Do you have a philosophy about money? People say things like "Money is meant to be spent," "A penny saved is a penny earned" (maybe updated to be a dollar), "It's important to save for a rainy day," and "I'm spending my children's inheritances." Sometimes, of course, these are offhand remarks, but even so they may indicate overall attitudes about money.

Even without an explicit philosophy, many people approach financial decisions within some basic framework of optimism, fatalism, or risk avoidance. Sometimes this philosophy has developed because of childhood experiences of poverty or difficult times in young adulthood, or the reverse, a lifetime of financial ease or a lack of responsibility. Different people react to financial stress in different ways. Think about your personal financial philosophy as you answer the following questions:

>> Do you know how much money is in your checking account, savings account, investment portfolio, pension fund, and other assets? Or do you leave that to someone else to manage?

>> Do you carry a lot of cash, or do you use credit cards for most purchases?

>> Do you buy a lot of products online or from television advertisers?

>> Have you ever regretted a major purchase bought on impulse?

>> Do you like to shop?

>> Are you or have you been in serious debt?

>> Do you know much money you are receiving (or will receive) from Social Security or a pension?

>> Do you know how much money your home (if you own it) is worth in today's market?

>> Do you know how much you pay in taxes and maintenance?

>> Do you have a regular household budget? Do you live within it?

>> How often do you get a new car?

>> Are vacations or travel an important part of your life?

>> Do you have current or future financial obligations to other family members, such as your grandchildren's education?

>> Would you be able to maintain these obligations if you were to start spending more on your own care?

>> Do you want to be able to leave money to children, grandchildren, or other people?

>> Do you want to be able to leave money to cultural, religious, or other institutions that you have supported?

TIP

A financial adviser can help you work out just what your assets are worth (you may be surprised to find you are worth more than you think) and create different options for accessing and spending this money. Different housing options have different cost profiles. Setting up a budget based on the costs that different housing options will require is a good way to determine what extra money you may have or how much you may need to trim from your current budget.

REMEMBER

To accommodate a lifestyle you prefer, you may have to start now to set priorities and limits. You should be comfortable with the financial plan as a basis for determining how much you can spend on future care without jeopardizing other important factors in your life.

Creating a Plan Based on Your Profile

The personal profile you have sketched in the preceding section, along with other items that are important to you, can offer guidance as you move forward.

For example, someone who belongs to several social and community groups, likes to meet new people, has generally good health, has no dependents (other than, perhaps, a spouse), and has sufficient financial resources to set aside for care may well consider assisted living. The facility may be nearby or in a setting closer to adult children or siblings (who, in this scenario, are financially independent). Check out Chapter 8 for more information on assisted living.

A person with a similar profile may not like group living and would prefer to spend the money on home modifications and home care assistance if necessary.

On the other hand, someone who already needs help with chronic health conditions, is struggling economically, and doesn't have many contacts outside family may find a multigenerational living arrangement worthwhile. In this scenario, the rest of the family can benefit as well from the contributions. This option can also involve a nearby setting or a move, depending on where family members live and who moves in with whom. It may even involve the creation of a new home to match the new household's needs.

For someone who suffers from serious health conditions and may need more care in the future, the options are more limited. More family or paid assistance will be required, either at home or in a skilled nursing facility (SNF). Home- and community-based services can provide a basis for the needed care, but if 24-hour care or care requiring special expertise is needed, these services won't suffice. A skilled nursing facility (or the extended-care section of a continuing-care retirement community) may be the most appropriate option (see Chapter 16).

REMEMBER

Between these two extremes, of course, lie many possibilities and options. I consider these in other chapters in this book. But in evaluating specific settings and services, keep the personal inventory in mind as the framework for decision making. Someone else's decision may be perfect for that person. You want to make a decision that is right for you.

Drawing a CareMap to Visualize Your Profile

Making lists is an important step in the process of creating a personal inventory. But it's not the only way. A new tool — called a CareMap — is available online at `https://atlasofcaregiving.com/caremap/`.

The idea of a CareMap grew out of an extensive research project conducted by Atlas of Caregiving that documented, using mostly high-tech tools, what a family caregiver did every minute of a full day. One of the techniques that proved to be most useful is also the simplest. All you need is a sheet of paper and a pencil. A video can show you how to draw simple icons to represent people and services. There is also a digital version online for those comfortable with computers. You may want to ask someone to help you as you get acquainted with the idea.

Although planned for family caregivers, the idea is easily adapted to the person planning for the future. Starting with you at the center, you draw your home, adding people who help you daily, periodically, or infrequently, and people you help. You can add pets who both provide emotional support and need care. You can add people who live close by, at a middle distance, and those who are farther away. Needed services like doctors, transportation, and food delivery can also be added. At the end you have a picture that shows what exists in your life and, equally important, what's missing.

In Figure 2-1, Lucy lives with a dog but gets help from her daughter, Sharon, who lives nearby. Lucy reciprocates by babysitting her grandson Bobby. Lucy's son, Joe, lives too far away to help frequently but does send money to help with medical and household expenses, such as a housekeeper who comes once a week. Lucy has a friend, Maria, who both provides emotional support and looks to Lucy for advice. Lucy has other friends in a prayer circle. She uses city transportation to shop and go to medical appointments with Dr. Lew.

In this CareMap, the heart icon stands for the healthcare services Dr. Lew provides to Lucy. The hand icon indicates that the person helps someone else in the family (as Lucy helps her grandson Bobby). The smiley face icon stands for friendship, and the dollar symbol tells you that Joe, Lucy's son, lives too far away to provide hands-on help but contributes financially. The housekeeper has an icon for household chores, and the ellipsis (. . .) is used to mean "other" (in this CareMap, transportation). You can find more icons at the Atlas of Caregiving website, or you can create your own if you use paper and pencil.

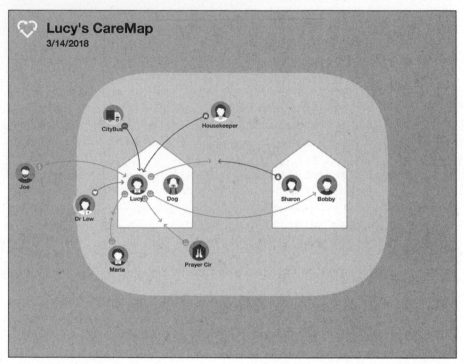

Illustration courtesy of Atlas of Caregiving

FIGURE 2-1:
The CareMap brings your lists to life and can be saved and revised as needs change.

Chapter **3**

Finding Services

T he options for the future are varied and sometimes complicated. The good news is that a lot of information is available from many different sources. The bad news is that the information is often incomplete or inaccurate, driven by marketing agendas, and hard to apply to your personal situation.

With the suggestions I provide in this chapter and some judicious selection, you can find reliable sources of basic information to get started. You can narrow your search to the sources most likely to be helpful. Even then, you should double-check the information to make sure you have accurate facts and figures. All this research can be a lot of work, so you may want to ask a friend or family member to help you with this process.

TIP

Each of the chapters on a specific topic — assisted living, for example (see Chapter 8) — also has suggested resources. You can go directly to that chapter and then come back to this one for more general resources, or you can do the opposite — start here and then go to the specific chapter.

Where to Turn for Help

If you're in the market for a new car or washing machine, what do you do? You probably look online for product information and perhaps user reviews, go to a dealer to see the different models, and maybe ask friends and family for their recommendations. You look at the product, find out what it has and doesn't have, what it costs to buy it and have it delivered, and what the manufacturer's warranty covers. Then you decide which option best fits your needs and your budget. This is typical consumer behavior.

Housing, healthcare, and other options you're considering only loosely fit the consumer behavior model. Although some aspects are similar, developing a future plan involves many other considerations, such as what type of person you are and what type of lifestyle you want to have in the future (as I discuss in Chapter 2).

For one thing, in healthcare you often don't know the cost until after you've used the product — for example, had a hospital stay or outpatient tests. You may not know that certain hospital doctors are outside your insurance network and will bill you separately. You may not realize that a hospital stay "for observation" doesn't count toward the three-day Medicare requirement for short-term rehabilitation in a skilled nursing facility (SNF). You have a better idea going forward in assisted living or a nursing home, but even then, many costs are hidden. And your choices are more lasting and carry greater weight in your life than that new washing machine.

REMEMBER

In your research, finding out what's not included is just as important as learning what is included. Don't take anything for granted; ask and document the answers, and jot down the name of the person you spoke to. Also don't forget that things may change over time. For example, a physician who accepted your insurance or was in your health plan's network may no longer be available. Research should be an ongoing process to make certain you have the most current and accurate information.

You should read between the lines or specifically ask about what isn't transparent. For example, a basic fee for an assisted-living facility may not include charges for additional aide services, or if they are mentioned, the likelihood of your needing them may be downplayed. Health-insurance coverage may not include some expensive prescription drugs or assistive devices such as customized walkers; its coverage of home healthcare or rehabilitation services may be limited in terms of the time and providers you can use. Long-term care insurance may present difficulties in accessing benefits by denying claims and delaying decisions.

One aspect of consumer behavior does fit both the product model and the services you're researching: the importance of being informed, inquisitive, and at times skeptical. The more you know, the less likely you are to be surprised. Preferably, your surprises should be on the positive side, not of the "Why didn't someone tell me this?" variety.

In the next section, you find some preliminary tips to help you begin and organize your search. The sections that follow offer information about federal programs, state and local programs, and community-based services.

Organizing your research

When looking for care options, the three major routes are the Internet, phone, and personal visits. Often, you'll be searching multiple sites, making numerous phone calls, and visiting various facilities. You'll probably ask people you know about their experiences. How can you keep all the information straight? The following sections provide some tips to help you find and keep the information in an easily accessed way.

Web searches

You can keep track of information you find on the web in one of two ways: either digitally or via a paper filing system.

>> **Digital filing:** If you are technically adept (or have a techie in your family), you can set up a system of folders on your computer to store information in different categories. Or you can bookmark sites that you visit frequently.

>> **Paper filing:** If you're a paper person, set up a notebook or filing system that becomes your information bank. Print out pages from useful sites. It can be incredibly frustrating to try to find something you know you have read somewhere but can't find again. Be sure to include the web address on the page printouts for future reference.

TIP

During web searches, use different search words to help guide you to multiple sites. And always check that the sponsor of the website is reputable and reliable. Verify the information with an authoritative source. Note whether the article or web page is dated to make sure the information is current.

REMEMBER

Web addresses may disappear into cyberspace. If you encounter this problem, try searching for the organization by its name. Unless the organization has disappeared along with its website, you can usually find the new web address. Sometimes organizations change their names or merge with other organizations and the new website may not contain all the pages you remember from the old websites.

Phone calls

Before you place a call for information, plan your questions in advance so you know specifically what you want to ask. Make a written list of your questions, and write down the answer to each question as you get it.

After each phone call, mark the date, time, and person you spoke with, as well as contact information and any notes from the phone conversation. Keep these hard copies in your research files in case you need to contact a person again or want to follow up.

You may have to go through several phone referrals to find the person who is best able to answer your questions. Be persistent.

Personal visits

When you visit an office or facility, bring a written list of questions. Fill in the answers to your questions during your visit and keep the list in your research file so you can compare different service providers at a glance.

On your search, you may visit different types of service providers. To determine eligibility for services, each place requires certain types of documentation, such as a birth certificate, a passport, or other proof of citizenship, or a health insurance card, so plan ahead, make copies of everything you need, and file the papers with the other information you gather about each service. Make sure you bring all the relevant documents to the meeting.

Federal government programs

Federal agencies — primarily the Centers for Medicare & Medicaid Services (CMS), but also other agencies such as the Administration for Community Living, the Administration on Aging, and the Social Security Administration — are good places to begin. (Medicaid is a federal-state program, so it is important to look at both the federal rules and your state's program.) Throughout this book I refer to specific online links, but here I give an overview of some of the main resources.

Medicare and Medicaid

Even though Medicare doesn't cover long-term care, it's an important resource for the medical care that people receiving long-term care services and supports (often abbreviated as LTSS) need. Some of the short-term benefits — for example, for home healthcare or rehabilitation services — may fill gaps while more viable long-term solutions are arranged.

CMS, part of the U.S. Department of Health and Human Services, oversees Medicare. Its website, www.medicare.gov, is the primary resource for beneficiaries and families.

If you're enrolled in Medicare, you receive by mail a handbook titled "Medicare and You," which is updated every year. Although the cover says it is "an official U.S. government handbook," the inside cover warns that it isn't a legal document. For legal guidance, you need to go to the relevant statutes, regulations, and rulings, which can be hard to find and tough reading for a nonlawyer. The handbook is also available online and in an e-book format. You can also speak to a Medicare agent by calling 1-800-MEDICARE (1-800-633-4227). If you use a smartphone, use the numbers rather than the letters because the "E" won't connect.

WARNING

One common scam directed at Medicare beneficiaries is a phone call from someone claiming to be from Medicare and asking for personal information. Medicare does not make uninvited phone calls to beneficiaries.

Medicaid is the federal-state program that provides healthcare and long-term care for people with low incomes and assets or very high medical costs. Eligibility and services vary by state. Much of the information on the Medicaid website, www.medicaid.gov, is designed for regulators and policymakers, although it includes links to state sites, which have more specific information for residents. This is just a place to start; you'll need to dig into the information on the state Medicaid website and other sources.

TIP

See Chapter 11 of this book or check out AARP's *Medicare For Dummies* by Patricia Barry (Wiley) for more detailed information on Medicare and Medicaid. These sources cover the basics, including the differences between Original Medicare and a Medicare Advantage plan. If you need help choosing a Medicare Advantage plan, you need to do further research on local plans.

Other federal agencies

Aside from Medicare and Medicaid, the following federal agencies can provide information you may find useful in your research:

>> **Administration for Community Living:** In 2012, the U.S. Department of Health and Human Services created an umbrella organization, the Administration for Community Living (ACL), to bring together various federal agency resources to coordinate policy and reduce fragmentation in policies on disability and aging. The main website is www.acl.gov, and the ACL has many resources on long-term care at https://longtermcare.acl.gov/.

>> **Administration on Aging:** The Administration on Aging (AoA) is part of the ACL. AoA supports what is often called the *Aging Network* of agencies and professionals. It was created in 1965 with the passage of the Older Americans Act and provides support services, nutrition services, preventive health services, the National Family Caregiver Support Program, elder-rights services, and services to Native Alaskans, Native Hawaiians, and Native Americans. Its website is www.acl.gov/about-acl/administration-aging.

>> **Eldercare Locator:** The Eldercare Locator, a free service of the AoA, is a basic go-to site for locating resources in your community. Its website is https://eldercare.acl.gov/Public/Index.aspx. You can access an online chat forum, or you can call 1-800-677-1116 for information.

>> **Area Agencies on Aging:** The more than 600 Area Agencies on Aging (AAAs) provide information and referrals to services such as adult daycare and senior-center programs in their region. To view a map of AAAs, enter your city and state or zip code at www.n4a.org/about-n4a/?fa=aaa-title-VI, or click on the Eldercare Locator link near the bottom of the page for more information. Some state associations of AAAs also have maps of their locations within the state.

>> **Social Security Administration:** The Social Security Administration (SSA) administers Social Security benefits, which may be an important part of the financial side of your plan. The agency's website at www.ssa.gov lets you check or estimate your retirement benefits online and get other information. All Social Security benefits must now be paid by direct deposit, so if you or your parent or other relative is receiving Social Security benefits, it should be by direct deposit. If you have moved or plan to move, be sure to inform the SSA by going to www.ssa.gov/myaccount or calling 1-800-772-1213.

TIP

AARP's *Social Security For Dummies* by Jonathan Peterson (Wiley) provides more detail on all aspects of Social Security.

>> **USA.gov:** This site is the main federal government portal at https://USA.gov. It has a section on senior citizens' resources, which has links to a variety of federal agencies and a separate listing of many state resources, including lesser-known ones such as the "National Farmers Market Directory," prepared by the U.S. Department of Agriculture: www.ams.usda.gov/local-food-directories/farmersmarkets.

>> **National Disability Rights Network**: Every state and territory has one protection and advocacy agency (P&A) responsible for protecting the rights of individuals with disabilities. See this website for a state-by-state listing: www.ndrn.org/en/ndrn-member-agencies.html.

State and local programs

Different states assign aspects of long-term care to different agencies. Finding the right state agency for the information you need can be challenging. For example, Medicare is Medicare wherever you are (although there are some local variations in determining payment to providers) and Social Security is one system, but Medicaid in Florida is the Florida Agency for Health Care Administration whereas in Wisconsin it is ForwardHealth. More important than the name is the variation in Medicaid from state to state.

After you have located the right agency (and if possible, the right person in the agency), make sure to keep a record of how to find it again. Check out the following list for state agencies that are relevant for future care planning:

>> **Departments of aging:** Every state has an agency devoted to services for older adults, often linked to services for people with disabilities. Like Medicaid, however, what the agency is named varies, although not as much. Although the most common name is Department (Office, Division, Commission) of (for, on) Aging, other variations include the Division of Elderly Affairs (Rhode Island) and the Aging and Long-Term Support Administration (Washington). The National Association of States United for Aging and Disabilities has a state-by-state listing of offices at www.nasuad.org/about-nasuad/about-state-agencies/list-members. These agencies have information about senior centers, food programs, counseling, and other services, both state-funded and in partnership with federal agencies.

>> **County and city departments of aging:** Many counties and cities also have Departments of Aging that contract with local community agencies to provide services. It may be easier to get information from a local agency than from the state, although that may depend on the level of staffing. These are the same agencies described in the preceding section as Area Agencies on Aging.

>> **Advance directives:** The federal Patient Self-Determination Act, enacted in 1990, requires hospitals and other providers (including psychiatric hospitals and other mental-health providers) and health plans to maintain written policies and procedures with respect to advance directives — documents that spell out what kinds of treatments you do or do not want if you are not able to speak for yourself.

The providers must ask whether a patient has an advance directive; in practice this means that if you're admitted to a hospital, someone (probably the admitting clerk) will ask you whether you have an advance directive. If you do, that information should go in your medical record. The federal law does not specify what form the advance directive should take; that's up to states (see Chapter 17 for more details). The advance directive usually includes the name of the person you have chosen to speak on your behalf if you are unable to express your wishes.

Caring Connections, an arm of the National Hospice and Palliative Care Organization, has state-specific forms you can download at www.aarp.org/advancedirectives.

>> **Medicaid:** Every state has a Medicaid program for low-income people that provides a basic package of services as defined by federal law (see Chapter 11 for more details). Each state, however, determines its own optional services and criteria for eligibility for different types of services. Home- and community-based services are optional and may be covered under a waiver from the federal government that allows states to spend their funds for these services or through other approaches. Some programs have long waiting lists.

Community-based organizations

Public programs are important sources of information, but you may find that information from nongovernmental sources answers more of your immediate questions. These sources may be national organizations concerned with issues related to aging, national disease-specific organizations with local or regional chapters, service organizations in your community, and others. Some organizations do advocacy, some provide services, and some do both. Some are primarily focused on the older person or person with disabilities; others serve both the person and their family members.

Many of the public agencies will refer you to these local resources, but I recommend doing an environmental scan of your own. A state or city Department of Aging, for example, may have lists of community agencies that it funds, but its list may not include other organizations, such as faith-based groups or volunteer organizations.

TIP

There is no comprehensive list of these organizations, and there are hundreds of them, so you'll have to do some detective work (again, a friend or family member can help). But most of the major national organizations can also direct you to local resources. Some disease groups have several organizations providing information, so you should compare the sites to see which one offers the most relevant information for you.

Here are a few sites to get started:

>> **AARP** (www.aarp.org): From the home page you can go to several different subject categories, such as health, work and jobs, retirement, home and family (which includes caregiving), and money (click the "Menu" icon at the upper-left corner of the page). Each of these sections provides information and directs you to other resources.

>> **Alzheimer's Association** (www.alz.org): This site has links to local chapters, which offer educational sessions, support groups, and other services. The main site has information about Alzheimer's disease and other dementias, including research and treatment.

>> **American Diabetes Association** (www.diabetes.org): The website has links to local chapters, information on prevention and treatment, and services.

>> **American Heart Association** (www.heart.org): The AHA has information about heart disease and stroke, treatments, and prevention.

>> **CancerCare** (www.cancercare.org): CancerCare's website provides free professional support services to anyone affected by cancer. The organization has educational programs for patients and caregivers, counseling services, and limited financial assistance. Services are available online and by phone.

>> **National Council on Aging** (www.ncoa.org): Through its BenefitsCheckUp tool, NCOA has information for older adults on accessing benefits such as help paying for medications or food. The tool is organized by state or zip code.

>> **National Hospice and Palliative Care Organization** (www.nhpco.org): This organization has information about end-of-life concerns and links to help you find providers of both types of services.

TIP

Small organizations may not have staff to respond immediately to your requests. You may have to call back a few times to get the information you need. Be patient but persistent.

This list is only a glimpse into the multiple resources available through voluntary health organizations and advocacy groups. Search the Internet by disease and by area of interest (treatment options, financing, research, and more) to drill down into your specific areas of interest. All the chapters in this book on specific aspects of long-term care (financing, for example, or family caregiving) have many more suggestions.

WARNING

Don't be misled by sites that promise cures or easy ways to finance long-term care. The Internet is a hotbed of literally incredible offers and fraudulent schemes.

A VIEW OF MEDIA REPORTING ON HEALTH

Many people get a lot of their information about healthcare from television or newspapers. News reports are often orchestrated by big companies and their public relations firms. So, be wary of news reports that use the words *cure, miracle,* and *breakthrough.* The questions most often left unanswered in these reports are whether there are alternative options, whether the treatment is available or is still in an experimental phase, the cost, who is promoting the information, and whether there is a conflict of interest. Check with your doctor before buying into these drugs or treatments.

A website that provides expert analyses of news reports and press releases is Health News Review (www.healthnewsreview.org). The site has tool kits about interpreting medical studies and other ways to get behind the headlines.

Taking Your Research to the Next Level: Site Visits for Housing

One of the most important decisions to make in your future plan is where to live. No matter how much information you have collected, the real test of whether a place can meet your needs comes only from your direct experience. Websites, brochures, phone calls, and interviews set the stage by giving you basic information about costs, eligibility, services, and the like. But when it comes to deciding if and where to move, only a site visit will give you that final piece of information. You can follow up visits by checking that the sites meet federal and state regulations.

TIP

The chapters in this book on assisted living (Chapter 8), nursing homes (Chapter 16), and multigenerational family housing (Chapter 6), as well as those specifically addressed to the lesbian, gay, bisexual, and transgender population (LGBT) and veterans (Chapters 18 and 19, respectively), all have advice about what to look for.

Tips for your tours

When you visit a facility, ask questions — lots of them. Write down the answers and the name of the person who gave them to you. Whatever your specific questions, try to adopt the attitude of being an interested but not convinced consumer.

But in addition to asking questions, be a good observer. Try to get an overall impression of the place. Borrowing a term from real estate jargon, does the place have *curb appeal* — that is, is it attractive from the outside? This doesn't mean luxurious or showy. Facilities have personalities, just like people, and you can often get a sense of whether that personality is warm and welcoming just from the way you feel when you enter it.

Then focus on individual elements such as the type of accommodation for mobility or low vision, how residents and staff interact, and the noise level both inside and out. Can you see yourself (or your parent) in this place? If so, what about it appeals to you? If not, what bothers you? It is important to speak to current residents and staff to get a true picture of what your experience at the facility may be like. Try not to make snap judgments, but also trust your instincts.

REMEMBER

Don't be swayed by one person's opinion. Listen to all the pros and cons, and then make your decision with your family, considering all the evidence and your own evaluation.

Federal and state regulations

Both the federal and state governments regulate long-term care services and facilities. The standards are set by agencies that pay for services, monitor quality of care, and establish rules for licensing staff. It is important to understand what standards are monitored and how a facility or agency measures up to the requirements. Particularly important is the number of problems noted by government surveyors or through public complaints.

» **Home care agencies:** There are different types of home care agencies with different regulatory oversight. For a home care agency to be paid by Medicare and Medicaid, it must be approved by CMS (Centers for Medicare & Medicaid Services). These agencies provide skilled nursing care, personal care, and therapies from professionals such as physical, occupational, and speech, and respiratory therapists. Social-work services are also available.

TIP

Home Health Compare (www.medicare.gov/homehealthcompare/search.html) is a CMS website that gives you information on specific agencies and how they are doing with meeting federal standards. Many but not all states license home care agencies that provide personal care services. Check the website of your state department of health to see whether all home care agencies are licensed and what they require in terms of background checks and training. See Chapter 15 for more detail.

REMEMBER

Most states do not regulate companion agencies that provide nonmedical services such as preparing meals, homemaker services, and personal care, although the number that do monitor them is increasing. You'll have to exercise due diligence about the agency's practices regarding background checks of employees, training, and other issues.

» **Assisted-living facilities:** The federal government doesn't have standards for independent living or assisted-living facilities. (A final CMS rule of January 2014 sets standards for states that include assisted-living facilities in their Medicaid home- and community-based services waivers. States have a transitional period to ensure that they meet the standards.) These facilities are subject to various state regulations, which include building and safety codes. Some are licensed under different categories of congregate living. Because they do not provide medical services (except in a specific nursing unit), they are not generally regulated by departments of health. (See Chapter 8 for more details.)

>> **Nursing homes:** Nursing homes are subject to federal and state regulation, with specific requirements about staffing, training, prevention of abuse and neglect, reporting incidents of poor quality, and other standards. A CMS website, Nursing Home Compare, allows you to search by facility name (www.medicare.gov/nursinghomecompare/search.html). (See Chapter 16 for more details on nursing homes.) State governments also regulate nursing homes, and many department of health websites also provide information on the results of their surveys. This information is also available on Nursing Home Compare.

>> **Beneficiary and Family-Centered Care Quality Improvement Organizations (BFCC QIOs):** As part of the CMS structure, each state has a designated BFCC QIO that is responsible for ensuring and improving quality of care and for reviewing complaints. (A separate set of organizations called QIOs work with providers to improve quality.) If, for example, you feel that you're being discharged from a hospital too quickly, you can appeal the decision to the local BFCC QIO.

TIP

There are two BFCC QIO organizations — Livanta and Kepro — that cover different regions. Most people don't know about these organizations, but they can be very helpful in resolving problems. This website will tell you which organization covers your state: www.qualitynet.org/dcs/ContentServer?cid=1228774346765&pagename=QnetPublic%2FPage%2FQnetTier4&c=Page. You can also look up Livanta (www.livanta.com/bfccqio.html) and Kepro (www.keproqio.com) to see the review process.

>> **Long-term care ombudsmen:** Ombudsmen (the term comes from Swedish) investigate complaints and negotiate solutions to problems in nursing homes and assisted-living facilities. You can find information at http://ltcombudsman.org/about/about-ombudsman.

TIP

You may also find the following CMS websites useful:

>> **Comparing hospitals:** www.medicare.gov/hospitalcompare/search.html

>> **Comparing physicians:** www.medicare.gov/physiciancompare/

>> **Comparing dialysis facilities:** www.medicare.gov/DialysisFacilityCompare/search.html

You can see a directory of equipment suppliers that participate in Medicare's competitive bidding program at www.medicare.gov/SupplierDirectory/.

WARNING

These or other comparison sites are useful as a starting point, but they don't provide all the information you need, and the sources on which they base their reviews may be incomplete or outdated.

Chapter **4**

Making Decisions: A Family Affair

U nless you live in total isolation, the decisions you make concerning the future affect other people — family, friends, coworkers, and others. You may already depend on some of these people, and they may depend on you. Although the ultimate choice should be yours, getting to that point may involve some discussion and negotiation. Be open to what others may say. Compromise may be the best way to proceed.

Talking through these decisions with other people can sometimes be uncomfortable, but I strongly encourage you to do it sooner rather than later. The decisions don't have to be implemented immediately, and you will be better prepared if you have a road map. You may encounter detours and roadblocks, but if you have a destination in sight, you can work around them.

In this chapter, I discuss some of the issues you may consider as you discuss all the options with others, and I suggest some ways to resolve disagreements, whether they are based on the current situation or have long-standing roots.

Holding Family Meetings

Perhaps you have held family meetings throughout the years to discuss job changes, divorce, moves, problems in school, budgets, and other family matters. Or perhaps yours is a family where the very idea of sitting down together to talk about a major life change would be a totally new and probably anxiety-producing experience. If so, don't be put off by the novelty of the idea. Planning for the future entails decisions that you shouldn't make alone, whether the plan is for you or for a parent or other relative.

TIP

For more advice on holding a family meeting, go to the Family Caregiver Alliance's guide at www.caregiver.org/caregiver/jsp/content_node.jsp?nodeid=475.

Who should be included?

If you created a personal inventory as I recommend in Chapter 2, you have a list of your close family members and friends. Review it and see whether you want to add anyone or take anyone off the list. If you didn't go through this exercise, now is a good time to do it.

This list gives you a starting point for people to include in your plan. But not all them need to be part of every aspect of your decision making. Limit your initial discussions to the people most directly involved in your life, or the life of your parent or other relative. This is your inner circle, or core group. People who you believe would want to be involved but can do so only on a limited basis form an outer circle. People can move from one category to another as the discussions proceed and as needs arise.

REMEMBER

When making plans, involving the person who is at the heart of the discussion is essential. If it is you, then you are already the center. But if it is a parent or other relative, he or she should be the primary person in every discussion. In some situations, that may not be possible — because of advanced dementia, for example — but for most situations, the person himself or herself is the critical factor. That doesn't mean that everything this person says is the final answer; it just means that the discussion should be *with* the person, not just *about* him or her.

Spouses or partners, of course, should be involved, as well as adult children. Sometimes people who are more distantly related — cousins, nieces, and nephews, for example — are important members of the group. If the person you are planning for is your parent and you have siblings, count them in (even if the relationships between you and them or between them and your parent aren't ideal).

TIP

Try to keep the inner circle to a manageable number — perhaps five or six. But don't leave out anyone who really should be involved. If you have many children or siblings, they should be included. They may not accept your invitation to participate and you may need to deal with that later on, but the invitation should be open.

When should you get together?

Legions of columnists and other advisers encourage people to have serious discussions like these at holiday times. The rationale is that it is more likely that the whole family will be together at these times. But is this really the best time to have a serious talk about sensitive matters? Keep in mind that holidays are also times when family members are distracted by taking care of children and planning for the next event on the agenda; they may just want to enjoy the occasion. In some families, holidays are particularly stressful times when past jealousies and slights come alive again. If alcohol is on the menu, it may be a disinhibiting and unhelpful factor. Instead of burdening a holiday with this discussion, I recommend setting aside a specific time for a serious and thoughtful discussion, without any distractions.

TIP

With FaceTime, Skype, Zoom, and other technology, it is possible to have a meeting without everyone being in the same room. Businesses do it all the time, and it can work for families too.

TIP

If you anticipate disagreements and personality conflicts, consider inviting a neutral observer, such as a clergy member, social worker, or family friend who understands the family dynamics. This person is not a decision maker but can try to make sure that all points of view are heard in a respectful way. He or she can also keep the discussion on target and not let it get into a rehash of old family history or perceived injustices. This is not an occasion to debate whether "Mom always loved you best." The goal is not to arrive at a quick decision or to settle old disputes but to reach a consensus, even if that consensus is only an agreement to keep talking.

You also need to consider where to hold the meeting. It may be your home or your parent's, someone else's home, or a different place altogether. Whoever is host should supply plenty of snacks. Alcohol is not a good idea. It does loosen the tongue, but with unpredictable results.

What should be on the agenda?

Unless a crisis has occurred to precipitate the meeting, then present it as a preliminary discussion, not a done deal. You may say to your adult children, for example, "This winter has made it clear to me that I really can't keep up the house and grounds the way I used to. I'm thinking about moving — maybe to assisted living, or maybe just to a smaller house or apartment. I've done a little research, but I want to get your opinions." Or you may say, "Since your father died, I've been really lonely in this big house. I think it's time to make a move, but I'm not sure what to do. I don't want to move in with any of you, but it would be nice to be closer."

To your siblings you may say, "You all know that Mom had a few bad falls recently. Her doctor is concerned that the next one may be even worse. Mom can speak for herself, but she asked me to start the discussion with you. She wants to stay here in the house she has put so much love into and that we all grew up in. But is that the best choice?"

REMEMBER

You probably don't want to follow a formal agenda and parliamentary procedures, but establishing some ground rules is a good idea. Here are some examples:

>> Describe the purpose of the meeting and what you hope to accomplish.

>> Make it clear that everyone will have a chance to speak and that all views are important.

>> Encourage questions and concerns.

>> Let participants know that personal gripes and problems are off-limits.

>> Set a time limit for the meeting. Meetings that go on endlessly are unlikely to resolve issues.

>> Near the end of the designated time, sum up (or ask someone else to do it) and make a list of the issues that need to be resolved, who will gather more information, and when you will meet again.

For example, if the meeting is to discuss a change in your own or your parent's medical condition, and this may mean additional help is needed, you may want the agenda to include the following:

>> A concise description of the medical condition and recommended treatments (it is helpful to have a doctor's summary as well as a plain-language interpretation).

>> Any preliminary research you've conducted. Don't set yourself up as the expert, but try to counter opinions that you know are not based on fact.

>> What the course of treatment will mean in terms of its physical impact on you or your parent and the extra help that will be needed (someone to help with household chores, someone to manage finances, someone to communicate with doctors).

>> Likely length of treatment.

>> Financial implications (what insurance will cover, what will have to be paid for out-of-pocket).

>> What may be down the road, such as the need for full-time help or a move to assisted living.

>> Next steps and who will take on specific tasks.

The most important part of the agenda is not the specific items you put on it, but the nonjudgmental and open-minded atmosphere you create. Even if no decisions are reached, you will have set the stage for further meetings and discussions. All too often a family meeting is something that happens in a hospital, with professionals guiding the discussion, with a focus on end-of-life care or nursing-home placement. Starting the process long before that and on your own terms is better.

REMEMBER

Unless you must make an immediate decision (and you should try to avoid that), one meeting isn't going to resolve the issue. The outcome of the first (and maybe the second and third) meeting should be a good discussion of the possible choices, with unanswered questions put on the table. Everyone should have an opportunity to speak and to be heard. Closing off discussion prematurely only causes problems later. Of course, this is easier said than done in families with a history of poor communication, but that is not a reason to put off meeting.

TIP

Although planning includes consideration of end-of-life issues, such as legal issues and healthcare, in my view it is best to separate these emotion-laden discussions. It is hard to go back and forth between discussing the merits of assisted living and the kinds of treatments one would want in a terminal illness. But both are important, and one can set the stage for the other. Use your judgment and your knowledge of family dynamics to decide where to start.

Being Considerate of Others

It's tempting to think about a plan as all about yourself, or Mom, or Grandma. But in reality most plans affect others, either in implementation or in the ultimate consequences. Be sure to think ahead and include these considerations in the plan.

Time and energy are two big components of helping and are two of the biggest complaints that family helpers have when comparing what they're doing to other family members' contributions. When discussing how a future plan should be laid out, make sure to allocate responsibilities and to keep everyone informed. The following sections go into more detail to help you prevent any pitfalls.

Allocating responsibilities

Knowing who can do what is imperative to making a long-term care plan work.

Making a list of responsibilities

As early as possible, perhaps after the first family meeting, ask each person in the core group to construct a list of what he or she would be able to do to implement the proposed plan. The tasks can be time-limited, such as helping clean out a house, sell or donate unwanted items, and plan a move. It can be long-term, such as providing primary care one day a week, one weekend a month, or some other period. It can be monetary, including paying for home modifications, some home care assistance, or a designated amount for the overall budget. Or it can be an offer to have your parent move in with you or to move in with your parent.

Many people are reluctant to get involved because they fear it will become an overwhelming task, as it surely is if only one person is responsible. Limiting participation to specified contributions — whether they are the person's time or money — is a better way to encourage involvement.

REMEMBER

When you have everyone's lists, compare them and see whether tasks are self-allocated in a generally fair and workable way. The goal is not to arrive at an exactly equal division of labor or financial contributions; this is not like dividing a pizza pie. Rather the goal is a fair distribution of participation, one that considers the different participants' other responsibilities, assets, locations, and other factors. Some people will draw the line at personal care; others cannot afford to contribute as much money as the more affluent members of the group. Everyone should be at least comfortable with the result. And the main person — you or your parent — should also feel that this arrangement is acceptable.

It is possible, and maybe even likely, that the preliminary allocation of tasks doesn't work for some reason — everyone wants the same job, for example, and some jobs are not spoken for. In that case, time limits may be helpful — "If you do the transportation this month, I'll do it next month, and we can work out a schedule after that." Or some jobs may require paid help. Better to spend some money to hire someone, if you can afford to, than to leave the job undone or done by an unwilling person. And in some families, there are people who just won't do anything; they may give a reason or they may not. Perhaps a private conversation with these people to try to understand what is going on — which may not have anything to do with the issue at hand — will result in some cooperation. Or it may not. Whatever the outcome, if these people are or should be in the inner circle (siblings, for example), keep them informed about all medical updates, financial decisions, and other key factors. Many good plans have been derailed by a family member who claims, "Nobody told me what was going on."

Of course, as time goes on and needs change, the agreement may have to be revisited. But if the concept of sharing is clearly embedded in the arrangement, changes are more likely to be negotiable. Sharing is a concept we are taught as children; it is just as important in later years.

Taking on financial responsibility

Whoever has the responsibility of dealing with financial affairs should understand the seriousness of this task. It is more than paying monthly bills and balancing a checkbook. It involves keeping detailed records of how the money is being spent. This may seem unnecessary in families with good relationships, but it is prudent in every case. Work with an accountant or another financial adviser, if feasible, to set up a way to record income and outlays. Major financial decisions, like taking out a reverse mortgage or buying an annuity, should be discussed with the core family group. (See Chapter 12.)

The will should be up-to-date and its provisions shared openly with the core group. The names of the person who is designated as healthcare proxy and the alternate should also be shared. The point of all this record-keeping and sharing of information is not to sow seeds of distrust. In fact, it is the opposite. When everything is in the open, people are less likely to mutter about where the money is going and who may be taking advantage of the situation.

Being the medical record keeper

If one person is designated to accompany you or your parent to the doctor and to monitor health conditions, that person should also share important information with the core group. If possible, get permission to share this information. All members of the core group do not need to know every test result or blood-pressure reading, but they do need to know about major changes or problems. Without this ongoing medical information, others won't understand the severity of an illness or a cognitive decline. Many family disagreements about end-of-life decisions start from inadequate information much earlier during the illness. Partly this problem comes from some doctors' unwillingness to give bad news, but the person closest to the situation may also be reluctant to accept or share this bad news.

Timely sharing of medical information can also inform discussions of palliative care and hospice and make it more likely that these options are instituted early enough to make a real difference in care.

TIP

If you are a family member, a healthcare professional may say to you, "I can't tell you that because of HIPAA." First, HIPAA (the federal Health Information Portability and Accountability Act) does not prevent a healthcare provider from sharing relevant medical information with a person who is involved in providing, managing, or paying for care if the patient does not object. So, if you are the person in the hospital or at the appointment, make sure that you have made it clear who has permission to receive medical information. Also make clear any people you do not want to have this information. It is essential for good care that everyone knows what to do, why it is important, and what to look out for. For more information, see the Next Step in Care guide at www.nextstepincare.org/Caregiver_Home/HIPAA/.

Bringing in the outer circle

Friends and family members not in the core group can play an important role when you need help. They can run errands, shop for food, cook or bring meals, provide transportation, and do a million other things that need to be done but are hard to fit into a busy primary caregiver's life. Most of all, these people can do what they are best at doing: spending time, revisiting the past, talking about current events, taking walks, watching television, playing cards, listening to audiobooks, or doing whatever both people enjoy.

REMEMBER

In moving to an assisted-living facility, keeping in touch with people from the old neighborhood or community can be important for health and happiness. Many people have difficulty making friends in a new setting, and some assisted-living residents are reluctant to start new friendships because they anticipate that the time together may be short. It is comforting to see old friends and to introduce them to the new people in your new home. They may have a lot in common.

TIP

Many people in the outer circle will want to help, but putting goodwill and time together can be a chore in itself. Two websites have systems for organizing the outer circle:

>> **Lotsa Helping Hands** (www.lotsahelpinghands.com) has tools and calendars to help organize volunteers.

>> **Share the Care** (https://sharethecare.org) has a handbook and advice about starting a group in your community.

You can also create your own system through a designated website or other means.

For the outer circle, it is important to set limits on what is expected and acceptable and what is not. For example, if someone who comes to read to your parent should cancel, that's a disappointment, not a major problem. But if that person has volunteered to take your parent to a doctor's appointment, that's a different level of responsibility. Have a list of alternates, but if someone cancels frequently, don't ask that person to do an essential task.

WARNING

To be a member of the outer circle in good standing, people should accept the basic terms of the plan you have developed. Friends may think they are helping by criticizing the way the primary caregiver or the home care aide does things, or by telling you that they have read about a miracle drug that will get you back on your feet in no time, or even an investment that will guarantee an amazing return. This is the kind of help you do not need. People who undermine relationships or care systems are using a vulnerable person's needs as an opportunity to display their often-misguided expertise. Put them into the outer, outer circle.

Dealing with Conflict

Family conflict is at the heart of the world's great literature, from the Bible to the present. Think of King Lear. How much better off he would have been had he discussed his plans for divesting his kingdom with his daughters instead of royally announcing his decision. Few families today have a kingdom at stake, but sometimes high drama can come from very small stakes.

Mediators and counselors

If, after all your preparations and forethought, conflict cannot be resolved, it may be time to call in a mediator or counselor. This person can be a professional; clergy, social workers, psychologists, and family therapists all have training on how to handle conflict. It is important that the person be, and be seen by all as, an objective adviser, not someone hired to convince the others to agree to a plan.

Some mediation techniques are the same as I discuss earlier for holding a family meeting. They include setting ground rules for discussion (no negative personal comments, no interrupting, and time limits). Talk about feelings is allowed, but only using "I" statements. That is, "I felt left out of the discussion," not "You left me out of the discussion."

Sometimes individual counseling can help someone deal with the situation itself and the conflict it has engendered. Often these conflicts have roots in childhood or adolescence. Although you may feel that you have moved on and no longer feel these old hurts, they sustain surprising power over time.

Consensus and compromise

When a family is totally at odds over some issue, whatever the ultimate decision, there should be no winners and losers. If the process has further alienated some family members and made it less likely that there will be a meeting of minds — much less a meeting in person — then everyone loses. And witnessing family fights can be detrimental to younger family members, even to children, who may not understand just what all the unpleasantness is about.

REMEMBER

When conflict erupts, as it often does, try to keep the animosity level low. Everyone will have to live with the decision, often for years, as well as their behavior during the conflict. It is about long-term care, after all, and that may mean a very long time. The goal should be consensus and compromise, not victory.

2

Choosing Where to Live

Evaluate how you can modify your home for safety and accessibility so that you can stay where you are for as long as you like.

Consider the many aspects, including finances and privacy, that make multigenerational living a success or failure.

Look at all the objects you have accumulated and start the process of downsizing, which can improve your quality of life now and ease moving later.

Find out what independent living, assisted living, and other forms of community living can offer you.

Use guides and checklists to help you evaluate your community. A lot of your quality of life depends on what community resources are available.

Consider transportation alternatives that can keep you connected to friends, family, and the community. Discover the signs to watch for to determine when it's time to stop driving.

IN THIS CHAPTER

» Remaining in your home in your community

» Preventing falls and burns

» Making a home safe and accessible

» Lining up people to help in the home

» Planning for bad weather and other emergencies

Chapter **5**

Staying in Your Home

Studies show that most people want to stay in their current homes. But modifications may be necessary to accommodate changing needs, and you may need people and services to help with many tasks that you or your parents are no longer able or willing to do.

In this chapter, I guide you through some of the options available for home modification and obtaining outside help. I also review plans you should have in place to prepare the house and your family for a disaster such as a hurricane or flood or a more common event such as a power outage.

Staying at Home in Your Community

The common desire to stay in the same home is often called "aging in place." This is a term most often used by professionals and policymakers, although not by older adults themselves. It may be misunderstood as being unable to leave your home or having other negative implications. When people say they want to stay at home, they often are thinking not only of their physical home but also their familiar surroundings.

When you think of staying in your home, think, too, of your community. In fact, the federal Centers for Disease Control and Prevention (CDC) has a broad and complicated definition of aging in place: "the ability to live in one's own home and community safely, independently, and comfortably, regardless of age, income, or ability level." This definition adds conditions to the circumstances under which aging in place should occur. The person has to meet all three conditions: be safe, comfortable, and able to live independently. Living independently may mean living alone without any outside help, or it may mean living alone only if outside help is available. The critical element is being able to choose what you do and when you do it.

Sometimes these conditions conflict. The home may be quite comfortable but not safe. Or the home may be safe, but only with help. Or all those conditions may be met, but you or your parents don't have enough income or assets to support the arrangement.

The CDC's definition also includes living in your community. This adds another layer of complexity. What exactly is a community? What if the home is safe but the neighborhood is not? What if the person doesn't have a community of people nearby who are able to help as needed? Living alone shouldn't mean living in isolation. What seems to be a straightforward definition turns out to be complicated. You can do a lot to make sure all these elements are in place, but some things are beyond any individual's control.

This chapter focuses on ensuring that the home is safe and comfortable and on accessing home-based or local services routinely and in emergencies. I save larger issues related to the community and options for community-based services for Chapter 9.

Dealing with Two Major Hazards

An important first step in deciding whether staying in the same home can work is taking a hard look at the home. Looking past a cherished home's attractive features and focusing on its flaws and hazards can be hard to do. Having someone with fresh eyes with you as you survey the premises can be helpful, preferably someone with experience in home modification for older people, such as a physical or occupational therapist, a geriatric care manager, or a contractor who has done similar jobs.

REMEMBER

If you're trying to improve the home for a relative, be aware that older people often downplay concerns about safety and resist change. Be tactful but firm. Safety is not the only issue, but it is a prerequisite for enjoying a good quality of life.

Falls and burns aren't the only sources of injury at home, but if you address them, you'll likely prevent other kinds of injury as well.

Preventing falls

Your first priority should be preventing falls. Falls are among the most common accidents in homes. Older people are at risk for falls because keeping your balance as you age is more difficult, and it's harder to readjust your feet to regain your balance if you slip. Arthritis can limit your range of motion. Many older people suffer bone loss, or osteoporosis. Hips are the most likely joints to be injured because people tend to fall on their sides.

Falls are often the first step in a cascade of decline that ends up with a hospital stay and eventual placement in a nursing home or death. Fortunately, many fall-prevention measures are easy to take and are not expensive.

Here's a checklist for falls prevention adapted from the National Center for Injury Prevention and Control, a division of the CDC. The full list is available at `www.cdc.gov/steadi/pdf/check_for_safety_brochure-a.pdf`. Another valuable CDC publication for family caregivers is available at `www.cdc.gov/steadi/pdf/STEADI_CaregiverBrochure-a.pdf`.

>> **Floors:**

- When you walk through a room, do you have to walk around furniture? If so, make a clear path by moving the furniture.

- Are there throw rugs on the floor? If so, remove them or use double-sided tape or a nonslip backing.

- Are there papers, books, towels, shoes, magazines, boxes, or blankets on the floor? Pick them up and keep them off the floor.

- Do you have to walk over or around wires or cords (like lamp, telephone, or extension cords)? Coil or tape cords and wires next to the wall. You may need an electrician to put in another outlet.

>> **Stairs and steps:**

- Are shoes, papers, or other objects on the stairs? Remove them.

- Are some steps broken or uneven? Have them repaired.

- Does the stairway have a light? An electrician should install an overhead light and light switch at the top and bottom of the stairs. (Use an energy-saving type of light bulb so it doesn't need to be changed as often.)

- If there's carpet on the stairs, make sure it's firmly attached to every step.

- Make sure that handrails are not loose or broken and that they're on both sides of the stairs.

- To make seeing the stairs easier, paint a contrasting color on the top edge of all the steps. For example, use a light color paint on dark wood.

» Kitchen:

- Are often-used items on high shelves? Move them to lower shelves (about waist level).

- Is your step stool unsteady? If you must use a step stool, get one with a bar for support. Never use a chair as a step stool.

» Bathroom:

- Tubs and shower floors are often slippery. Put a nonslip rubber mat or self-stick strips on the floor.

- Install grab bars inside the tub and next to the toilet. Make sure you have this done by someone who knows how to place them correctly and securely. The screws should be installed in the studs in the wall, not in the tiles, or the grab bar will pull loose.

HANDLING CLUTTER AND HOARDING

Your survey of the home may have uncovered an unpleasant secret. Perhaps unread newspapers and magazines have accumulated, the refrigerator is full of rotting food, or the cats have taken over the bathroom. This behavior is not just difficult to look at, but it also can be a fire and safety hazard. Some of this accumulation is clutter. Bending down to pick up papers may be difficult for a person with arthritis, or a person with vision problems may not be able to read the sell-by date on foods. But sometimes the accumulation of stuff rises to the level of hoarding, which is a more serious problem.

Hoarding interferes with ordinary life by making it impossible to use the space as intended and impedes access in an emergency. You may be tempted to overlook the problem because one good cleaning would get rid of the worst of the mess. But it's not something that should be ignored, and if you get rid of the piles of what you call junk and your relative considers priceless, he or she will only refill the space as quickly as possible.

There are many theories about what causes this kind of behavior, which may be related to depression, anxiety, prior losses, or other mental-health issues. Hoarding is one manifestation of obsessive compulsive disorder (OCD). Dealing with hoarding requires consultation with experienced mental-health and home-organizing professionals who can negotiate the cleanup in nonjudgmental ways. A useful article prepared by the University of California-San Francisco is available at scienceofcaring.ucsf.edu/health-public/recognizing-and-addressing-hoarding-significant-senior-health-concern. Another resource is the International OCD Foundation at hoarding.iocdf.org.

>> **Bedroom:**

- Is the light near the bed hard to reach? Make sure a sturdy lamp is close to the bed.

- Is the path from the bed to the bathroom dark? Put in a night-light, preferably one that turns itself on after dark.

Preventing burns

Burns are a common problem in the home. Even a minor burn can lead to infection and serious consequences. Older people literally have thinner skin that's more susceptible to scalding from hot water or burns from electrical appliances. To keep older people safe from burns at home, make sure that you:

>> Replace electrical cords that are broken or cracked.

>> Replace electronic devices, heaters, or appliances that overheat, spark, or smoke.

>> Use a power strip rather than an extension cord.

>> Keep electrical appliances away from water.

>> Unplug small appliances such as toaster ovens and coffeepots when not in use.

>> Keep a three-foot zone of safety around the stove, oven, and microwave.

>> Use microwave-safe cookware.

>> Set the water temperature to a maximum of 120 degrees Fahrenheit (this may be a job for a plumber or apartment building staff).

>> Use a humidifier that sprays cool mist rather than hot steam.

>> Have smoke alarms installed and change the batteries twice a year. You can use changes to and from daylight saving time as your reminder.

WARNING

Smoking in bed is still a common cause of fires. Do everything you can to prevent this dangerous habit.

A comprehensive brochure with guidelines for preventing burns from the Hearst Burn Center at New York Presbyterian Hospital is available at nyp.org/pdf/burn_center/Burn_Safety_Prevention_Older_Adults_englishWEB.pdf.

Modifying a Home

When you've completed your safety checklist and made all the easy fixes and repairs, you may find that problem areas still exist. Some may be unsafe conditions, but others may be barriers that make it difficult for you or your relative to move about freely and to enjoy the comforts of home that make him want to stay put in the first place. This section covers modifications that can be made to an aging person's current home to allow him to continue his present living arrangement.

TIP

For more information on this topic, check out the AARP HomeFit Guide Downloads, Worksheets, and Resources at www.aarp.org/livable-communities/info-2014/home-fit-resources-worksheets.html.

Categorizing types of home modifications

Many houses and apartment buildings were constructed before universal design features were common or in some cases required by guidelines for remodeling and new construction under the Americans with Disabilities Act (ADA), passed in 1990. Ramps in public places, doors marked for wheelchair entrance, and buses with lifts and special seating for people with disabilities have become so common that they are scarcely noticed (unless of course you're the person with a disability who needs these accommodations). Yet the need for similar accommodations in private homes is less visible although equally important.

The Rehabilitation Engineering and Assistive Technology Society of North America (RESNA) puts home modifications into three categories:

>> **Accessibility:** Accessibility modifications allow a person in a wheelchair or with disabilities to move easily throughout a structure, such as with widened doorways, lowered countertops and sinks, grab bars in the tub or shower, and light switches and electrical outlets at waist height.

>> **Adaptability:** Adaptability covers changes that can be made more quickly, without having to completely redesign the home or use different materials for essential fixtures.

>> **Universal design:** These features are usually built into a home, including appliances, floor plans, and fixtures that are flexible, sturdy, reliable, and easy for all people to use. A guide to universal design can be found at universaldesign. ie/What-is-Universal-Design/The-7-Principles/7-Principals-.pdf.

These categories are important because they involve different levels of planning, implementation, and cost. For example, adapting a home is the least complicated type of modification. Grab bars and outdoor ramps are examples. Making a home accessible, however, may involve structural changes and complying with building code and ADA requirements. Universal design may come into play when you are completely remodeling a home or building a new space.

Checking out accessibility

General home safety issues (see the earlier section "Dealing with Two Major Hazards") are important for all older people living on their own. But other specific features can make the home easy to use — or not — for people who have disabilities or are aging. Start in the kitchen and bathroom and think about the particular problems you or your parent may face in accessibility:

» Are cabinet knobs or pulls easy to use? Pulls are generally considered easier to use than knobs.

» Are stove controls easy to use and clearly marked?

» Are faucets easy to use? Universal design faucets have one lever, not two knobs to turn. This makes mixing hot and cold water easier.

» Can the oven and refrigerator doors be opened easily? Is the freezer easy to reach?

» Is the kitchen counter height and depth convenient? Most kitchen counters are too high for a person in a wheelchair.

» Is there room to move around the bathroom and a place to put towels and shampoo in easy reach?

» Is the shower faucet easy to use? Turning on the shower and getting the right temperature can be difficult. A new showerhead or faucets may be needed.

» Does the height of the toilet seat make getting up difficult? A raised seat may help.

In closets and storage spaces, check the following:

» Does the closet contain items that have just been put there to get them out of sight? Move them so that the closet is easier to access for coats, hats, umbrellas, and boots.

» Can items in the closet, like a coat on a hanger, be removed and replaced easily?

» Can the use of storage space be improved with closet shelf systems?

Doors and windows may need the following updates:

>> Are the doors wide enough to accommodate a walker or wheelchair? The standard for a wheelchair is 36 inches. Most door openings are narrower.

>> Are the doors and windows easy to open and close?

>> Are the door locks sturdy and easy to operate?

Evaluate the electrical outlets and safety devices:

>> Are electrical outlets easy to reach?

>> Is the area around outlets free of clutter?

>> Are the outlets properly grounded to prevent shock?

>> Can you hear the doorbell in every room?

>> Is the telephone readily available for emergencies? A land line may be more reliable in an emergency than a cellphone.

>> Is there an alarm system? If so, is it easy to use? If not, consider whether one is needed.

TIP

The preceding information is only a partial list. The University of Southern California Leonard Davis School of Gerontology has an extensive resource list at `https://homemods.org/resources/`. Also see the AARP HomeFit Guide for a questionnaire to help you plan when you remodel: `www.aarp.org/content/dam/aarp/livable-communities/documents-2015/HomeFit2015/01%20Is%20My%20Home%20HomeFit.pdf`. One part of the HomeFit guide has suggestions for remodeling for people with vision, strength, and mobility problems.

Some items that need correcting can be done by you or a friend or family member, but if you have determined that major changes are necessary — for example, widening doorways or replacing kitchen cabinets or appliances — you probably need to find a contractor to tackle the modifications. Head to the next section for advice on finding the right person for the job.

TIP

Remodeling is a messy and often frustrating experience. The first phase, demolition — even if it's limited to one room or area — is unsettling. Delays are common. It may be a good idea to move your relative to another setting while the work is being done, especially if you expect a lot of dust, noise, and disruption.

Finding a contractor

How do you find a reliable and knowledgeable contractor? If you have already worked with a contractor and were pleased with the results, then you have a head start. Ask this person to go over the problem areas with you, suggest fixes, estimate the cost, and tell you how long it will take to do the work.

TIP

Most people with accessible homes have neither built their own houses nor undergone extensive remodeling. Ask for recommendations from friends or neighbors who have had similar work done. Check online referral sites for recommendations. Then ask a few contractors for estimates and for people to call for references. Some home builders work with certified aging-in-place specialists, a program developed in partnership with AARP. Visit www.aarp.org/livable-communities/info-2014/7-steps-to-hiring-a-contractor.html for worksheets and more information.

Before hiring a contractor, check with the local Chamber of Commerce or other agency to see whether any complaints have been filed against the company. Make sure the contractor is licensed to perform the work and can obtain any building permits required. Finally, ask for a written agreement that stipulates a small down payment and schedule of payments, with the final payment to be made only when the work is completed and approved.

WARNING

A frequent scam carried out against older people occurs when a "contractor" scans a neighborhood for a likely target and offers to do needed (or unneeded) repairs or home modifications. The person asks for a large down payment and either disappears or does only a token amount of work. If you're thinking of home modifications for older relatives, be sure to warn them about this scam.

WARNING

Attempting any major repairs, especially if they involve climbing ladders or using power tools, is dangerous. Some people want to save a few bucks by doing the jobs themselves, but they need to be reminded that the cost upfront is much less than the aftereffects of being injured.

REMEMBER

If you or your relative lives in an apartment building or housing complex, you need to contact the management to make some changes, particularly in corridors and stairways and even within the apartment itself. Co-op or condo residents may be required to obtain approval from their governing board too.

Getting help paying for home modifications

TIP

Many home modifications, such as ramps and lighting replacements, are relatively inexpensive. But when you start widening doors and installing new kitchen equipment like a refrigerator with side-by-side doors, the costs add up. In the bathroom, installing a roll-in shower can be costly although important for someone who cannot move from wheelchair to tub. Eldercare Locator, a federal agency funded by the Administration for Aging (AoA), suggests these resources for financial assistance:

>> Some funds for home repair may be available through Title III of the Older Americans Act. They are distributed through the local Area Agency on Aging (AAA). You can find your nearest AAA by calling Eldercare Locator at 800-677-1116 or going online at https://eldercare.acl.gov/Public/Index.aspx. These funds are likely to be limited, however, and best suited for relatively small jobs.

>> Rebuilding Together, Inc., a national volunteer organization dedicated to assisting low-income seniors, may be able to direct you to a local affiliate. You can contact it at www.rebuildingtogether.org.

>> Some types of home modification — those determined to be medically necessary — may be covered by Medicaid (for eligible low-income people), depending on the state you live in. For example, a roll-in bathtub or shower for a person in a wheelchair may be covered. A doctor's order may be required, and some Medicaid programs limit eligibility to certain diagnoses or ages. Check with your state's Medicaid office for details.

>> If the home is mortgaged and has substantial equity, a home equity loan may be available from the bank. However, this loan will increase the mortgage payment.

REMEMBER

Whether major improvements and their associated costs will substantially improve your or your relative's safety and quality of life is a personal decision. You may decide that aging in place is not really feasible after all and that a move to assisted living or another setting is the best choice (see Chapter 8). If you do decide to stay, going through the important process of evaluating the home and making those small changes that can prevent accidents will make it much safer.

NOT COVERED UNDER MEDICARE

Don't look to Medicare for help in covering remodeling costs. According to the Medicare Rights Center, a national nonprofit organization at www.medicarerights.org, "Medicare will never cover home modifications (like the installation of a stair lift or grab bars near the toilet or tub) or assistive devices (like large-button telephones or flashing doorbell signals for the hard-of-hearing)." However, the services of an occupational therapist to teach a person how to use the devices or modifications may be covered.

Seeking Help at Home

Creating a safe and comfortable environment is only one factor in staying in your home. Many older adults need at least some help at home. Some people need just a little assistance with transportation and shopping, for example, while others need a lot of help with personal care such as bathing and dressing. People with complex chronic conditions usually need help with managing medications, operating medical equipment, monitoring symptoms, and similar tasks. In the following sections, I help you consider whether family members can provide those important services or whether you need to consider hiring trained professionals.

Allocating tasks to family

At least 80 percent of assistance at home is provided by unpaid family members. A first step for providing help at home is to allocate tasks to family members and/ or friends. Talk to them to find out who's available and willing to help and what limitations they have. If several cooperative family members are involved, the tasks can be divided. One person may be able to spend several afternoons a week shopping and preparing meals, while another can manage medications and doctor visits. A friend may be able to pick up prescriptions from the pharmacy or drive to religious services.

Drawing a CareMap (see Chapter 2) will give you a snapshot of all the people in your life who can help and the services they can provide. Don't forget to add the friends who say, "Just call me if you need help." When given a specific task, they may be quite happy to help.

TIP

When you arrange a plan for allocated tasks, make (or have someone help you make) a master list of family helpers, their phone numbers, their tasks, and the schedule. Put the list in an easy-to-find place, such as on the refrigerator, to help the person being assisted remember who is coming when. Also be sure to distribute the list to family and helpers so everyone knows what tasks are being taken care of.

REMEMBER

Community-based agencies such as volunteer groups, social-service agencies, and faith-based groups have services that are often helpful. These arrangements can be complicated, but if everyone is willing to be flexible, the necessary tasks can be accomplished. Chapter 20 offers some guidance for family caregivers in these situations.

Searching for services

When family members and friends can't provide all the help that is needed, paid home health or companion services provided by agencies or hired privately can fill the gaps. One factor in your decision to stay in your home may be the availability — and affordability — of these services. Home care comes in many varieties and from many different sources.

REMEMBER

Medicare (Original Medicare and Medicare Advantage plans), Medicaid, private health insurance, and long-term care insurance have their own rules and criteria for providing services. Some people are covered by more than one policy. Chapter 15 covers the details of home care services and working with insurance plans, but as an introduction, here are a few key points to remember:

>> Medicare home healthcare is intended to be part-time or intermittent (not constant). The goal, according to Medicare, "is to provide treatment for an illness or injury." The Medicare home health benefit "pays for you to get certain healthcare services in your home if you meet certain eligibility criteria and if the services are considered reasonable and necessary for the treatment of your illness or injury." See www.medicare.gov/coverage/home-health-services.html for more information.

To be eligible for this benefit, you must have a need for skilled nursing — that is, the kind of care provided by a nurse or physical therapist. Personal care provided by an aide is included only when this need exists.

>> Medicaid for low-income people provides long-term home healthcare, including aide services, but eligibility and availability vary by state. Many states have created Medicaid Managed Long-Term Care plans (MMLTC), which are implemented by private companies.

>> Private employer-based insurance generally follows Medicare rules.

>> Home care services are generally available through long-term care insurance but vary by policy, and there may be waiting periods and other limitations.

>> Hiring workers privately is also an option that gives you more flexibility but also more responsibility.

Having reliable, competent, and friendly home care workers can make a big difference in someone's ability to age in place, but working out a suitable arrangement takes time and effort — and often money.

Finding help for other chores

In addition to family, friends, and paid home care workers, you may need additional help in taking care of pets, maintaining the yard, cleaning the gutters, and all the other chores that become difficult to do. If these regular maintenance tasks aren't taken care of regularly, the home can quickly deteriorate, leading to safety problems as well as expensive repairs. Serious problems, such as a leaking roof or frozen water pipes, can create havoc. Chores that involve climbing, shoveling, heavy lifting, and other strenuous activities are best done by someone younger and stronger.

TIP

Some community agencies and religious organizations have volunteers who will help with these chores. Ask the organizations you belong to or senior centers for suggestions. Local schools or universities may also have community service programs for students. Some heavy or risky chores should be performed only by trained workers. If you hire people to help, make sure that they give references and do the job competently.

Putting technology to use

Technology is all around us, and *assistive technology* — devices and adaptations that are designed to help people who are aging or have disabilities function independently — can make a big difference in a person's ability to stay at home safely. Assistive devices come in all sizes and shapes and can be cheap or very costly. Earlier in this chapter, I mention some common assistive devices — grab bars, handrails, and raised toilet seats. Other common devices are hand-friendly tools for opening jars or gardening, TV remote controls with big numbers, and Personal Emergency Response Systems (PERS), the kind immortalized and satirized in the TV commercial, "I've fallen, and I can't get up!" In the healthcare world, telehealth — distance monitoring of chronic conditions like daily weight checks on a person with heart failure — is growing, especially in rural areas.

How far you're willing to go to bring assistive devices into your life is a personal choice. Inventors and investors have identified people staying at home (and their adult children) as a huge market for these products. The products include mattresses that sense every movement and can relay information about how many times the person gets up to go to the bathroom or the kitchen, monitors that track a person's movements in the home, and GPS devices that can locate a person with dementia if she wanders. A robot that can make a bed, cook a meal, and even carry on a conversation is not yet on the market, but if there is a demand, it will certainly be produced. The movie *Robot & Frank,* which described an aging man's reluctant adaptation to a robot, is a fantasy, but fantasies are sometimes early glimpses of reality.

Buying an assistive device is only the first step. You have to learn how to use it and perhaps teach an older adult or an aide how to use it. Some devices that seem simple are not. For example, a cane is probably the most common assistive device. Yet it should be the right length and used on the correct side of the body. (*Hint:* It's not the side where the pain or injury is.) And as you move up the scale toward devices with moving parts and controls to set, the need increases for adequate instruction and someone to call when there are problems. Constant monitoring means constant responses, most of which will turn out to be false alarms. If you're the responder, it can become all too easy to ignore that flashing red light or annoying beep.

Looking for technological solutions to the problems of aging overlooks a basic human need for contact with other people. And while technological devices offer to provide peace of mind, the devices themselves can fail and at best require someone to respond whether there is a real emergency or just a faulty sensor. That in itself can be a major responsibility.

TIP

Consider assistive devices, but focus on the ones that will make a difference and that don't add burdens to your life. AbleData.com (www.abledata.acl.gov), a project of the National Institute for Disability and Rehabilitation Research, has information about products and resources.

Preparing for an Emergency

Disasters happen — hurricanes, floods, heat waves, blizzards, tornadoes, fires, power outages, building collapses, acts of terrorism. An aging person, even one who can live safely at home in ordinary circumstances, is particularly vulnerable when the home environment is threatened and when water, power, gas, or telephone service is interrupted. People who live alone are at particular risk, especially if they are isolated from their neighbors or community agencies. Quite simply, they are more likely to die because nobody checks up on them because no one knows who they are.

Fortunately, disasters are relatively rare, but they can be catastrophic. Preparing for these events is no guarantee but can make the chances of survival and safety much greater.

TIP

Preparing for a disaster is a major part of staying safely in the home. The Federal Emergency Management Association (FEMA) and the Red Cross have lists of ways to prepare, which you can see at www.ready.gov/make-a-plan and www.redcross.org/prepare/location/home-family.

Creating a support network

The first step is to create a personal support network, a list of people and agencies you or your parent can call on for help in an emergency. The list should include preferably three people, and each one should know what particular problems you or your parent may have, such as getting down stairs if there is no elevator. If a home care agency is providing workers in your or your relative's home, the agency should know about the emergency plan. The members of the support network should live or work close to the older person, and they should know who the other people on the list are and how to reach them. Communication in an emergency is often disrupted, and the more people who are in contact, the more likely help will be forthcoming.

You should also find out what agency to contact in your community — it may be the police, the fire department, a special disaster hotline, or some other place. Some agencies have lists of people with special needs. Of course, none of this guarantees that you will be at the head of the line if evacuation is necessary, but it certainly doesn't hurt.

TIP

If you or your parent lives in apartment building or housing complex, let the management or superintendent know that in case of an emergency, you would need certain help (backup oxygen supplies, for example). Many buildings keep lists of people with special needs (and their pets) just for that reason. Some communities suggest that people with disabilities or age-related problems register with the local fire department or police station.

Making an emergency plan

REMEMBER

FEMA and the Red Cross advise people to create an emergency plan that includes the following:

>> **A location for you and your relative to meet:** This spot may be right outside the home, if it's safe, or in a more distant location. Finding each other in a disaster can be difficult without a destination. Generally, community centers and schools are the most easily identified meeting places. If your community has designated shelters for emergencies, those are good places to reconnect.

>> **Contact information for family members, members of the support team, home care aides, and others:** Your list should include all the people who are part of your daily or weekly life. Make sure that you have cellphone numbers and alternate ways to reach them. Keep a copy of the list where it is easy for you to find, and give a copy to all the people on the list so that they can get in touch with each other.

>> **Escape routes and safe places:** Knowing how to get out of a building safely and quickly is essential in some kinds of emergencies. Just as a flight attendant informs passengers to identify the nearest emergency exit (which may be behind you), identifying the safest way to get out of a home is essential. There may be specific instructions for some types of emergencies, such as going to the basement or a closet with no windows in case of a tornado warning.

>> **A plan for pets:** Take them if you must leave, but be aware that emergency shelters may not be able to accommodate them. The support network should include someone who can board the pets temporarily.

Power outages are not as dramatic as major disasters when evacuation is necessary, but they are more common and can create serious risks. It's not just that the lights are out and the TV doesn't work; toilets can't be flushed and food in the refrigerator may spoil. Here are a few tips:

>> If electricity is needed to operate home medical equipment, have a backup system ready to use.

>> Find out whether your electricity provider has a registry for people who depend on power for medical equipment. You may be able to be placed on a list for expedited repairs.

>> Have several working flashlights on hand as well as extra batteries.

>> Don't use candles.

>> Fill the bathtub with water so that if the power goes out, there will be water to flush the toilet.

>> Keep the refrigerator door closed.

>> Keep a land line; it may work in storms when cellphone service isn't available. And keep your cellphone charged. If possible, have both lines available to call for help or to check on service restoration.

For more tips, see the American Red Cross brochure "Disaster Preparedness For Seniors By Seniors," prepared by 12 seniors in Rochester, New York, after their experiences during a two-week power outage. It is available at `www.redcross.org/images/MEDIA_CustomProductCatalog/m4640086_Disaster_Preparedness_for_Srs-English.revised_7-09.pdf`.

Putting together a disaster kit

A key part of a disaster plan is preparing a kit of essential items that can be easily located and taken with you. The basic items can include but are not limited to:

>> Bottled water and nonperishable food items

>> Flashlight and extra batteries

>> Battery-powered radio

>> First-aid kit and manual

>> Photocopies of health insurance and other identification cards

>> Prescription medications, eyeglasses, and hearing-aid batteries

>> Sanitation and hygiene items (moist towelettes, toilet paper)

>> Clothing appropriate for the climate

REMEMBER

Both the kit and the plan discussed in the preceding section should be reviewed regularly and changed if needed.

Chapter **6**

Under One Roof: Generations Living Together

Remember the Waltons, the large fictional family from the 1970s TV show? Whatever struggles they faced in an isolated rural community in the Great Depression of the 1930s, their strong three-generation family ties saw them through. Viewers saw multigenerational living through a lens of nostalgia and loved it.

An option for families is to mimic the Waltons and consider living together as part of a long-term arrangement. (If your family can't get through Thanksgiving dinner without hurt feelings or an argument, then this chapter may not be for you.) Multigenerational living is becoming more common, and it can work. But it takes considerable thought, planning, and negotiation. Some of the aspects you have to consider are space, money, and personal boundaries. This chapter guides you through the key decision points.

Multigenerational Living: Everything Old Is New Again

If you were born after 1940, you probably grew up in a nuclear family: mother, father, 2.3 children. Maybe grandparents or other relatives lived nearby but not under the same roof. Although the nuclear family seemed the norm for middle-class Americans, it was actually an aberration lasting only a few decades. For most of human history, family members of all ages lived together, and they continue to do so in much of the world. In the United States, large social and economic changes have not only redefined family — think of blended families, same-sex marriages, and children born to surrogate mothers — but have also revived multigenerational living with some modern adaptations.

Why different generations are living together

Each family is different and has its own story, but several reasons contribute to the appeal of generations living together.

TECHNICAL STUFF

Economics is probably the major driver of multigenerational living. Unemployment, loss of housing, credit card debt — all the uncertainties of a changing economy have driven many families together to share resources and space.

Another reason to share a home is the changing needs of aging relatives. Living together can alleviate the strain on family caregivers who must maintain their own home and that of a parent or other relative. The needs of older people who can't live safely by themselves often can be addressed more easily and economically in a shared household than if they lived in a separate home. And as an advantage for the younger generations in the home, older people can contribute to the household economy and help with some tasks, particularly child care. These arrangements may especially benefit children as they get to know their grandparents intimately and not just on holidays and visits. The whole family may grow much closer as a result of the shared experiences. But these positive outcomes are not guaranteed and do require effort and patience.

On the flip side, prolonged education and poor job prospects have created the *Boomerang Generation,* young people who have not established households of their own and have returned to feather their parents' formerly empty nest. This generation includes those who have married and divorced, or who had children while unmarried, and move home with the grandchildren in tow. This way, younger people have a place to live, can establish themselves financially, and can help their aging parents at the same time.

As immigration from Asia and Latin America to the United States has increased, cultural traditions from these regions have encouraged families to live together just as immigrants of earlier generations from Eastern and Southern Europe did. For some families, the arrangement is a matter of economics. For others, the older generation may not speak English well and may need assistance in many areas, especially healthcare. Many want to live in multigenerational families because they value older generations' wisdom and traditions. Although living together across generations is a cultural norm for many, it is not without problems as the younger generation takes on more Americanized habits and beliefs. Many people who grew up in these multicultural, multigenerational households were enriched by the experience but also felt conflicted about their desires to be independent and successful in a different culture. Remember that not everyone who comes from a cultural or ethnic background follows the same beliefs and practices, including a preference for multigenerational living.

Defining family households by generation

The Pew Research Center, which studies social and demographic trends, identifies several different types of households. Which one describes your family now and which one would describe it if you all lived together?

» **One generation:** A one-generation household consists of people of the same age group: a married or cohabiting couple, a single person, siblings, or roommates. These people are not necessarily young. A married couple may be in their 80s, and older siblings may live together.

» **Two generations:** A two-generation family household includes a parent or parents and their child or children under age 25. It may include stepchildren from different marriages. A two-generation household can also be made up of a person over 60 and a parent in his or her 80s or 90s.

» **Multigenerational:** A multigenerational household can include

- **Two generations:** Parents or in-laws and adult children (or children-in-law) age 25 and older; either generation can "head" the household.

- **Three generations:** Parents or in-laws, adult children (and spouse or children-in-law), and grandchildren.

- **Skipped generations:** Grandparents and grandchildren whose parents are dead or unable to care for them. These are sometimes called "grandfamilies."

- **More than three generations:** The ages in the household can range from infancy to extreme old age.

THE GROWTH OF MULTIGENERATIONAL HOUSEHOLDS

In 1940, one quarter of Americans lived in households with at least two adult generations, usually parents and grandparents, as well as minor children. By 1980, that share had declined to 12 percent — the intervening decades were the high point of the nuclear family. But in 1980, that trend started to reverse, and since then the share of all Americans living in two-generation households has continued to increase. According to the Pew Research Center, in 2014 an estimated 60.6 million Americans, or 19 percent of the total U.S. population, lived in a household that contains at least two adult generations or a grandparent and at least one other generation. The Pew Center attributes this growth to the rising share of immigrants in the population and the rising median age of first marriage. Although this shift affects all ages, it is particularly significant for older adults and 25- to 34-year-olds. In a broader age group — 18–34 — living with parents was more common than other arrangements for the first time in 130 years. Another measure of this change: In 1900, only 6 percent of people 65 and older lived alone, whereas 27 percent currently do. However, people are living much longer than they used to but with many chronic health conditions. Older people who live alone are less healthy and often feel more depressed than their counterparts who live with a spouse or others.

REMEMBER

The more generations living together, the greater the opportunities for sharing knowledge and history. Many families find that they enter the arrangement for economic or caregiving reasons but remain in it because they enjoy the closeness of family interactions. But possibilities for friction and dissension also exist. The multigenerational households of older times were not necessarily happy with the arrangement or unaffected by intergenerational or interpersonal strife. The topic of who inherited the family farm in 19th-century America can be just as contentious as current disputes over homes and other assets. Addressing early on the ways in which everyone's needs will be met and clearly stating everyone's responsibilities will go a long way toward ensuring a cooperative arrangement. In later sections I suggest specific ways to accomplish this.

Considering family reactions before making a decision

A move to intergenerational living typically involves the entire family. If you're planning to combine households, think of how the other people in your life — spouse, children, siblings — are affected by this decision. Having an in-law, a grandparent, or grown children living in your home is not the same as having them visit. Whether you are having an aging parent move in with you or you are the older person about to move into your child's home, ask yourself the following questions:

>> Will the other people in my life have to give up space to accommodate another person?

>> Will children still feel free to bring friends home?

>> Will family members have additional responsibilities?

If you're considering bringing a parent into your home, how your siblings react is a particularly sensitive issue. A lot depends on your prior relationship and their relationship with your parent. One sister may feel relieved not to have to take on the responsibility; a brother may worry that being in your home may undermine his relationship with your parent. Money — a topic that I discuss later in this chapter — is often a contentious issue between siblings. When dealing with siblings, consider the following questions:

>> Who is going to be financially responsible?

>> If the person you're bringing into your home plans to contribute to the household and then retires or suddenly can't contribute for other reasons, will the financial responsibilities change?

>> Will a parent's contribution to buying a home or supporting a household take money away from an expected inheritance?

>> If the move involves the sale of the parent's home, how will the proceeds be used?

REMEMBER

These issues are all best addressed at the outset, although they may have to be revisited as circumstances change.

If you're the older person moving in with an adult child, ask yourself the following:

>> What are my main concerns?

>> Will constantly being around grandchildren and their behavior annoy me?

>> Will I be able to accept the help that is part of the package?

>> Am I concerned that my son or daughter has never been a good money manager and may not use my financial contribution wisely?

These issues are best discussed before you make a move.

TIP

The following is perhaps the most important question you need to ask yourself before going further in your fact-finding: Is this something I want to do or something I feel I should do? If it's something you want to do, and the primary person you're concerned about also wants to do it, then you have a good beginning. If it's something you feel you *should* do, that doesn't mean it's a bad idea. Just take a good look at your worries and negative feelings. You may be making some assumptions about what it will be like that won't be borne out. Talk to others in this situation to see how they have handled the changes. A trusted family friend or counselor may be able to help you sort out your feelings and to help allay your concerns. But if this honest appraisal results in increasing rather than relieving your anxiety, this may be the time to acknowledge that the arrangement isn't going to be successful.

Where Should We All Live? Considering the Options

Sometimes the choice seems obvious: You live in a big house with plenty of room, and your parent or other relative has only a limited amount of space. Of course, your mother will come to live with you. Or the reverse may be true. Your mother is the one rattling around in a big house, and you desperately need more space.

TIP

But the move (by either of you) may involve living not just in a different home but in a different part of the country. Leaving everything familiar and adjusting to the new location may be difficult. A trial period may help determine whether this option is reasonable for the long term.

Another option may be for both of you to find a new home that has more accessible features and is in a convenient location for everyone. Some adult children and parents sell their homes and pool their money to buy a new home with room for both generations. A new home gives everyone a fresh start and minimizes some of the difficulty in adding more people to an already established household.

Some builders are responding to this market by offering homes that have separate entrances, two master bedroom suites, a den or family room that can be converted to a bedroom and bathroom on the first floor, and other flexible areas. Universal design features, such as wide doorways and few steps, are often part of the package, appealing to both the older generation and younger families with small children.

No solution is perfect, and the advantages and disadvantages for each family vary. Before you make a decision, consider all the pros and cons of each option. In the following sections, I guide you through the considerations of having a parent move in with you, moving in to your parent's home, and the financial matters you'll need to arrange.

Having a relative move in with you

When the right choice seems to be having a parent or adult child move into your home, considering how the space will work and how family roles will change is paramount to making the decision.

Organizing the space

If you're thinking about bringing a parent or other relative to live with you, making sure that the space in your home is adaptable should be a priority. Features of the home that are second nature to you — steps down to the laundry or up to the bedroom, a front door that is hard to open, kitchen cabinets that are hard to reach — may be difficult for an older person to navigate. The lighting may be fine for you but not for a person with poor vision. Here are some other aspects to consider:

>> Is there enough available space for all the equipment and personal belongings that your parent may bring? Review all the things that will have to come to your house before the move, and try to keep big items to a minimum. The grand piano or massive armoire may have to go, but try to accommodate prized possessions such as collections, artwork, or other valued items.

>> Does the floor plan allow sufficient privacy for everyone? An open floor plan is conducive to family togetherness but also limits the space available for each person to find a special spot to read, write, watch TV, or take a nap.

>> Are modifications needed for safety or accessibility? This is discussed in Chapter 5, so look at those suggestions.

>> Are pets going to accompany your relative? If so, how will you integrate them into your household, especially if you already have animals to care for? Your dog and your mother's cat may get along very well, but don't count on it.

>> Is there sufficient space for you to have meals together, at least some of the time? Sharing mealtime is one of the benefits of multigenerational living, but given today's hectic schedules and limited space, it may be difficult to arrange. Having a dining space that is easy to use makes it more likely that meals will be shared with one or more family members, even if everyone is not available.

Remodeling your existing home to accommodate an older person may be a possibility. Some modifications can be relatively modest, such as providing an entrance with no steps or adding grab bars. So-called mother-in-law apartments or accessory units have been around for a long time and can be added or incorporated into the existing structure. This allows the older person to have private space, often including a kitchen, but still be part of the family. Remodeling can be expensive, however, and may not add to the home's resale value. It may also be useful for a limited time if the older person needs more help or can't be left alone. Making minor modifications to the home for safety and accessibility may be more affordable than a larger renovation project.

One variation on this idea is a self-contained structure that is built on the premises but not connected to the main house. Informally called *granny pods*, these units come in small, medium, and large sizes (a typical size is 12 feet by 24 feet) and can be set up in a backyard. They have water, plumbing, and electricity. The selling point for many people is the incorporation of technology, which can monitor the person's vital signs, filter air contaminants, and do all sorts of other activities. The prices range from $85,000 to $125,000.

REMEMBER

Zoning regulations and building codes may place some restrictions on both accessory dwellings and granny pods. Check with the municipal office on land use and a contractor to find out the rules and the process to apply for a variance if necessary.

Changing family roles

With all the best intentions, bringing an older family member to live with you requires some major adjustments as family roles and responsibilities change. The nonprofit Family Caregiver Alliance offers some valuable suggestions at www.caregiver.org/home-away-home-relocating-your-parents. Here are some key points to consider:

>> Think about how comfortable you are with becoming the head of household when the household now contains the parent who has always been in charge. And how will the parent feel about ceding control?

>> Be prepared for resistance from a parent who may no longer feel (or be) in control and may fear losing independence. Involving your parent and all other affected members of the family in decision making is a good strategy. Try holding family meetings and, for those who won't express their views candidly in a meeting, one-on-one conversations.

>> Consider how your parent can contribute to the household, apart from financially. Child care is one common opportunity (as long as the parent is able to keep up with the child). Another is preparing special meals on occasions. Some older people have special skills that can be drawn upon — perhaps making repairs, gardening, mending clothes, or keeping scrapbooks up to date. Most older people want to feel useful, and giving them an opportunity to help out is usually appreciated.

>> Devise ways to accommodate your parent's interests, routines, and food preferences without unnecessarily disrupting your own lives. If the move involves joining a different religious congregation, make the introductions early. Find out about community activities that your parent can attend.

>> Be especially sensitive to how your children react to having an older relative in their home. Many children are enormously enriched by living with a grandparent, learning family history, and asking about "the old days." At the same time, they may be embarrassed in front of friends by their grandparent's old-fashioned ideas or attitudes. If the older person has symptoms of dementia, explain what is going on to the children, and give them tips about how best to respond to repeated questions or other signs of memory loss.

Preparing to move into your parent's home

Instead of having your older relative move in with you, you may consider moving in with that person. You may be struggling to pay the rent for a small apartment while your parent has plenty of space. This may be a more viable option if you live near each other and you would not have to move to another community, perhaps even to another part of the country.

Most of the considerations that I discuss in the preceding sections apply to this kind of move as well, so be sure to consider how they apply in your case. Here are some additional factors to think about:

>> Moving more than a short distance may require you to give up a job or personal relationships. Is this something you are prepared to do?

>> Moving in with a parent involves a different psychological adjustment than is the case when your parent moves in with you. If you are moving back to the home you grew up in, be aware that you may fall back into similar patterns, even though you are now an adult.

>> If this potential move is prompted by a parent's illness or accident, you may assume that the move is temporary, but it may be difficult to alter once you are in residence.

>> If you'll be moving with a partner and/or children, consider how they will adjust to the new situation and how your parent will adjust to them.

If, after considering all the implications, the move seems like the right thing to do for all you, then you need to plan carefully, considering all the features that have to be in place.

Making fair financial arrangements

Depending on your financial circumstances and personal relationships, arranging to pay for the additional costs of a multigenerational family may be easy or difficult. For most people, it's a matter of considerable sensitivity and may bring up deep-seated feelings about what is valuable, what is not, and what expenses should be assumed by one or another party. If you're the adult child, you may feel it is your responsibility to pay for everything, even if you don't have sufficient resources or you have competing demands. If you're the parent, you may feel the same way or quite differently. Many older people say that they don't want to be a burden, and they often mean that as a financial burden. And then there are siblings, often living at a distance and watching this arrangement with both relief and suspicion.

REMEMBER

The advice from financial planners, social workers, attorneys, and others is consistent: Make money matters transparent and as equitable as possible. This doesn't guarantee that there won't be conflict, particularly with siblings, but it does help to minimize it.

Here are some specific steps you can take:

TIP

>> **Determine a set contribution.** Sit down and figure out how much you and your parent or child can or is willing to contribute toward household expenses and whether that money will be designated for a specific purpose, such as rent, food, utilities, or household help. Having at least most of the contribution as a fixed sum makes the arrangement more predictable and less threatening to someone who may be accustomed to saving every penny for a rainy day. If you're moving into your parent's home, clarify what you're going to contribute financially and who is going to pay bills and monitor expenses.

Be sure to put the agreement in writing. This will help avoid misunderstandings later. The agreement can always be changed.

>> **Set aside fun money.** Make sure that the contribution allows for some personal money to spend on small luxuries, clothing, gifts, or any other purpose. This is not an allowance, because it is their money and they have discretion to save it or spend it.

>> **Set up bill paying.** Set up an efficient and reliable way to pay bills, whether that is online or by check. Some recurring bills, such as rent or mortgage payments, can be deducted from your account automatically. Monitor the accounts carefully. Your parent may have paid all the bills before, or that may have been a spouse's job. Your role should not be to take away all financial responsibility, unless the parent is unable to do any independent financial management. You should discuss any major financial adjustments or needs.

>> **Consider getting a power of attorney for parents.** If they agree, you may want to obtain power of attorney (POA) for financial affairs. This can cover all

financial matters or be limited to specific needs. Consult an attorney for advice. Even if your parent is fully able to manage money now, an unexpected medical event may occur, in which a POA would be important.

>> **Check on Social Security and other income.** Make sure Social Security payments or pension payments are deposited automatically in your parent's bank account. Also make sure the Social Security Administration has the person's current address. You can check at www.ssa.gov/myaccount or call 1-800-772-1213.

WARNING

>> **Watch out for scams.** Older people are often the targets of phone or Internet scammers who announce sweepstakes winnings that never happened, solicit money for charities that don't exist, and offer other once-in-a-lifetime opportunities to cash in. Warn your parent about these scammers, and if one happens to slip through your warning net, alert authorities and the bank or credit card company about it.

>> **Fill in family members on the arrangements.** Involve siblings or other relatives such as nieces and nephews in a discussion about financial arrangements. Let them know what everyone is paying for (in general, not necessarily in dollar amounts) and contributing (again, in general). If they offer to contribute or to take over your responsibilities for a vacation period, make sure there are no strings attached. Also make sure they really understand what they will have to do if they take over your job, even for a week or two. If you feel that other relatives will use this time to pressure your parent for money or changes in the arrangement, don't accept the offer.

>> **Consider a personal-care agreement for parents.** If you have to give up your job or cut back on hours to accommodate your parent's needs, consider consulting an attorney about setting up a personal-care agreement. This document sets out the amount your parent will pay you and the hours that will count toward your salary. But understand that it's not a substitute for your regular salary, and no benefits are attached. Some courts have looked askance at agreements that pay family members their prior or even higher salary as a way to transfer assets without incurring tax penalties. The amount should be consistent with what you would pay to a paid home care worker.

>> **Update the will.** Make sure the older and younger generations have an updated will with clear instructions about the disposition of any property or assets as well as items such as jewelry, artwork, or other pieces that may have sentimental as well as monetary value. Sometimes people promise the same item to several different people, forgetting what they have said to another person.

>> **Designate a healthcare proxy.** Along with a will, the older person should have an updated advance directive and healthcare proxy naming someone to make healthcare decisions in case she cannot do so herself. You can find more about healthcare proxies and advance directives in Chapter 17.

Making the Move

You've decided. Multigenerational living, with its pros and cons, is a good solution to your needs. You've done all the planning, designing, remodeling, and negotiating. Now it's time for the move. Moving is one of life's major stressors, way up there with illness and divorce, so take time to organize this event.

TIP

The Family Caregiver Alliance has a helpful and exhaustive checklist for downsizing a home in preparation for a move. You can find it at `www.caregiver.org/downsizing-home-checklist-caregivers`. Also look at AARP's Downsizing the Family Home at `www.aarp.org/downsizing`, and the accompanying workbook, to walk you through the process. But in the following sections I cover some key points.

Note: If you or your parent has accumulated lots of stuff over the years and is determined to keep it, you may have to deal with a hoarding problem. For advice, see Chapter 5 for more on hoarding.

REMEMBER

Most of the moving process consists of the same steps you would go through if you were moving to a new home, new town, or even overseas. Moving from a familiar place to the unknown, and giving up all the familiar surroundings, can be hard, even if the move is welcomed and appreciated. Be patient and sensitive to feelings of sadness and the memories associated with the home and its contents. Allow time to do things right.

Getting started

Start the process of decluttering well ahead of the move. Doing it in small steps — a few hours a day — makes it less upsetting and reduces the chances that important items will be discarded by mistake. Do the following to make the process go smoothly:

>> Shred canceled checks and other unneeded papers that have personal information. Check with an accountant about what records need to be retained.

>> Toss outdated food.

>> Take unused or expired medications to a pharmacy for instructions on safe disposal. Some pharmacies have postage-paid bags you can use to mail the drugs for proper disposal.

>> Donate clothes or household items that won't be needed in the new home.

>> Collect all important papers and keep them in one place. These may be deeds, wills, birth certificates, passports, discharge papers from the military, or other legal documents. These are hard to replace and may be necessary to obtain benefits or for other reasons.

>> If children, siblings, or others have used the home as a storage unit for their high school or college textbooks, memorabilia, and other items with meaning only to them, ask them to reclaim and remove them. They may decide that these things are not so valuable after all and add them to the discard list, or they may be thrilled to have them back again.

Planning ahead

The more you do ahead of time, the easier the transition will be down the road. Be sure to

>> Start a notebook or computer file folder for the move. Include to-do lists, phone numbers, appointment times — anything that you may forget but will need at some point.

>> Get estimates from moving companies. Better rates are available for nonpeak times (the middle of the month, for example).

>> Make a floor plan of the new home, with accurate measurements and placement of doors and windows, so that you know exactly how much space there will be.

>> Measure any big pieces of furniture (bed, chest of drawers, tables) and decide where they should be placed by the movers.

>> Make plans for pets to be moved and accommodated in the new home.

>> Refill prescriptions in advance.

>> Obtain or order any medical equipment that will be needed so that it is delivered and in place when the move happens.

Sorting and packing

Use these tips to help make the packing stage of the move easier and quicker:

>> Go through one room at a time, starting with the easiest. Sort the items into piles: definitely save, possibly save, donate, and discard. You and your relative may have disagreements about what goes where. Try to compromise, but make sure that all truly unneeded and unusable items are discarded.

>> Make packing an event to bring family and friends together. Having a group together takes away some of the anxiety and creates a positive atmosphere.

>> Label everything with its destination.

>> Make sure you keep all the items needed during the move in one place: keys, medications, clothing, legal documents, checkbook, cellphone, first-aid kit, cash, and your moving notebook (which I recommend in the preceding section).

Settling in

New connections will have to be made: membership in a new congregation, and a new doctor, dentist, dry cleaner, and barber or hair stylist are all important to feeling at home. Introduce your parent or child to neighbors and friends. Tour the community together to check out shops, libraries, and other services.

After all the boxes have been unpacked and the furniture rearranged, take some time to get accustomed to the new arrangement. What didn't work out exactly as planned? What adjustments need to be made? Don't try to do everything at once.

Checking In over the Long Haul

Finally, check in with everyone at least once a month and perhaps more frequently to see how the new arrangement is going. What is working well? What is not? What unexpected challenges have arisen? Living with extended family means paying attention to each person's needs and feelings so that the family bonds are strengthened, not shredded.

Dealing with all the changes that can occur over time requires frequent reappraisals. Open communication is the key to identifying problem points and taking appropriate steps before they escalate. Sometimes multigenerational families live in harmony for many years. And sometimes, with all the best intentions, this solution just doesn't work out. If that happens, it should not be considered a failure but recognition that sometimes living apart may bring families closer together than living under one roof.

IN THIS CHAPTER

» **Understanding downsizing's emotional aspects**

» **Making downsizing part of home adaptations**

» **Taking the first step**

» **Going ahead with a move**

Chapter **7**

Downsizing for Now and Later

E very day brings a new deluge of ads for consumer goods — by mail, newspapers, and magazines, and increasingly through messages on our computers and cellphones. America has been called, with good reason, a consumerist society.

But there is another trend that emphasizes a minimalist style of living, with fewer material possessions and accumulations from the past. The examples range from books and websites that stress the joy of decluttering and the ease of living in "tiny" homes (really tiny, as in 100 to 400 square feet) to its ultimate expression in the Swedish practice of "death cleaning" — ridding yourself of your belongings while you're alive.

Is there a middle ground? This chapter is designed to help you find it for yourself or your parent. *Downsizing* is the term most often applied to this process, but I think of it as *rightsizing,* a term borrowed from the business world, sometimes to justify getting rid of jobs and therefore employees. In this case it's just getting rid of things.

REMEMBER

You may or may not be thinking of a move. If you are, then downsizing is not only appropriate, it is essential and best addressed as early as possible. If a move does seem probable, give yourself six months to a year to plan and to do the job carefully and without undue stress. But even if a move isn't in your immediate plans, downsizing can make your home safer, more comfortable, and more welcoming. The goal of downsizing is to find the right balance between your desire to keep your belongings and memories and your need to have a comfortable, safe, and decluttered home. Whether you move now or later, you'll have already done the hard work of choosing what matters most to take with you.

The Emotional Aspects of Downsizing

Most of the work of downsizing involves sorting, organizing, decision making, and disposing of the things you no longer need or want. Hard enough, but unless you recognize the emotional toll this process can take, it will be even more difficult. It's not just the items with obvious personal history such as wedding photos or grandparents' silverware; it's often ordinary items that bring back memories of childhood or places that you visited. Allow some time to reflect on these memories before deciding whether the items they are attached to stay or go.

Some people attach emotional value to items that represent unfulfilled goals. The sewing machine reminds Mom of the projects that she never got started and Dad the expensive woodworking tools that he can never figure out how to use. These lost opportunities may loom larger than items that are attached to completed projects.

People who experienced hard financial times may collect things that once were hard to come by but have no real use now such as monogrammed towels or heavy suitcases. The personal profile in Chapter 2 may help you determine what characteristics define your personality, including your attitudes about money. These may play a role in downsizing.

While you're going through items, think about who in your family would want them. If there is conflict about distribution, it may be time for a family meeting led by a trusted friend or professional.

The positive side to downsizing can't be overlooked. In the newly streamlined space, you can reposition furniture, highlight items you value highly, and in general make an old space both familiar and new. And there's the practical benefit of making it easier to clean and to find things that always seem to be missing — your glasses or keys, for example.

TIP
In the award-winning AARP's *Downsizing the Family Home* (Sterling), home and lifestyle columnist Marni Jameson offers helpful advice on both the practical aspects of downsizing and the emotional impact of the process. She and her brother managed their parents' move from a family home laden with 50 years of

memories to an assisted-living apartment. Her expertise and experience can be useful for someone planning to stay or move.

TIP

One way to keep memories alive is to take photos of objects that you don't want to keep but don't want to lose altogether. The photos can be put into digital form and shared with family and friends. Perhaps a young techie in your family can take on this task, or you can use a commercial service.

WARNING

If the home is filled with garbage, piles of papers and bags, evidence of pest infestation, animal waste, unworkable toilets, or unsafe stairs, this is not ordinary clutter. It is likely a case of hoarding, which requires expert mental health attention as well as organizational assistance. According to the Mayo Clinic, "A hoarding disorder is a persistent difficulty discarding or parting with possessions because of a perceived need to save them. . . . Hoarding often creates such cramped living conditions that homes may be filled to capacity, with only narrow pathways winding through stacks of clutter. . . . People with hoarding disorder may not see it as a problem, making treatment challenging. But intensive treatment can help people with hoarding disorder understand how their beliefs and behaviors can be changed so that they can live safer, more enjoyable lives." Hoarding is difficult to address because the person is often dealing with loss, trauma, and long-buried issues. A useful article prepared by the University of California-San Francisco is available at scienceofcaring.ucsf.edu/health-public/recognizing-and-addressing-hoarding-significant-senior-health-concern. Another resource is the International OCD Foundation at hoarding.iocdf.org.

Downsizing and Home Renovations

A good time to think about downsizing is when you're considering renovating your home to make it more accessible (see Chapter 5). Look at the spaces you're considering adapting: the bathroom, kitchen, or stairs, for example. Removing hazards and opening areas for easy access can be the first salvo in the downsizing effort.

REMEMBER

Don't just toss the removed items in another area where they may cause new problems. Take stock of what's been removed and what can be disposed of right away and what you want to save or give away. Chances are items have accumulated in these spots because the locations are convenient, not because the items have a purpose there. Combining decluttering with a process that improves the living space may defuse the emotional response.

Getting Started

Where to start downsizing? The following sections describe a few important steps.

TIP

If adult children still use your home or garage as a storage facility for their belongings, ask them to help your downsizing project by removing their possessions. Explain that you're working to streamline your home to make it safer and more accessible, and that their belongings should live with them. When they see how difficult it can be to make decisions about their school papers and other memorabilia, they may be more tolerant of your own challenges in downsizing.

Putting together important papers

A good first step in downsizing is looking for the important papers that you'll need to keep and those that can be discarded. Among the critical papers to keep are deeds, mortgage statements, birth and marriage certificates, tax records, passports (check to see whether they are still valid), diplomas, and military service records. Keep all these together in a safe place and let family members know where they are.

Assemble legal papers that are important right now (or can become important in a medical emergency). These include advance directives, including those naming healthcare proxies, do not resuscitate (DNR) orders, durable power of financial attorney, a will, a list of current medications, and other medical records (see Chapter 17 for more information on these documents). These should be kept in a safe place as well, but should be readily available in an emergency. AARP's *Checklist For My Family* by Sally Hurme (American Bar Association) offers lists of what to keep and for how long.

TIP

Check with your accountant or tax attorney to find out how long you should keep tax records. There are different rules for different situations, and you want to be sure that you can discard (shredding is advised) some old records.

Sorting and decision making

After you've gone through the important paperwork and the kids have taken their things, don't stop the momentum. It's time to sort through the bigger stuff.

TIP

The Family Caregiver Alliance's checklist for caregivers on downsizing a home (www.caregiver.org/downsizing-home-checklist-caregivers) recommends four categories, each designated by a colored tag or sticker. In this scheme, green=save, orange=possibly save, blue=donate/sell, and red=discard. You can label boxes and garbage bags with the different colors. The goal is to begin to determine where different items will be going. Don't make the mistake of tagging everything green for save; that defeats the purpose. And if there are no red tags for discard, you aren't facing reality.

Start small. Pick one area — a drawer or closet, perhaps, or a seldom-used bedroom. This technique puts some boundaries around your tasks and reduces feelings of being overwhelmed. You may find things you've forgotten existed, and some you swear you've never seen before. If you've gotten along without them until now, don't put them in the "save" pile!

When you've done all you can do in your small designated area, make sure you immediately get rid of all the items tagged or boxed for discarding. The temptation to move things from red to orange or even green can be very strong. If something should be discarded, then discard it as soon as possible. Out of sight, out of mind. If the items are big, you may need to arrange a special trash pickup. If something is going to be donated, donate it immediately. (See the next section.)

Continue going through your house room by room, or closet by closet and file cabinet by file cabinet. As you move through different areas and rooms repeating this process, you may come across items you want to give to particular individuals. You can do this in two ways: give the person the object now with an explanation of why you think it would be meaningful to him; or add the designation to your will so that the person will get it later. Many wills just set out a process for determining how family items are divided so that it is as fair as possible.

Consider how other people may react to this gift and whether other items that you find will be appropriate for them. You should be prepared for the possibility that the friend or relative you have carefully chosen to receive an item you consider precious won't want it.

Richard Eisenberg's article "Sorry, Nobody Wants Your Parents' Stuff," based on his own experiences (www.forbes.com/sites/nextavenue/2017/02/12/sorry-nobody-wants-your-parents-stuff/#4b157de724ed), includes advice from professionals in the antiques and collectibles market. They point out that the heavy furniture that our parents' generation valued is out of style. The "Ikea Generation" rules. There are always exceptions for items that have special value, either because of what they are or who owned them. And there's always the possibility — remote, to be sure — that your Civil War–era quilt will be hailed on *Antiques Roadshow* as a national treasure.

REMEMBER

While you're thinking big, be sure to also think small. When emptying kitchen cabinets of unusable utensils, it's a good time to check for outdated food and medications. Freezers often contain packages with no label or date; discard safely. Check with a pharmacist about how to dispose of drugs. This is a process that should be repeated at regular intervals.

Donating or selling items

You may be surprised to find that sometimes it's hard to donate and even harder to sell things. If you have artwork, first edition (or rare) books, or expensive jewelry that you don't wear anymore, your first step is to have these items appraised by a knowledgeable dealer. You can also look on the Internet for auction or sale prices for comparable pieces.

But be prepared. The artist whose works you bought 30 years ago may have become famous . . . or faded into obscurity. Or maybe it's the frame that's valuable, not the artwork. Your great-grandfather's collection of campaign buttons may be valuable or not. Your father's toy train set may bring a handsome price (especially if you have the original box), or it may just be another example of a mass-produced product. Upright and console pianos, once prized possessions in middle-class homes, are hard to get rid of now. If you have a piano in reasonably good condition, or one that can be brought back from disuse, ask a piano tuner for schools or organizations that may be able to use it.

If you donate the items, you need the value for your tax return. You can find an Internet site that values items. And if you're going to try to sell them, you need the value to set a fair price or a price that you will accept.

TIP

In the happy event you turn up something with considerable value and you decide to keep it, you should add it to your homeowner's insurance policy.

TIP

Check with local service agencies, such as the Red Cross, the Salvation Army, homeless shelters, and others, to find out whether they accept donations of household items and, if so, what kinds. They may have specific requirements and may or may not pick up the items. They may take kitchen utensils, for example, but not bedding. Libraries may take books in good condition for book sales, or they may not. Donating items to a service organization that you support is a good way to show the group that you value their contribution to the community. They will appreciate your gesture, and you will feel good about the donation.

You can try to sell items that you don't need in your newly streamlined home, including furniture and tools, individually on a website such as eBay or Craigslist, with the understanding that you may have to deal with many responses that don't result in a sale. Or you can give some of them to a consignment shop that displays and sells the items for a percentage of the sale price. Or you can hire an estate sale company, even though this is not, strictly speaking, an estate sale.

Another option is a yard or garage sale, if someone in the family has the time and energy to organize it. Don't underestimate the time it takes to organize a sale. You have to examine each item, decide on a price, label everything (even those things you don't want to sell in order to make sure no one walks away with them!), place them strategically, advertise the sale, and then have someone to handle sales and another person to monitor the crowd.

Hiring professional help

TIP

For a big downsizing project, consider hiring a professional organizer and a cleanup crew. They can help you plan the project, keep the process moving, involve you in major decisions, and help manage the emotions that inevitably arise. The National Association of Senior Move Managers has a booklet describing their services, which include rightsizing and relocation: www.nasmm.org/education/ Guide_To_Rightsizing_and_Relocating.pdf.

Making the Move

You may have started the downsizing process with every intention of staying in the same home, but perhaps over time it has become clear that it's time to move. Chapter 6 on moving to a multigenerational home has some tips that apply to moving (as well as downsizing). But working with a moving company presents its own challenges.

Moving companies are regulated by states; this website will take you to your state's rules: www.relocation.com/library/moving_guide/state_regulations.html. If you're moving to a different state, federal rules are described in the Department of Transportation's Federal Motor Carrier Safety Administration website at https://www.fmcsa.dot.gov/protect-your-move. You can also check the Better Business Bureau and, of course, the reviews on consumer websites.

Whatever company you choose, keep in mind this advice from the Family Caregiver Alliance's fact sheet at https://www.caregiver.org/downsizing-home-checklist-caregivers:

>> Be sure you have a written contract from the moving company and a clear idea of coverage for lost or damaged possessions.

>> Get a firm time for their arrival, at both the old and new residences.

>> Check inventory lists.

>> Check payment options: credit card or check?

» Have someone assigned to meet the movers at the new residence. Be sure they have a key! If this is a facility, be sure the manager is expecting you.

» Ensure that all boxes are properly labeled.

» Use the "open first" boxes to set up the bedroom and bathroom immediately.

» Prepare to spend a few days unpacking and organizing. Get someone to help if you can. Work as quickly as you can to make this new home feel homelike.

Chapter **8**

Assisted and Independent Living and Other Group Settings

t's a common problem: Your house is too big and costly to maintain. Or your kids live across the country and you want to live closer to them and your grand-kids. Or you're the kid, and your parents need more help than you can give them. But no one wants to give up privacy and independence. Whatever your situation, assisted living may seem like a very good solution. And the ads stress how pleasant and easy life can be in a place called, say, Gracious Living Manor. But you have a lot to think about before taking such a big step.

When choosing whether assisted living is the way to go for your situation, there are many considerations. This chapter guides you through all that comes with assisted living: the services, options, costs, and more. I also cover pitfalls to steer clear of and alternative group-living arrangements. But first, it helps to know exactly what assisted living is, so read on.

REMEMBER

You or your parent are looking for a home, not a hotel or a temporary place to stay. Whether the ultimate choice is assisted living or some other group arrangement, or to age in place, it should be a decision that is based on your needs, preferences, and resources.

What Is Assisted Living?

Assisted living is a term that is often used as though everyone understands it in the same way. But that's not the case. Assisted living is just a generic term like *hotel* or *automobile* that covers a lot of options. Before getting into the specifics, I like to start with a simple definition: Assisted living is a residence where groups of people share meals and other activities and where individuals can receive personal assistance to maintain their independence. People who choose assisted living typically would have difficulty living completely on their own but do not require constant medical attention.

You can also think about assisted living as an intermediate step in long-term care. It's in the middle of the spectrum of long-term care, which often goes from independent living to assisted living to nursing-home care. Independent living can be in your own home (see Chapter 5) or the entry level of assisted living or in special housing for older people. About 70 percent of residents in assisted living come to the facility from their own house or apartment.

In this section I cover a more formal definition of assisted living, what services are included, which healthcare options may be provided, and tips for finding a facility to provide a broader understanding of all that assisted living covers.

Interpreting industry and government language

Most definitions of assisted living come from industry or government sources and emphasize different aspects of this setting. It's important to keep the source in mind when you gather information. For example, Argentum (formerly the Assisted Living Federation of America), a trade organization, says, "Assisted living is a housing and healthcare option that combines independence and personal care in a residential setting." This is a good definition as far as it goes, but it doesn't tell you what personal care means and what healthcare services are likely to be offered.

The Eldercare Locator (https://eldercare.acl.gov/Public/Index.aspx), a free service connected with the federal Administration for Community Living (ACL), has an even more specific definition: "Assisted-living facilities offer a housing alternative for older adults who may need help with dressing, bathing, eating, and toileting but do not require the intensive medical and nursing care provided in nursing homes." This definition, while accurate, doesn't include younger adults who may want or need the kinds of services available in assisted living. It also underestimates the importance of the social aspects of assisted living.

Living with a congenial group of people with whom to share meals, activities, and conversation is a potential benefit, since social connections have been shown to improve health and well-being as well as to reduce medical costs. Keep in mind, though, that it is sometimes hard to make new friends in assisted living because residences experience a lot of turnover. Most people stay in assisted living for only 22 months, according to the 2010 National Survey of Residential Care Facilities. Nearly 60 percent move on to a nursing facility, a third die, and the rest move home or to another location. *Note:* The 2010 survey has not been updated and has been replaced by a survey with a different name — the National Survey of Long-Term Care Providers. The Centers for Disease Control and Prevention (CDC) website has several recent reports on aspects of assisted living at www.cdc.gov/nchs/nsltcp/index.htm.

State governments, which license group residences, call assisted-living facilities by different names. Some examples of state licensing categories are *residential care facilities for the elderly* (California), *residential facilities for groups* (Nevada), and *personal care homes and assisted-living facilities* (Pennsylvania).

TIP

You may also come across the acronym *ALF* in your search. It is shorthand for assisted-living facility, not the character in the TV series popular in the 1980s. Similarly, *ALP* is an abbreviation for assisted-living program, not a mountain.

Owners of assisted-living facilities tend to shy away from that term in the name, preferring more appealing names like *village, community, manor,* or any phrase that evokes a secure and invigorating lifestyle.

REMEMBER

Your state's name for assisted living is not as important as its licensing requirements and its monitoring activities. Some states have detailed standards about what counts as assisted living and what must be provided, as well as building and safety regulations. States may require training for staff, background criminal checks, and other safeguards. Regulations in other states are less definitive. The National Center for Assisted Living, a provider organization, has information about state offices at www.ahcancal.org/ncal/about/Pages/StateAffiliates.aspx and a state regulatory review at www.ahcancal.org/ncal/advocacy/regs/Documents/2017_reg_review.pdf. Another important publication is the National Center for Assisted Living's "Guiding Principles for Assisted Living" at www.ahcancal.org/ncal/about/Documents/GPAssistedLiving.pdf. This guide offers a good check on the kinds of information that providers should be giving you as a prospective resident, including contracts, finances, and resident transfers.

TIP

When you check out your state's regulations, find out whether it has a bill of rights for assisted-living residents. Most states have such a document and generally require facilities to post it and give copies to residents. These documents may be lengthy. Some of the items include the right to privacy, to confidentiality of personal and medical information, to have private communications with a physician or attorney, to practice the religion of one's choice, and to be given notice about transfers or fee increases. Some are negative rights, such as the right not to be coerced or required to perform work. However, not all the documents tell residents how to complain if they feel their rights have been violated. One way is to contact the state's long-term care ombudsman, who is responsible for investigating complaints in nursing homes and assisted-care facilities. You can find the ombudsman in your area at www.1tcombudsman.org/ombudsman. Or you can contact the National Consumer Voice for Quality Long-Term Care at www.theconsumervoice.org.

Getting to know what assisted living offers

REMEMBER

All assisted-living facilities, however defined, offer three main components:

>> **Shelter:** Residents are given a place to live, usually a private unit or apartment.

>> **Meals:** Food is provided, although not necessarily three meals a day.

>> **Staff:** The facility staff provide the assistance that comes with the name. In addition to managers and activity directors, most facilities have aides or attendants to help with bathing, dressing, getting around with a cane or walker, and other daily tasks.

TIP

When it comes to services provided by staff, you may frequently hear the term *ADLs.* It stands for *activities of daily living,* which are the actions people take for granted until they can't do them by themselves anymore — dressing, bathing, going to the bathroom, and feeding themselves. ADLs have a companion term — *IADLs,* or *instrumental activities of daily living* — that includes tasks like making phone calls, managing money, managing medications, shopping, and cooking. People in assisted living may also need help with these responsibilities.

Assisted-living facilities may be located in cities and look like ordinary apartment buildings. Some are in suburban locations with lots of open space. There are fewer assisted-living sites in rural areas.

Some assisted-living facilities are luxurious and provide a wide range of services and amenities. At the other end of the spectrum, some facilities have small staffs and offer limited assistance.

REMEMBER

When you're considering an assisted-living facility, be sure to ask about staffing: how many, training, special skills, and background checks. If the management seems evasive, probe further. The response will give you an idea of whether this is a place you want to consider further or avoid.

Assisted-living facilities may be large or small. About a third of all facilities are considered large (25 or more beds), but they have more than 80 percent of all assisted-living residents. About 82 percent of all facilities are run by for-profit organizations, some of which are national or regional chains. The rest are run by charitable or religious organizations or by state, city, or local governments.

In general, larger facilities have more staff and can offer more activities. This benefit may be offset by frequent staff changes and a more impersonal management style. Your preferences about small-group living versus a large residence should be part of your decision. If you or your parent have always lived in a private house with few close neighbors, it may be difficult to adjust to large-group living, even if you have your own apartment. Or a new environment may be just what you are looking for.

A CDC analysis comparing smaller and larger assisted-living facilities found that in 2016, in larger facilities, more residents were age 85 and older, and a higher percentage of people needed personal care assistance. Residents in smaller facilities were also more likely to be receiving Medicaid. The percentage of residents who had fallen in the previous 90 days increased with the bed size of the facilities. For more detail, go to www.cdc.gov/nchs/products/databriefs/db299.htm.

ASSISTED LIVING: BORN IN THE 1990S

Before the 1990s, you would have had a hard time finding an assisted-living facility. The forerunners of today's facilities did exist, but they were generally called *board and care homes* and were run by religious or fraternal organizations. The big growth of assisted-living facilities in the mid-1990s stemmed from a downturn in nursing-home placement, the desires of an aging population for a housing alternative that stressed independence, and entrepreneurial opportunities in filling this residential gap.

An AARP Public Policy Institute report found that in 2010, the United States had more than 53,000 facilities with more than 1 million beds. (The terminology of *beds* probably stems from nursing-home or hospital usage.) Not all facilities are fully occupied, however. Assisted-living facilities are spread unevenly across the country, with largely rural states having the lowest capacity. In the past few years, growth has slowed somewhat as some older people have been unable to sell their homes to pay for assisted living and some operators expanded too quickly and misjudged the market.

Checking out healthcare services

The healthcare services offered in assisted living vary considerably. Most common is assistance with administering medications. Some states require staff with specialized training to help with this task. Some assisted-living facilities have medical staff, usually a nurse, available 24/7 on-site; others have a part-time nurse or someone on call.

Compared to practice 20 years ago, assisted-living facilities are now accepting people with more serious chronic conditions. The National Center for Health Statistics, a government agency, reported in 2010 that 82 percent of assisted-living facility residents had Alzheimer's disease or dementia, high blood pressure, heart disease, or a combination of those conditions. Some assisted-living facilities have adapted to the greater healthcare and assistance needs of these residents, while others have not. The 2016 CDC survey described in the previous section found that among residents of smaller facilities (4–25 beds), the prevalence of Alzheimer's disease and depression was higher, but the prevalence of cardiovascular disease was lower.

REMEMBER

If you have a chronic condition that requires frequent monitoring and checkups, be sure to ask whether you can continue to see your own doctor or what alternatives will be available, especially if you're moving to a new area.

REMEMBER

Alzheimer's disease and other types of dementia are conditions that require specific care and are a huge factor when making a long-term plan. A 2012 MetLife Mature Market Institute survey of long-term care costs found that about half of assisted-living facilities provided Alzheimer's and dementia care, but 61 percent of them charged an additional fee. Sometimes the special units or programs within a facility are called *memory care*, perhaps to avoid the stigma of dementia. If memory care is important in your plan, be sure to ask about the staff qualifications and training, types of programs available, and opportunities for interaction with other residents. Also ask whether behavioral interventions are used instead of psychoactive drugs, which should generally be avoided. And care for people with dementia should be more than keeping them from wandering; it should include activities designed to stimulate their minds and keep them active.

Finding more information on assisted-living facilities

Your goal is finding the right assisted-living situation, one that offers the right balance of independence and privacy with the kinds of assistance you need now and may need later. After you know more about assisted living, you can begin your fact-finding process.

TIP

You can get information about specific assisted-living facilities from many sources. A lot of marketing information stresses the *living* aspect of assisted living and glosses over the *assisted* part. It's hard to find out how friendly the staff is, whether management is responsive to concerns, and all the other quality-of-life questions that matter so much. You have to ask about and observe these aspects for yourself. But you can learn a lot from some basic resources, including the following:

>> **Eldercare Locator:** This federal resource (https://eldercare.acl.gov/Public/Index.aspx) is a good place to start. It directs you to your nearest Agency on Aging for assistance. There is also a basic introduction to assisted living at https://eldercare.acl.gov/Public/Resources/Factsheets/Assisted_Living.aspx.

>> **State websites:** State websites are important because you can generally find which assisted-living facilities have a lot of health and safety violations or don't offer what you're looking for. You can then eliminate these from consideration. Some states also have good consumer information, specific to that state, on their Office of Aging or Health and Human Services websites. Note, though, that these agencies have different names in different states.

>> **Your state's long-term care ombudsman:** This individual investigates complaints about assisted-living facilities and nursing homes. Check with that office, usually located in the State's Office on Aging, to find any complaints about a specific facility and how they've been addressed.

>> **The Commission on Accreditation of Rehabilitation Facilities:** This nonprofit organization lists continuing-care retirement communities that meet its survey standards about business practices, philosophy and physical environment, and some aspects of assisted living. You can contact it at www.carf.org/ccrcListing.aspx.

>> **Argentum** (formerly the Assisted Living Federation of America): A membership organization of assisted-living providers, this group has a website at www.argentum.org/about-argentum/state-partners/ where you can search for its state partners.

>> **Internet sites:** When you search on the Internet for "assisted living," you can find ads for specific facilities as well as companies that offer to help you find a facility in your area. Sometimes these companies are endorsed by celebrities, which isn't a guarantee of quality. Personal assistance from "care" or "family" advisers may be available. Facilities on these lists typically pay to be included, so not all options may be offered to you.

>> **Friends or relatives:** People you know who are currently in or have lived in assisted-living facilities are a good resource for information on local facilities. Keep in mind, though, that one person's good or bad experience may not convey the whole picture.

>> **Doctors and other healthcare professionals:** Talk to doctors and nurses with experience in providing care to assisted-living facility residents.

TIP

Use more than one resource, because no single one is likely to have all the options. Be aware of the criteria for including the assisted-living facilities and the sponsorship of the list. And none of these resources can tell you what it's really like to live there. You should address questions about quality of life in your visits to various facilities. I suggest some specific questions in the later section "Beyond the Brochure: What to Look For When You Visit."

Evaluating the Cost of Assisted Living

REMEMBER

Now the big question! How much does assisted living cost? No surprise, this question isn't easy to answer. But it's important, because you or your family will have to pay most of the costs of assisted living. There are two big costs to consider: the entry fee and monthly costs.

>> **Entry fee (sometimes called a community fee or security deposit):** Some but not all assisted living facilities require an upfront cost of admission. This cost varies considerably across the country and by type of apartment or unit and other factors. Some fees may be a few thousand dollars; other high-end facilities may have a starting point of $100,000. Many people use the proceeds from the sale of their homes to finance the entry fee. It is important to check facilities' policies on the entry fee.

>> **Monthly fee:** Monthly fees fall into a range, but on average the cost of assisted living for a one-bedroom, single-occupancy unit currently is around $3,750 a month, or $45,000 a year. Genworth Financial, Inc., an insurance holding company, conducts an annual comprehensive survey of assisted-living costs. You can find the 2017 survey and information by state at www.genworth.com/about-us/industry-expertise/cost-of-care.html.

TECHNICAL
STUFF

The median figure includes both higher and lower rates. For example, in the 2017 Genworth survey, the annual cost of assisted living in Georgia was $33,000; in Texas, $42,000; in Washington State, $55,920; and in Alaska, $72,000. (The cost of living is generally more expensive in Alaska and Hawaii.)

CHECK THE FACILITY'S FINANCIAL HISTORY

Whether the assisted-living facility is a nonprofit or a for-profit organization, find out about its financial history and stability, planned improvements or needed maintenance to the physical plant, possible mergers with other organizations, or other economic factors that may affect your decision. Some assisted-living chains have gone into bankruptcy because of inadequate capital investment and ongoing financing. You should ask for an audited financial statement and ask your accountant or financial adviser to help you interpret the information. CARF, a private accrediting organization, has a free June 2016 "Consumer Guide to Understanding Financial Performance and Reporting in Continuing Care Retirement Communities" at http://www.carf.org/About/FAP/.

REMEMBER

Assisted living is largely private pay, meaning that you have to come up with the money on your own. Some specific services are exceptions, which I talk about in Chapter 11 on Medicare and Medicaid, and long-term care insurance (see Chapter 12) may cover some costs. You may be able to obtain some financial assistance. But for the most part, your own dollars will pay for assisted living. Some portion of the fees may be tax-deductible, so check with your accountant.

Choosing from the menu of cost plans

Stand-alone facilities typically have a selection of plans that are based on the type of services included. While the cheapest option may be attractive for many, the additional costs, particularly for added personal care, can become burdensome. Be realistic about what you or your parent may need. Keep in mind that additional services may be added when needed rather than being included upon entry to the facility.

If the assisted-living facility is part of a continuing-care retirement community (CCRC), which provides a wide range of living arrangements on one campus, then services and costs will probably be tiered. Generally, they fall into the following three categories. (A fourth model, which is essentially a rental agreement, may also be available.)

>> **Type A, extensive or life-care contracts:** This service plan provides housing, residential services, and amenities, including unlimited use of healthcare services, at little or no increase in monthly fees as a resident moves from independent living to assisted living to nursing-home care. The trade-off is usually a higher entry fee.

>> **Type B, modified contracts:** Often with lower monthly fees than Type A contracts, these plans include the same basic services, but only some healthcare services are included in the monthly fee. The resident pays for additional services beyond a minimum, perhaps at a discounted rate.

» **Type C, fee-for-service or à la carte contracts:** These include the same basic services as Type A and B contracts but require residents to pay for all health-related services on an as-needed basis. These contracts may have lower entry and monthly fees for the independent living portion of the stay, but there is a risk of higher nursing-home expenses.

The higher the entry fee, the more likely it is that monthly charges will not increase. And the reverse is also true.

Which plan to choose depends partly on your current and foreseeable needs but also on your emotional and financial tolerance for risk. With Type A and Type C contracts, you get the same apartment and same basic services, but the difference will show up if — more likely, when — you need more assistance.

To get some idea how these options vary, Table 8-1 shows the range of fees by contract type for a selected group of continuing-care retirement communities.

TABLE 8-1   ### Range of Fees by Contract Type for Continuing-Care Retirement Communities

Fee	A: Life Care	B: Modified	C: Fee for Service	D: Rental
Entry fee/security deposit	$160,000–$600,000	$80,000–$750,000	$100,000–$500,000	$1,800–$30,000
Independent living monthly fee	$2,500–$5,400	$1,500–$2,500	$1,300–$4,300	$900–$2,700
Assisted living monthly fee	$2,500–$5,400	$1,500–$2,500	$3,700–$5,800	$4,700–$6,500
Nursing care monthly fee	$2,500–$5,400	$1,500–$2,500	$8,100–$10,000	$8,100–$10,700

Table source: U.S. Government Accountability Office, "Older Americans: Continuing Care Retirement Communities Can Provide Benefits, but Not Without Some Risk" (June 2010).

REMEMBER

Part of the entry fee may be refunded after you leave or die. This may vary by type of contract. Make sure it's spelled out in the contract.

Asking questions to create a monthly budget

REMEMBER

After you have narrowed your search to a few likely possibilities, you should ask for more specific costs. Here are some basic questions suggested by the National Center for Assisted Living:

>> What is included in the basic monthly cost? Ask for written information.

>> Does the residence have a written schedule of fees for extra services? If so, request a copy.

>> Under what circumstances may the fees change? How much notice is given for fee increases?

>> Is a security deposit and/or an entrance fee required? What is the refund policy?

>> Can service agreements and/or contracts be amended or modified?

With this information, you can create a budget for monthly costs that includes

>> Basic services, whatever model you choose

>> Potential additional services, such as

- Personal laundry

- Medication assistance

- Entertainment and field trips

- Transportation

- Telephone

- Cable television

- Internet service

- Beauty shop or barber

- Special diets (if available)

- Other charges

In coming up with a budget, be sure to consider what costs you'll no longer be paying (rent or mortgage, home insurance, snow removal, gardener, housekeeper) and what costs will simply be transferred to a new provider (telephone, cable television). Most meals will be provided (depending on the plan), but you may still want to eat at a restaurant occasionally.

REMEMBER

Keep in mind that costs are more likely to go up than down. This is especially true as more personal care and medical services become necessary.

Beyond the Brochure: What to Look For When You Visit

Of all the steps you can take in looking into assisted-living facilities, the most important is your visit. I should say your *visits,* because you should go more than once, both on planned visits and on unannounced drop-ins. An unplanned meal-time visit can give you essential information, not just about the food but also about the atmosphere in the dining room. Try to visit an activity to gauge the level of participation and enthusiasm. What you see, hear, taste, and smell can tell you more about how the facility actually runs than a whole folder of brochures, lists, and websites. Above all, talk to the residents. If the management discourages this, it's a bad sign.

REMEMBER

Ask as many questions as you can think of. But also trust your instincts. Is this a place you can see yourself or your parent living? Do you get a good feeling from the residents and the staff? Don't ignore small warning signs that may alert you to bigger problems. And don't be rushed into a quick decision.

The following sections walk you through what to look for when visiting an assisted-living facility, both in the common areas and in the individual residential units, as well as noting how a continuing-care concept works.

Making notes about the common areas

The staff member who takes you on a tour will be sure to point out the highlights of the furnishings, the dining room, the grounds (assuming the facility is not in the middle of a city), and all the available amenities. These things are important, but also take a close look around the public areas to find the answers to the following questions:

>> Are they clean and litter-free?

>> Are the bathrooms clean and well stocked?

>> Do the walls look freshly painted?

>> Is there good natural light?

>> Is the temperature comfortable?

>> Are there comfortable seats for residents and visitors?

>> Are all the areas accessible for people with mobility problems?

>> Are there elevators?

>> Do you see residents with canes, walkers, and wheelchairs? If not, you may assume that none of the residents need this equipment, but it may be that people with disabilities stay in their rooms and don't feel welcome in the public areas.

>> Are exits clearly marked?

>> Can you eat when you want, or are mealtimes set?

>> Is there an easy give-and-take between staff and residents?

>> Do you feel welcome as a visitor?

>> If you or your parent is used to ethnic foods or has religious restrictions about foods, can the facility provide appropriate meals?

Checking out the residential units

You should also visit a typical apartment or unit. Make sure you see more than the model apartment, which may have special amenities that are not always part of the basic package. The residential unit is where you or your parent will spend a lot of time, so you want to be sure that it is big enough and can accommodate the personal items you'll want to bring. Also find out the answers to these questions:

>> Is there a 24-hour emergency call system that is easy to use?

>> Is there space in the bathroom for someone to assist with bathing?

>> Is the kitchen (if there is one) well laid out and easy to use?

>> If there is no kitchen, is there a place to keep food?

>> Are the telephone and television easy to operate?

TIP

AARP has a good summary checklist of questions to ask when you visit and spaces to note the answers and your reactions. The checklist allows you to enter comments about more than one visit. You can find it at http://assets.aarp.org/external_sites/caregiving/checklists/checklist_assistedLiving.html.

Investigating continuing care

Assisted-living facilities may be stand-alone sites or may be affiliated with a hospital or nursing home or integrated healthcare system. Many assisted-living facilities are part of a continuum of care that starts with independent living and moves through assisted living to nursing-home care, called a continuing-care retirement community.

TIP

The CCRC promise of never having to leave to go to a separate nursing home temporarily (for a minor illness or accident) or permanently may seem like an attractive option. Many people, however, fail to investigate the nursing-home level of care as extensively as they do the entry level of independent or assisted living. The management may not be as eager to show you the nursing-home setting as the dining room or activity center, but ask to see it anyway. One thing to observe: Are there visitors from the assisted-living section? Sometimes people moved to the nursing home become isolated from their friends still in assisted living.

Pitfalls to Avoid

When deciding whether assisted living is the right place for you or your loved one, watch out for some common problems. After you make the commitment to locate to an assisted-living facility, make note of the pitfalls in the following sections and have a plan ready.

Unnecessary trips to the ER

Assisted-living facilities are understandably concerned about responding appropriately to medical emergencies. But that doesn't mean that every fall or fever requires an ambulance trip to the emergency room, with a long wait and then a likely ambulance ride back to the facility. These episodes are stressful and frustrating. Often the problem can be monitored or treated in the facility with a doctor visit the next day.

REMEMBER

Everyone at the facility should have a clear understanding of your (or your parent's) preferences about going to the ER, whom to contact should you be unable to communicate, and under what circumstances you would want cardiopulmonary resuscitation (CPR) to be administered if your heart stops. You should ask your doctor about the risks and benefits of CPR for someone with your or your parent's health conditions. Your wishes should be documented. All staff should be aware of your preferences. Most states allow an out-of-hospital do not resuscitate (DNR) order, if that's what you want. Without this document in place, an ambulance attendant is required to perform CPR.

Additional costs or a move after a hospital stay

Sometimes a hospital stay is necessary, and sometimes a resident's condition changes. Often when older people are discharged from a hospital, they need additional time and help to recover. The hospital stay itself can lead to a temporary loss of function and cognitive problems, especially if you have been on pain medication or had anesthesia. Some assisted-living facilities insist that the resident hire a private aide to help, or even suggest that the resident can no longer stay in the apartment and must move to a nursing home. The circumstances under which this can take place should be spelled out in the contract and should allow for an independent medical assessment. This process may also be part of the state's bill of rights for residents.

TIP

According to the federal Fair Housing Act Amendments Act of 1988, which prohibits discrimination against people with disabilities, facilities should make a "reasonable accommodation" to the new needs. However, some residences may refuse, citing state regulatory requirements, and courts may agree. In that case, you can seek legal help from a consumer advocacy group or a private attorney. A court may require the facility to continue to provide services while the case is being decided.

Exclusion from social activities or dining room seating by other residents

One of the most difficult situations in any group-living arrangement occurs when one group of residents bands together to exclude another resident, perhaps because he or she is showing signs of dementia, has poor table manners because of a neurological disorder, is unable to participate fully in some activity, or for no clear reason at all. Staff have to be sensitive to these situations and try to negotiate an acceptable balance. This may never happen to you or your parent, but it would be helpful to know how staff handle these situations.

Failing to read the contract

Probably the most common mistake people make when signing up for assisted living is to fail to read the contract very carefully. Don't be one of them. Read the contract. Really read it, fine print and all. Ask your attorney, financial adviser, or a trusted friend or family member — or all three — to read it. This is your chance to ask any final questions and to make any final changes.

TIP

Consider adding your state's bill of rights for assisted-living residents to the contract. And certainly read both documents to make sure that nothing in the contract contradicts what is in the bill of rights.

Independent Living and Other Options for Group Living

Perhaps you don't need the level of care provided at assisted-living facilities. Or perhaps the idea of living with a group of strangers, whose backgrounds may or may not be similar to yours, doesn't appeal to you. You would rather spend time with people who share some aspect of your history or experiences.

What options are there? You have a few, but finding the right one is often a challenge. The five main choices are independent living for seniors, affinity communities, cohousing arrangements, house sharing, and group homes. In general, none of them have the same range of services as in most other assisted-living facilities, but exceptions exist. These alternative settings vary, depending a lot on the organization that started them.

Independent living for seniors

Independent living covers a wide range of options — including Naturally Occurring Retirement Communities (NORCs) and Villages (Chapter 9). Most definitions of independent living include any housing arrangement designed or adapted for people aged 55 or over. Some are low-income or subsidized senior housing, and some are high-end retirement communities, complete with golf courses and other amenities. In a continuing-care retirement community, independent living is the first level. Whatever the arrangement, the emphasis is on providing a safe and barrier-free environment where basic services are provided to people who can manage with little or no assistance.

Affinity or niche communities

Affinity or *niche* communities are for people who have common backgrounds, usually because of prior employment. Special types of affinity communities also exist for lesbian, gay, bisexual, and transgender individuals (LGBT), discussed in Chapter 18, and for military veterans (Chapter 19). There are approximately 100 of these niche communities around the country. The most famous is the Motion Picture & Television Country House and Hospital in California. In existence since 1940, it has been the last residence of many film legends. The 2012 movie *Quartet* depicted a fictional version of a residence where aging musicians continued their craft and personal friendships and disputes. This movie was based on Casa Verdi in Milan, where 60 retired musicians live and practice.

Some affinity communities are based on more typical kinds of employment. For example, there are communities for volunteer firefighters, unionized letter carriers, university professors and administrators, and others. Costs are generally lower because they are subsidized by the founding organizations. The best way to find out whether you would fit into one of these communities is to ask the union or professional organization that represents the interests of retired workers to guide you.

TIP

Affinity communities may be based on other shared interests beyond employment, such as travel, sports, or hobbies. Ask yourself: Is this connection really important to me? Do I want to spend most of my time with people who feel the same way I do, or who worked in the same industry? It may be a wonderful match or a little too much of one thing.

Cohousing arrangements

Cohousing is a community-development effort as well as housing arrangement. It may be initiated by a group of neighbors or friends. Some cohousing projects are started by housing developers. Cohousing is different from NORCs, which are discussed in Chapter 9. In NORCs, people have aged in place, and service programs can be created around their existing neighborhood. The Village concept, also discussed in Chapter 9, is similarly built around existing communities. Cohousing is a designed community.

An idea that started in Denmark, this option involves a group of friends or neighbors who live in separate houses and manage their own finances but work together to design and manage their own community. According to the Cohousing Association of the United States, cohousing has six defining characteristics: participation in the planning process, neighborhood design, common facilities, resident management, nonhierarchical structure and decision making, and no shared community economy (members aren't paid for their contributions to the community). There are entry fees and monthly charges.

The potential benefits include the mutual support that members can provide and the village-like atmosphere that is part of the cohousing philosophy. Opportunities for multigenerational living are also important for some families with grandparents or other older relatives. There are, of course, downsides. Cohousing can be expensive, especially if you don't use all the common services. Privacy is limited, and the community may have more or less stringent rules, especially about selling property.

TIP

The Cohousing Association's website has a directory of communities by state. These sites are concentrated in Western states like California and Washington, but there are some examples throughout the country. And if you are energetic, you can start a cohousing project yourself. To help guide you, check out www.cohousing.org/what_is_cohousing.

House sharing

On a more informal scale, sometimes friends choose to live together and take care of one another as they age. There are even websites for older people looking to share housing. While this idea may be appealing, it takes a good deal of organizational and management skills to make it work. It also depends a lot on each person being mentally sharp, reasonably healthy, and cooperative in nature. This may be true at the outset, but people and circumstances change. Before entering a house-sharing arrangement, have everyone agree in writing on the basic house rules such as how the common rooms will be used, when and how bills will be paid, and any special considerations such as allergies, pets, and visitors.

TECHNICAL STUFF

So far this idea seems to appeal mostly to women who are single or widowed, although historically men who were separated from their families because of work or illness organized themselves into similar arrangements.

Group homes

Called, variously, residential-care homes, adult family homes, adult foster care, personal-care homes, and board-and-care homes, these are houses in residential neighborhoods that can usually accommodate a small number of people. Typically, the residents have a bedroom but not additional private space. The owners provide meals and some assistance with ADLs (activities of daily living). These homes are much less expensive than assisted living, but they don't provide the same range of services. In some states, Medicaid may pay for a group home for eligible people. If you're considering this option, make sure the home is licensed by the state.

TIP

Investigating this type of housing involves many of the same steps as looking at assisted living or other group settings. However, these are formerly private homes, operated by private individuals, and their reputation, credentials, and training are particularly important. As in assisted living, visits at different times of day are crucial. Some questions you may want to ask are about food preferences and special diets, whether pets are permitted, television and telephone access, and whether and when guests are permitted. See the Eldercare Locator booklet "Housing Options for Older Adults" at https://eldercare.acl.gov/Public/Resources/Brochures/docs/Housing_Options_Booklet.pdf for a list of questions to ask about group homes.

Chapter 9

Beyond Your Home: Living in a Community

Young families often look carefully at the surrounding community before buying a home or making a move. They investigate schools, recreation, shopping, parks, safety, commuting, and the ambience of a neighborhood. Although some of the elements to consider may differ, people who are thinking about a move later in life should look just as carefully at communities. Sometimes, however, the importance of a community is overlooked, precisely because it may be very familiar. Living in a community at one stage of life doesn't prepare you for what may be needed at a later stage.

This chapter is an overview of the strengths and resources that communities may offer and helps you decide whether your community, or a community you're considering moving to, has enough or the right kind of resources for you or your parent or other relative. It also describes naturally occurring retirement communities (NORCs) and Village networks.

Understanding Why Community Matters

Community is one of those words people tend to use freely but without being clear about what it means. Community can be a town or city or a neighborhood. It can be a legal designation for zoning, garbage pickup, or voting. It can be the members of a congregation, people who are the same age, or people of any age who share some important characteristic like a particular interest or a commitment to a social or political cause.

When considering where to live, think about *community* as the physical structures and services of a place as well as the interactions of people who live there. Both are important in thinking about what you or your older relative may need. The ability to live alone or with extended family may depend on the availability of services and the degree to which a community fosters mobility, healthy living, and social interactions. Strong communities help prevent social isolation by creating places where people can easily get around and have opportunities for interaction and engagement.

Communities that encourage residents of all ages to stay active, connected, and engaged are called *age-friendly* or *livable communities.* These places have evolved naturally or have been redesigned to meet the needs of their residents.

Defining age-friendly communities

Cities and towns around the world face similar challenges of aging populations and inadequate services. AARP's Network of Age-Friendly States and Communities and the World Health Organization (WHO) have developed a framework for age-friendly communities. See `www.aarp.org/livable-communities/info-2014/livable-communities-fact-sheet-series.html` for fact sheets that explain these concepts.

To find out more about the qualities of the communities in AARP's network, visit `www.aarp.org/livable` and search "domains of livability." WHO's report on the subject (which you can view at `www.who.int/ageing/projects/age_friendly_cities_network/en/`) defines age-friendly cities as those that

>> Recognize the wide range of capacities and resources among residents of all ages

>> Anticipate and respond flexibly to aging-related needs and preferences

>> Respect the decisions and lifestyle choices of residents

>> Protect people who are most vulnerable

>> Promote the inclusion of people of all ages in and contribution to all areas of community life

These elements are designed to make communities work for all ages, not just older adults.

AARP, which provides extensive guidance on age-friendly communities, has a similar definition: "A livable community has affordable, appropriate housing; adequate transportation; and supportive community features and services. Once in place, these resources enhance personal independence, allow residents to age in place, and foster residents' engagement in the community's civic, economic, and social life." You can find out more from AARP at www.aarp.org/livable.

These broad goals can best be achieved by concerted community effort. State and local policies regarding land use, transportation, and housing — many of which have been designed to attend to the needs of households with children — may need revision. AARP is working with local and state officials to ensure policies address the needs of residents of all ages. See www.aarp.org/content/dam/aarp/livable-communities/documents-2017/USCM-AARP-Aging-Report-1-17-17.pdf.

TIP

In addition, AARP has extensive materials, available at www.aarp.org/livable-communities/tool-kits-resources/, to be used by a coalition of community partners to identify problems and plan action. The tool kit has resources on walkability, housing, shopping, recreation and cultural activities, transportation, and healthcare services. This would be a good project for a citizens' group, but if you're looking at the community as an individual, the surveys alone can tell you a lot about what is available and what problems exist. For example, the survey on walkability asks questions about sidewalk maintenance, curb cuts (for mobility), and similar issues. You can fill out the surveys of interest to you and take the result to your municipal government, which is responsible for maintenance. Just reading through the surveys will give you new insight into the many aspects of community that you may have never thought much about.

Looking at livable-community initiatives

More than 250 communities have already signed up in the AARP Network of Age-Friendly States and Communities (developed based on the WHO model). The network is a prominent and successful model of how cities, counties, and states are becoming more age-friendly. You can learn more at `www.aarp.org/livable-communities/network-age-friendly-communities/info-2014/member-list.html`. Here are two examples:

>> **New York State:** New York was the first state in the nation to enroll in the World Health Organization's Global Network of Age-Friendly Cities and Communities and AARP's Network of Age-Friendly States and Communities. Through the New York age-friendly agenda, the state is helping older adults stay in their neighborhoods by building and preserving more than 8,600 affordable housing units; encouraging social participation by using technologies to help older adults navigate their health and healthcare needs; making streets safer for people of all ages; and creating a comprehensive plan to better protect older citizens from financial exploitation and foreclosure.

>> **Philadelphia:** Philadelphia joined the World Health Organization's Global Network of Age-Friendly Cities and Communities in 2011 and AARP's network in 2012. Transportation — safe, affordable, and reliable — is a critical component of the age-friendly plan, with improved safety and access for pedestrians and bicyclists as well as cars and increasing access to public transit. All city buses, trolleys, and trains are wheelchair accessible and have lower platforms to make boarding easier. New, high-density residential and mixed-use developments near transit hubs benefit residents of all ages. The Farmers Market at Frankford Transportation Center, where grocery stores are few and far between, brings healthy and affordable foods to low-income communities. And senior community centers and satellite centers host weekly events for older people, such as book clubs and art classes, at little to no cost.

TIP

AARP has extensive materials to help you evaluate your community as well as communities you're considering moving to. The Livability Index scores neighborhoods and communities across the United States for the services and amenities that impact your life the most. Find the tool at `https://livabilityindex.aarp.org`. It is a great conversation starter, but it shouldn't be interpreted as a final or comprehensive assessment.

Taking a Walk Around Your Community

Walking around your community is one of the best ways to find out what it offers and what it lacks. Use AARP's Walk Audit at `www.aarp.org/livable-communities/getting-around/info-2014/aarp-walk-audit-tool-kit.html`. Take a stroll and bring a notebook and camera. Document what you find.

TIP

Making a map of your community will help you understand how roads and buildings connect — or don't. The guide from the United Hospital Fund's NORC Blueprint project (available at `www.norcblueprint.org/uploads/File/Community%20 Mapping%20Guide%20revised%20050510.pdf`), shows you how to use tools like Google Map and GPS positioning to create a picture of your community's resources.

Looking at sidewalks and surrounding areas

Here's what you'll be looking for when checking on the safety of sidewalks and outdoor spaces:

>> Are the streets clean? Are trash bins provided at regular intervals?

>> Are the sidewalks smooth and level?

REMEMBER

Falls outside the home can be as dangerous as falls at home, so take particular note of sidewalks and streets that may be dangerous. Call your local agency in charge of streets and buildings to report any particularly bad spots.

>> Are there traffic lights in frequently crossed areas? Is there ample time to cross safely?

>> Are there curb cuts (areas cut out of the edges of a sidewalk) at intersections, making it possible to move a wheelchair or walker without having to lift it up? Do both sides of each crossing have curb cuts? Are the curb cuts visible to people with low vision?

>> In cold climates, are there regulations about snow removal from sidewalks? Who is responsible for keeping sidewalks free of ice and snow?

>> Are vehicle traffic rules enforced so that pedestrians do not have to dodge cars turning into a lane or speeding up to go through an intersection?

>> If there are bicycle paths, are they clearly marked, and do bicyclists and skateboarders pay attention to older people crossing the street?

>> Is any outdoor seating provided? It can be in parks, at bus stops, on traffic islands, or any place someone may want to pause and sit before moving on.

>> Does the neighborhood have well-maintained and safe green spaces?

>> Are there any public restrooms? Are they wheelchair accessible? Are they clean and conveniently located?

>> Are streets and public spaces well lit at night?

>> Is there a visible police presence?

>> Is the noise level high?

Checking for places to stop, shop, and chat

In recent years, communities have realized the value of creating places where people can work, play, and live. Just as in beloved historic downtowns, these are places where you can go by foot. That stands in stark contrast to most conventional development that has relied on auto transportation and sprawl to accommodate new growth in houses, shops, schools, and services. The coffee shop where everyone once met for lunch has been replaced by a fast-food counter or coffee bar, where computer users predominate. And now malls and shopping centers are fast disappearing, losing ground to online retailers and limiting community choices even more.

So when you're evaluating the opportunities for social interaction in a community, here are some suggestions of what to look for:

>> Are there places to eat that are easy to get into (ramps or no steps), have comfortable seating (tables that aren't crowded together), and have restrooms on the same floor?

>> Are there places where people can get together just to talk or take part in activities? Community and senior centers, libraries, and other public buildings can serve this purpose.

>> What shopping options are there? Are there grocery stores, stationery stores, pharmacies, dry cleaners, shoe repair shops, beauty salons, barbers, and banks within walking distance?

>> Are there well-maintained sidewalks?

>> Is there good signage and ample seating?

>> Are there active storefronts and places to window-shop?

>> Are there a variety of ways to get around, beyond just driving?

>> Perhaps most important, is this a place you want to come back to again and again? Do people seem to be moving as fast as they can to get away, or are they moving along at a pace that allows them to enjoy their outing?

REMEMBER

TIP

Visit www.aarp.org/WhereWeLive, where you'll find *Where We Live*, a series of books each featuring more than 100 innovative strategies that are in place to create age-friendly communities.

Rating your community

After you have mapped, surveyed, walked, and looked at your community from a fresh perspective, what conclusions can you draw? Try this simple technique:

Create a list of all the important topics you have reviewed and rate them on a scale of 1 to 10, with 1 being the best and 10 the lowest ranking. Leave a space for notes about why you came up with this rating.

Add up the ratings and see whether on average your rankings were at least above 5. Most likely your review will be a mix of good and bad points. If, however, the bad clearly outranks the good, then perhaps this community is not now and will not likely be a good place to grow old.

TIP

Even if the good outweighs the bad, the neighborhood can probably still use some improvements. Are there ways you can improve the lower rankings? For example, can you work with others to improve bus transportation? Or collaborate with the municipal government to add restrooms? Enlist others to help you; this is not a one-person responsibility or task. Considering what you liked about the higher-ranked areas may give you ideas.

Finding Community Services

In addition to what is visible within a community, an important part of an evaluation is what you can't see: the availability of services designed for older people. Some of these services are:

>> Adult day programs

- Social programs (offer meals and activities)

- Medical day programs (help with healthcare needs as well as social activities)

>> Case management (coordination of medical needs)

>> Group meals for seniors in a senior center, community center, or church

>> Exercise and physical fitness programs

>> Friendly visitor programs

>> Home-delivered meals

>> Hotlines

>> Legal services

>> Minor home repairs

>> Nutrition counseling

>> Telephone reassurance

>> Support groups

>> Transportation

Not every community has all these services, and they are particularly sparse in rural areas. You or a family member will have to investigate what is available and what restrictions are in place. Some publicly funded services called *home- and community-based services* are available only to people eligible for Medicaid (see Chapter 11 for a discussion of eligibility requirements). Other services are open to everyone but have waiting lists. Many services are free, but others charge.

The best place to start is your local Area Agency on Aging, which may be a city or regional office. This agency probably has information on all the publicly funded services available in your community. Find your local AAA at Eldercare Locator (https://eldercare.acl.gov/Public/Index.aspx).

Some medical facilities and home care agencies may have a staff person who can make referrals to community-based agencies. Often this person becomes involved after a hospitalization because of the high risk of readmission if services aren't in place to keep the person at home.

Beyond publicly funded services and medical referrals, many religious and charitable organizations offer services. Volunteers work with many agencies to visit older people at home, do minor repairs, shovel snow, pick up prescriptions from the pharmacy in bad weather, and just be a good neighbor. People who receive home-delivered meals often look forward to the delivery person's visit as much as they do the food itself.

Disease-specific organizations, such as the Alzheimer's Association or the Parkinson's Disease Foundation, have local programs that offer training, support groups, and other activities to people with the disease and their family members. The United Hospital Fund's Next Step in Care website has a guide to these resources as well as some helpful tips about finding out what is available. Go to www.nextstepincare.org/Links_and_Resources for details.

TIP

Before you call an agency, write down specific questions to ask, and be as concrete and detailed as possible. Take advantage of the fact that you have a real person on the line to talk to you. Get the names of people you find helpful, and ask to speak with them if you need to call again.

Think broadly about community resources. A museum may offer special classes or tours for older people or people with disabilities. Colleges and universities may have performances, classes, or other opportunities to stay engaged. Community centers offer programs for all ages and may have special events for older people.

CAN YOU HEAR ME NOW?

One of the least-addressed aspects of government and community services is the way they communicate with the people they serve, particularly older adults. The World Health Organization (WHO) guide to age-friendly cities has an age-friendly communication and information checklist. Following are some of the key points, applicable to many settings:

- Oral communication accessible to older people is preferred — for instance, through public meetings, community centers, clubs, and broadcast media.

- Printed information should have large lettering, and the main ideas should be shown by clear headings and boldface type.

- Telephone answering services should give instructions slowly and clearly and tell callers how to repeat the message at any time.

- Bank, post office, and other service machines should be well lit and easy to use.

- Most important: Plain language is best — use familiar words in short, straightforward sentences.

Professionals called *geriatric care managers*, who are usually social workers or nurses, may be able to advise you on what services are available and how they have worked out for other clients. Geriatric care managers charge fees, generally by the hour. The Aging Lifecare Association (formerly the National Association of Professional Care Managers) has a referral service at www.aginglifecare.org/ALCA/About_Aging_Life_Care/Find_an_Aging_Life_Care_Expert/ALCA/About_Aging_Life_Care/Search/Find_an_Expert.aspx?hkey=78a6cb03-e912-4993-9b68-df1573e9d8a. You can also ask local agencies for referrals. Geriatric care managers are particularly useful when you're not on the scene all the time, because they can keep tabs on the workers you have hired and make sure all is going smoothly.

Considering NORCs and Village Networks

Because most people want to stay in their homes and in their familiar communities, many communities have been taking on new characteristics. These communities have organized in various ways to meet the changed needs of aging residents. (*Note:* I'm not talking here about assisted-living facilities, which offer a form of group living created to provide personal care and other help, or independent living or cohousing arrangements. See Chapter 8 for a discussion of these options.)

Two options to consider are naturally occurring retirement communities (NORCs) and Village networks. They are different approaches to a common desire to age not only in one's own home but also in one's community. NORCs have a longer history than Villages, but both models are evolving.

With the information in the following sections as a starting point, you can make a more informed choice about aging in place in the community you know. If these options don't work for you, then consider one of the group-living arrangements described in Chapter 8.

Navigating NORCs

Many people who are aging in place live near others at the same stage of life. They may have bought their homes in the suburbs when they were starting out as young families, or they may have taken advantage of union- or government-supported apartment housing and never left. These communities are called *naturally occurring retirement communities,* or *NORCs.* No one planned these communities. The residents created them simply by aging in place.

Defining a NORC

The United Hospital Fund's Aging in Place Initiative (now taken over by the New York State Office for the Aging) describes a NORC as "a community that was not originally built for seniors, but that now has a significant proportion of older residents." Just what that proportion is varies by locality, but generally to be considered a NORC for government or philanthropic funding, a community must have at least 40 percent of its households headed by someone 60 years or older. There may be a minimum requirement of 200 people in that category.

REMEMBER

The demographic designation is only a start. To be able to serve residents, the NORC must offer services. Although the first NORC, established in 1986, was in a moderate-income housing complex in New York City, NORCs are now found in suburbs, rural areas, and small towns. Following are the two main types of NORCs:

>> **Housing-based NORCs:** Also called a *classic, closed,* or *vertical* NORC, these are located in a single age-integrated apartment building, a housing complex with multiple buildings under common management, or an area where several apartment buildings are clustered together.

>> **Neighborhood-based NORCs:** Also known as *open* or *horizontal* NORCs, these are typically one- and two-family homes in age-integrated neighborhoods.

What NORCs offer

NORCs coordinate a broad range of social and medical services to support the residents in the NORC designated area. They build on the strengths of a multidisciplinary team of social-service and healthcare providers, housing managers or representatives of neighborhood associations, and community residents, especially older adults. They may be affiliated with healthcare organizations in the community. NORCs do not charge for services and are funded by a mix of government funding and charitable grants.

The social-service, healthcare, and housing partners, such as an apartment complex's management, agree to organize and develop a mix of on-site services that respond to the residents' changing needs and promote community change in support of successful aging.

The NORC philosophy builds on involving residents in their own healthcare and engaging them in community resources so that they remain active and productive. Some on-site services include:

>> Social work and case-management services

>> Nursing services, especially for adults managing chronic conditions

>> Educational and recreational activities

>> Health prevention and education activities

>> Opportunities for community engagement

REMEMBER

NORC services aren't covered by Medicare or Medicaid, although social workers can help residents gain access to the services they are entitled to under these programs.

TIP

NORCs exist in at least 25 states, but there is no central database of NORCs. Check with your local Area Agency on Aging (call Eldercare Locator at 1-800-677-1116 for the number) or your state or city's Office of Aging for NORCs in your area. And much more information can be found on the United Hospital Fund's NORC Blueprint website, now taken over by the New York State Office for the Aging (https://aging.ny.gov/NORCBLUEPrint/NORCindex.cfm?Name=blueprint/index.html).

Joining a Village

The Village Movement started in 2001 in Boston's Beacon Hill neighborhood. Residents who were getting older but didn't want to move got together and decided to pool resources so that they can obtain services more cheaply. They also wanted a way to connect socially. They created an independent nonprofit organization and set membership dues that are used to leverage their buying power. They hired an executive director to respond to members' individual requests and to develop discount agreements with external preferred service providers. They called their new arrangements *Villages* to emphasize the old notion of people living in small communities helping each other and banding together to meet common needs.

There are now more than 200 Villages in the United States and more than 150 in development. Each Village is independent and develops its own services and activities. The Village to Village Network (www.vtvnetwork.org) is an organization that shares information and resources with participating members, and the website has a map with the locations of existing Villages.

In 2012 the Rutgers School of Social Work conducted a national overview of Villages to find out how they're organized, who the residents are, and what services are provided. Sixty-nine Villages responded. Most had been in existence for three years or less. Over three quarters had at least one paid staff member. Not surprisingly, the survey found a high level (nearly 90 percent) of older adults who were very or extremely involved. Most Villages are freestanding organizations. A few were part of a private social-service agency, a continuing-care retirement community or housing provider, or part of a care consortium.

Volunteers play a large role in Village management by assisting with group activities or administrative tasks. Staff provide some services, such as monitoring phone requests, coordinating requests for professional services, and organizing recreation and social events. The most likely services to be referred to outside providers are home maintenance and repair, home health and personal care, housekeeping, and legal and financial assistance.

All but three of the 69 Villages in the Rutgers survey reported charging a membership fee. An average annual fee for an individual was $430.75 and for a household was $586.91. Some discounted memberships were available with income thresholds. Most of the Villages are located in predominantly urban or suburban areas and serve high or middle-to-high income areas.

The typical Village has 96 members, predominantly white women over the age of 65. About half of the members live alone, and a quarter need help with household chores. If needed, the Village can help with referrals to physicians and home health aides, but the primary emphasis is on the buying power of the group for nonhealthcare services and the social support of the members.

IN THIS CHAPTER

» Talking about driver safety with older adults

» Honing your driving skills and adjusting your driving habits

» Making your car safer

» Determining when to give up driving

» Considering other ways to get around

Chapter **10**

Getting Around: Transportation Options

We can take for granted the independence, flexibility, and freedom of hopping in our car to get around: to run errands, visit friends, go to a movie, get to work. But as we age, our reflexes may not be as quick, our bodies not as flexible, and our vision not as keen, all making driving more challenging. This chapter covers how you can assess your driving habits, or those of your older relative's, and how you can introduce the topic of safe driving before it becomes a critical concern. You also discover ways you may adjust your driving habits and take courses to sharpen your driving skills. With new technology, you may be able to make your car safer or purchase one that incorporates more safety features. And if you limit or stop driving, there are transportation options to get you places: family and friends, public transportation, paratransit, car services, volunteers, and paid drivers. You find out about all that here.

Judging Whether Driving Is Still Safe

Older drivers are, by and large, safe drivers. They are more likely to wear seatbelts than younger drivers, and they are not as prone to speeding, driving under the influence of alcohol or drugs, or risk taking. They are less likely to text or talk on the phone while they drive. Still, when older drivers are involved in accidents, they are more likely than younger drivers to suffer serious trauma and to die.

WARNING

The reality is that aging changes reaction times, vision, and distance perception. In addition, medications may affect driving ability. The label on the pill bottle may warn, "Do not operate heavy machinery while taking this drug," but some people do not realize a car is considered heavy machinery.

Many older drivers adjust their own driving habits to take account of these changes. They drive less at night, stay closer to home, avoid driving in heavy traffic or bad weather, and drive more slowly. Even with these adjustments, older drivers may be at risk not just from their own driving but also from other drivers who create situations that require quick thinking and rapid responses. Think of how many near misses you have experienced or witnessed as drivers zip through stop signs or make left-hand turns without checking for oncoming traffic. Speedy reactions and your ability to anticipate events may have meant the difference between safety and harm for you or others.

Watching for warning signs of unsafe driving

You should give up driving, or ask an older person to give up driving, only if there are real and specific safety concerns. Age alone is not a reason to curtail driving. To find out whether there is a problem, watch for the warning signs in the following list. If you have concerns about an older relative, drive with them and note safety lapses with specific incidents and dates.

TIP

AARP, with the MIT AgeLab and The Hartford Center for Mature Market Excellence created a checklist of 28 warning signs for older drivers. You can use the items on the checklist to observe an older person's driving over time and monitor it for a pattern of warning signs and an increase in frequency. The full list is available at hartfordauto.thehartford.com/UI/Downloads/FamConHtd.pdf.

Here are what I consider to be the top warning signs that someone shouldn't be driving anymore, culled from the 28 signs:

>> Difficulty turning to see when backing up

>> Riding the brake

>> Signaling incorrectly

>> Parking inappropriately

>> Hitting curbs

>> Failing to notice traffic signs

>> Having trouble navigating turns

>> Moving into the wrong lane

>> Getting scrapes and dents on cars, garages, and mailboxes

>> Getting confused at exits

>> Confusing the gas and brake pedals

REMEMBER

The last item on my list — confusing the gas and brake pedals — is frequently cited as the cause of serious accidents involving older drivers, often resulting in injury to pedestrians and property damage.

If you see any of these signs (or even if you don't so far), thinking about options and, if you have an older relative, starting a conversation about safe driving makes sense. The next section helps you open that touchy subject.

TIP

A driver safety course, such as the AARP Smart Driver course, offered in classrooms and online at www.aarp.org/drive, can help drivers hone their safety skills and be more aware of their limitations and challenges. Taking the course with a friend (or you) may encourage your relative to take it as an educational experience, not as a threat to independence. Many states offer car insurance discounts to motorists who complete the course.

For more advice on how to assess someone's driving, AARP Driver Safety offers a free seminar called "We Need to Talk," developed based on information created jointly by The Hartford and the MIT AgeLab. The seminar is available in both English and Spanish and can be viewed online at www.aarp.org/weneedtotalk.

Starting the conversation

Talking about safe driving to a relative who may have taught you the rules of the road is not easy. Ideally, conversations about safety should start before there is a problem. Introduce the topic gently. This talk is best done in a nonjudgmental and nonthreatening way. A trusted person, whether it's a family member or someone else, can initiate this conversation. A spouse or adult child may be a good choice (or not, depending on the relationship). Older drivers seem to respond best to family or doctors. The strength of the trust between the two people is what counts.

While you want to address the topic before it's emotionally charged, if there is a valid safety concern, that conversation should begin now, and better before an accident than after one. Don't put off the talk simply because you're concerned about hurt feelings.

This will probably not be just one conversation but a series of talks. The most important part of the conversation will be listening and validating your relative's concerns.

Here are some ways to open the conversation:

> "I'm worried about your getting lost."

> "With so many bad drivers on the road, I'm concerned about your safety. Can we talk about what you can do to stay safe?"

> "I know you are on some new medications. Have you talked to the doctor about whether they affect driving?"

> "Do you think you may need new glasses? I noticed that you almost missed the exit sign."

Unless the situation is really an accident waiting to happen, use the opportunity to talk about classes to fine-tune driving skills such as AARP's as well as safe driving habits and ways to adapt the car (see more about these in the next section). Later in this chapter, I come back to the question of what to do when an older person absolutely refuses to make any adjustments.

If you and your older relative agree that driving doesn't feel as safe as it used to, a good first step can be to set up a driving evaluation. A comprehensive driving evaluation can be arranged through a local occupational therapy driving rehabilitation specialist. Occupational therapists can identify the physical, visual, and cognitive challenges the individual faces and can recommend ways to limit risks. Visit the American Occupational Therapy Association web page to find a specialist in your area: www.aota.org. A comprehensive driving evaluation can also be arranged through your state's department of motor vehicles. However, many older drivers may be wary of going to the DMV because it has the power to immediately revoke a license.

Making Your Car Fit You

Experts have found that as we age, changes in vision, flexibility, strength, range of motion, and height can make us less comfortable and reduce our control behind the wheel. There are adjustments you may be able to make to your car.

CarFit, an educational program developed by the American Automobile Association, AARP, and the American Occupational Therapy Association, can help educate drivers to become safe and comfortable in their cars. CarFit organizes community events at which technicians and volunteers discuss safe settings to make the car fit the driver. The service takes approximately 20 minutes. Go to `car-fit.org/carfit/RegisterCarFit` for information about events around the country.

TIP

If you're taking your older relative's car for CarFit, take the opportunity to have your own car checked out too. It may reveal some problems you were not aware of and may also make the experience more acceptable to your relative.

The most common adjustments are to mirrors, steering wheels, and seats. Some adjustments can be done easily, such as these:

>> Your line of sight should be at least three inches above the top of the steering wheel.

>> There should be 10 inches between your breastbone and the air bag in the steering wheel.

>> The center of the head restraints should be about three inches or less from the center of the back of your head.

Systems for emergencies, such as OnStar in General Motors vehicles, are also easy to obtain. They call for help, giving your location. Other systems are available for different manufacturers. They are paid for on a subscription basis.

REMEMBER

Performing regular maintenance on the car is critical. Set up, or have your older relative set up, a schedule with a trusted mechanic to go over the car at regular intervals, even if it's not being driven a lot.

Increasing safety with new technology

In addition to adjustments to make your car fit you, today's technology can help make a car (and its driver and occupants) safer. Your old car probably already has air bags and anti-lock brakes, and perhaps a GPS system that gives directions and alerts about approaching exits and turns. But there's more.

The Hartford and the MIT AgeLab, which has been a leader in driver safety for older people, convened a group of experts to review the past decade of research and innovations in driver safety. Following are the technologies they recommend:

>> **Smart headlights:** Adjust the range and intensity of light based on how far away the traffic is and reduce glare

>> **Emergency-response system:** Offers quick assistance in case of a medical emergency or collision

>> **Reverse backup camera and monitoring system:** Warns drivers of objects to the rear of the vehicle to help drivers judge distances and back up safely

- » **Blind-spot warning system:** Alerts you to oncoming traffic by a flashing light in your side-view mirror and a beep or steering wheel vibration

- » **Lane-departure warning:** Helps drivers avoid wandering into another lane

- » **Vehicle-stability control system:** Helps keep the car in the intended line of travel, especially when the driver underestimates the angle of a curve or encounters severe weather

- » **Assistive parking system:** Enables vehicles to park on their own or indicates distances to objects, making parking easier and reducing stress

- » **Voice-activated system:** Allows drivers to access features by voice command so that they can keep their eyes focused on the road

- » **Crash-mitigation system:** Detects when the car may be in danger of a collision

- » **Drowsy driver alerts:** Monitor the degree to which a driver may be inattentive and alert them to pay attention

Some of these devices may be standard in a new (probably more expensive model) car or can be installed by a car dealer. Generally, each manufacturer prices these technologies as part of an equipment package. For example, smart headlights may be part of an "all-weather" package because of their capacity to compensate for poor weather conditions as well as bends in the road.

Choosing a new vehicle

In addition to the new technology in the preceding section, when someone buys a new vehicle, the National Highway Traffic Safety Administration (NHTSA) recommends looking for features that consider the physical and visual challenge of aging:

- » High or extra-wide doors

- » Adjustable foot pedals

- » Large interior door handles

- » Oversized knobs with clearly visible labels

- » Support handles to assist with entry and exit

- » Large or adjustable-size print for dashboard gauges

- » Seat adjusters that can move the seat in all directions; the driver's line of sight should be three inches above the adjusted steering wheel

- » Dashboard-mounted ignition rather than steering column-mounted ignition

DRIVERLESS CARS

Proponents of driverless cars say that huge numbers of people who are older or have disabilities will regain their mobility and independence. Young people won't have to pay such high rates of insurance. Accidents will decrease. These driverless cars should also save fuel and ease congestion. Because they can sense when cars ahead of them are braking, as humans are unable to do, they can drive much closer to each other. But will people be able to overcome their ingrained fear of riding in a vehicle that doesn't have a human at its controls? And will car manufacturers be able to produce a fail-safe vehicle? Time will tell, but remember that when the first automobiles were introduced, the common cry was "Get a horse!"

Modifying vehicles

Adjustments such as pedal extensions or other adaptive equipment may require technical assistance. The American Occupational Therapy Association has a directory of driving-rehabilitation specialists at myaota.aota.org/driver_search. Also see the website of the Association for Driver Rehabilitation Specialists, www.aded.net, for professionals in your area who can diagnose driving problems and help drivers learn safer practices.

Having a disability can make driving an ordinary car difficult or impossible, so you may need a specially adapted vehicle. It may be a sedan or minivan with a wheelchair lift, a car with special steering or braking equipment, or any number of other adaptations. The NHTSA has guidelines on adapting motor vehicles for older adults and alternative guidelines for people with disabilities, which you can find at www.nhtsa.gov/sites/nhtsa.dot.gov/files/documents/adapting_motor_vehicles_brochure_810733.pdf.

A driver-rehabilitation specialist and a mobility-equipment dealer can help design the best features for you. The National Mobility Equipment Dealers Association can refer you to a dealer in your area at www.nmeda.com. A new vehicle modified with adaptive equipment can cost anywhere from $20,000 to $80,000.

TIP

Financial assistance may be available from your state government, nonprofit organizations, and some motor vehicle manufacturers. Some states waive the sales tax if you have a doctor's prescription, and the cost may be tax-deductible.

In considering a new vehicle or adaptations, the NHTSA suggests that you consider the following issues:

>> Does the vehicle have the cargo capacity (in pounds) to accommodate the equipment you require?

>> Is there adequate parking space at home for loading and unloading the vehicle?

>> What additional options would be necessary to operate the vehicle safely?

TIP

If a third party — an insurance company, a state agency, a nonprofit organization, or the VA — is paying for a new vehicle, adaptive devices, or other modifications, find out whether there are any limitations on what may be covered. Get a written statement on what a funding agency will pay before you or your relative agree to buy or make the changes.

REMEMBER

A driver's license may need to be modified to note any restrictions. And the insurance company should be notified of the adjustments.

Knowing When It's Time to Give Up the Keys

When all the safe driving courses, gentle conversations, and vehicle adaptations have failed to make you or your older relative a safe driver, then you need to act. It's not easy to give up the keys, but there are ways to make it work.

If it's for your older relative, AARP's "We Need to Talk" brochure indicates that car accidents, near misses, self-regulation of driving, and health changes provide opportunities for talking about driving. That brochure can help you with these conversations. Make sure to identify and practice alternative transportation (see the next section). And take special care to listen to the person's feelings about missing the freedom and independence when losing the ability to drive.

Note safety lapses you observed when driving together, indicating specifics incidents and dates. Keep the emphasis on safety and health. Say things like "I know you would feel terrible if someone was hurt when you were driving" or "Even if you were not at fault in a collision, you can be seriously injured or die." Concern for others may be a stronger motivation than concern for oneself. Tactfully mention, without dramatizing the point, that an accident would create a major financial and possibly legal burden. Acknowledge how difficult this transition is. With gentleness and concern, a decades-old driver can become a more or less willing passenger.

TIP

You may be able to enlist the support of a doctor to limit or forgo driving altogether, particularly if your relative has some medical or cognitive condition, such as Parkinson's or Alzheimer's disease, that affects driving. Your relative may be more willing to accept intervention if you identify the disease as the problem rather than the driver's skill. A person with dementia may get lost even in familiar places, in addition to the lapses in judgment that are often symptoms of this condition. The driving evaluations mentioned earlier in this chapter may provide a factual basis for the recommendation from a third party that it is time to give up the keys.

If all else fails, you may have to consider disabling the car, failing to renew the driver's license or having it revoked, canceling the insurance, or taking away the keys. Even these measures may not be enough, as some very determined older people will find ways around them, such as calling a mechanic to fix the car or driving without a license or insurance. Taking the car away is a final step.

Finding Alternatives to Driving

Housing and transportation are two basic needs, and they are often connected. In Chapter 9, you find more about how livable communities offer places where you can walk, bicycle, and access public transportation. They may have nearby stores and services you can walk to and bicycle-sharing services. But often people live in neighborhoods that aren't walkable, bikeable, or near public transportation. Housing in areas close to public transportation may be unaffordable for older people on fixed incomes. It's not surprising that so many older people don't want to give up their driving, which often results in feeling a lack of freedom and independence. Depending on where you or your older relative lives, there may be a few or many alternatives for getting around.

There are numerous options in addition to bicycles and walking:

>> Public transit (buses, light rail transit, trains/subways)

>> Paratransit (reservations-required vans or cars for people who cannot drive or who have disabilities)

>> Private transit (taxis, car services)

>> Specialized transit (programs organized by hospitals, senior centers, and religious or volunteer organizations to serve particular populations)

I discuss all these options in the following sections.

Public transportation and paratransit options

TIP

The National Aging and Disability Transportation Center, which is funded by the Federal Transit Administration and administered by Easterseals and the National Association of Area Agencies on Aging, has resources for consumers, including a guide to public transportation, at `www.nadtc.org/resources-publications/transportation-options-for-older-adults-and-people-with-disabilities/`.

Look into the public transportation options in your community, including buses, subways, and rail options. Check to see whether the public transportation in your community is set up for people with limited mobility. For some of the oldest transit systems in the United States (like in New York City), constructed before the Americans with Disabilities Act (ADA), access for people with disabilities can present a challenge. In its extensive subway system, not all stations are equipped with elevators, so a person who has difficulty with stairs may be able to get down to the tracks to get on a subway train but find that there is no elevator service at the destination station. Buses are now more likely to have lifts or ramps for wheelchairs or walkers and specially designated seats for passengers who are older or have a disability. Still, this adaptation isn't universal. And buses have designated routes and stops, which may or may not be convenient.

Get used to using public transportation before you need it. You can get a group of people together, or ask for volunteer help from students or family members or a nonprofit, to take a day tour of public transit to find out how to get around, pay the fare, signal for stops, and disembark.

Paratransit is another option. The ADA requires transportation agencies that provide fixed-route services (bus or train) to also provide paratransit services to people with disabilities who live within three-quarters of a mile from the fixed routes. These restrictions mean that not all older people will qualify for public paratransit services. Look for these standards:

>> **Availability:** Check the hours, such as during days, evenings, and weekends.

>> **Accessibility:** The transit comes to the door, or the bus stop is close by, and the vehicle is easy to enter.

>> **Affordability:** Fees are low enough for people on restricted budgets, with options for discounts.

>> **Destination:** Some services link only to specific places, such as going to the doctor or shopping; others are more flexible and go where the passenger wants to go within the service range.

>> **Assistance:** Check the types of assistance offered. Some services provide mechanical assistance (buses that have wheelchair lifts or ramps and special seating; paratransit drivers who assist passengers getting on and off).

>> **Information:** Find out about the routes and how to make arrangements to use it.

>> **Socialization:** While bus and van drivers should focus on the road, the way they greet passengers and help them on and off makes a difference. On a familiar route, passengers should feel free to chat, share their experiences, comment on the journey, and generally make the trip enjoyable. Some may prefer not to join in, and that should be respected as well.

You can use these standards to evaluate the options available in your area. Check online or by phone with the local government office that runs the public transportation system to obtain a map of the system, which may or may not have up-to-date information on accessibility features.

TIP

Area Agencies on Aging and Aging and Disability Resource Centers may offer fare assistance programs for eligible riders who can purchase vouchers at a discounted rate. The vouchers can be used to pay for services from participating transportation providers, including public transportation, taxi companies, or others.

Private options

Where public transportation isn't available or appropriate, some private services can fill the gap. Older people may balk at the expense of paid transportation, but maintaining a car and paying for gas and insurance is much more expensive than an occasional ride. Following are some of the more popular options:

>> **Family and friends:** Probably most older people get rides from family, friends, and neighbors from time to time. One person may offer to take you shopping or to religious services. Another may volunteer to go to the doctor and wait until the visit is finished. These are the traditional ways people who don't drive have been helped over the years, and they still work. Be aware of whether these volunteer drivers are themselves of an age or condition in which their driving capacity may be at risk.

>> **Taxis:** Taxicabs offer a common alternative to driving. Some cities restrict licensed cabs to picking up passengers on the street; others have some way to call from wherever you are. Some taxi companies have wheelchair-accessible vehicles.

» **Smartphone app car services:** The newest variety of car service, available in most cities, uses a smartphone app. Uber and Lyft are the most well-known. The app identifies your location and sends the nearest driver to pick you up. Fees are set in advance and paid for by a credit card on file. Tipping is optional. Uber has introduced Uber Health, a service available through some healthcare organizations, that arranges rides for doctor appointments. See www.uberhealth.com/ for more information.

GoGoGrandparent is a company that, for a fee, lets you order a smartphone app car service without the smartphone app. The rider calls a number, 855-464-6872, which relays the request to a dispatcher from a service such as Uber or Lyft: gogograndparent.com.

» **Car services:** This option is like a more upscale taxi. The cars are generally more comfortable, although more expensive than taxis. Some are wheelchair-accessible. If you set up an account with a credit card, you can be billed at the end of the month, which gives you a record of expenses.

» **Supplemental transportation programs (STPs):** STPs are nontraditional transportation services for older adults who don't drive and others who need assistance. Most STPs provide door-to-door rides, and some arrange for a driver to stay with passengers until they are ready to go home. Some STPs are organized by religious institutions or other community groups.

» **Volunteer programs:** Programs organized by faith-based organizations or private agencies often have a network of volunteers who provide transportation for shopping, doctor's appointments, and recreation. They may offer one-way, round-trip, or multistop rides, usually at no cost or on a donation basis.

» **Hiring a driver:** Some people may have the option of hiring their own driver when needed (as in the movie *Driving Miss Daisy*). It need not be a full-time position. If you hire a driver, make sure the person's driver's license and insurance are valid and up-to-date.

» **Transportation provided by independent or assisted-living facilities, Villages, or other residence- or community-based organizations:** These options have become increasingly important and desirable for older individuals and are often used to get to and from doctors' offices, entertainment sites such as movie theaters, and so on.

TIP

The Hartford's "Getting There" Worksheet is a systematic way of reviewing local options. It includes sections on family and friends, local programs that may offer rides, demand–responsive services or paratransit, private program services, taxis and car services, and mass transit. It provides a separate worksheet to determine costs. Measured against the cost of owning and operating a car, these costs may be much less. You can find the worksheets at hartfordauto.thehartford.com/UI/Downloads/FamConHtd.pdf.

For example, the section on family and friends, the top alternative to driving for older adults, asks these questions:

>> Are people available to provide rides at the times required?

>> To what extent are family or friends able or willing to provide rides?

>> Do people provide the rides willingly, or do they resent having to adjust their schedule?

>> Can the older person trade something for a ride (making dinner, taking the driver to lunch, paying for gas)?

TIP

You and your older relative can answer these questions yourselves. But to get the information for the public or other private options, you should do some research. To find out what is available in your community, check with the local Area Agency on Aging, the state Aging and Disability Resource Center, senior centers, health-care providers, and others who may know about options. Giving up the keys should lead to new ways of getting around, not the end of living fully in the community.

3

Legal and Financial Planning

Take a look at the differences in what Medicare and Medicaid cover in terms of medical and nonmedical care. Also consider whether you may be eligible for both programs or have private healthcare and long-term care insurance that can play a part.

Look at the pros and cons of long-term care insurance in today's market. I also review reverse mortgages, disability insurance, annuities, and life settlements.

Keep control of your finances by drawing up a will and perhaps a trust.

Chapter **11**

Unraveling the Rules of Medicare and Medicaid

You may be thinking about how Medicare and Medicaid will help pay for your long-term needs as you age.

Perhaps you've heard that Medicare doesn't cover long-term care. What most people mean by this declaration is that the federal Medicare program doesn't cover a long stay in a nursing home or 24-hour personal care at home or in an assisted-living facility. Medicare does, however, cover a short stay for rehabilitation therapy as well as many of the healthcare services you or your parent or other relative need to live safely at home and in the community.

Medicaid, a federal-state program for low-income individuals, does cover long-term care in nursing homes and many home- and community-based services, but its eligibility and other rules vary by state and set stringent limits on income and assets. Policymakers call people who are eligible for both Medicare and Medicaid by the awkward term *duals*. That means if you're eligible for Medicare and Medicaid, you can coordinate benefits from both programs.

Understanding the framework of these public programs is the first step in figuring out how they may or may not apply to you or your relative and how they may relate to other kinds of healthcare or long-term care insurance. Dive into this chapter to discover how these programs work.

REMEMBER

Medicare and Medicaid rules are subject to change. You can check www.medicare. gov, www.medicaid.gov, and your state Medicaid agency for information. Other sources of information are the Medicare Rights Center (www.medicarerights. org/), which has a help line for questions, and the Center for Medicare Advocacy (www.medicareadvocacy.org/), which has useful publications and updates on court cases.

TIP

As you start to navigate public healthcare programs, keep in mind that your State Health Insurance Assistance Program (SHIP) is a valuable resource. The SHIP advisers can guide you through the maze of Medicare, Medicaid, and other insurance plans. You may find that you're eligible for more than you realized. Find your state SHIP at www.shiptacenter.org/.

The Distinction between Medicare and Medicaid

Medicare pays for the medical care needed by someone who has a chronic condition or a disability but does not pay for the nonmedical services that person needs. (An exception is a recent change to Medicare Advantage plans, described later in this chapter.) Medicaid, however, pays for both for eligible low-income people.

REMEMBER

Here is an essential but still often misunderstood distinction between Medicare and Medicaid:

>> **Medicare:** A federal health insurance program for people age 65 and older and for younger people with certain conditions and disabilities. More than 59 million Americans are enrolled in Medicare.

>> **Medicaid:** A federal-state program that pays for healthcare and long-term care for low-income people who meet a certain threshold. Over 79 million Americans, including 8.9 million children, receive healthcare through Medicaid over the course of a year.

For more comprehensive information on Medicare, see AARP's *Medicare For Dummies* by Patricia Barry (published by Wiley).

Looking at Medicare Basics

Medicare is the main source of payment for medical care for adults 65 and older. If you or your parent live in your own home, assisted living, a multigenerational home, or some other non-nursing-home setting, you need access to medical service providers for primary care, preventive care, and management of chronic conditions; hospital care; post-hospital rehabilitation services and home healthcare; and emergencies, as well as prescription drugs and, for some conditions, durable medical equipment. Medicare generally pays for this necessary medical care.

In addition to Medicare eligibility parameters, the following sections also cover Medicare's two options: Original Medicare and Medicare Advantage plans. I also discuss Medicare's role in providing necessary medical care services.

WARNING

Beginning in April 2018, Medicare started issuing new identification cards to all eligible beneficiaries. The main difference is that your Social Security number (SSN) is no longer your ID number. This change is intended to prevent misuse of your personal information. But it has also given rise to new scams, mostly involving attempts to get you to pay for your Medicare card (it's free) and to get access to your personal information. Ignore any callers who claim to be from Medicare. Another change is that gender is no longer listed on the card. If you already have a Medicare Advantage, Medigap, or prescription drug plan ID card, those IDs are different from the SSN.

Are you eligible for Medicare?

If you or your parent is 65 or older, you're probably already enrolled in Medicare. Enrollment is automatic when you start collecting some form of Social Security benefits. If you are 65 or older and not yet collecting Social Security benefits, you can enroll in Medicare online, over the phone, or in person through the Social Security Administration.

Not everyone over 65 is automatically eligible for Medicare. You must be a U.S. citizen or a legal resident of the United States for over five years. Residents of Puerto Rico are eligible. If you (or a spouse) have worked at least a total of ten years (40 credits) and contributed to Social Security under the Federal Insurance Contributions Act (FICA) through your employers, you are eligible.

TIP

Earning 40 work credits means only that you don't have to pay monthly premiums for Part A services. Anybody who is a citizen or legal resident for at least five years can get Part B and Part D services by paying premiums for them like everybody else.

REMEMBER

The Affordable Care Act (ACA, also commonly called Obamacare) doesn't affect Medicare eligibility. If you or your relative is enrolled in Medicare, you don't have to do anything. The ACA did make some changes to Medicare: Some preventive measures such as mammograms and colonoscopies are now free, and a timetable has been set for closing the so-called doughnut hole in Part D for prescription drugs (discussed in the later section "Prescription drug coverage").

The U.S. Supreme Court ruling in June 2013 that struck down Section 3 of the Defense of Marriage Act has implications for Medicare eligibility. The Act had defined a *spouse* as a "person of the opposite sex," so the Court's decision opens Medicare eligibility and benefits to same-sex couples. The Department of Health and Human Services has begun to issue specific policy changes, including same-sex married couples' rights under Medicare Advantage plans to reside in the same nursing home. For more information, see Chapter 18 on LGBT issues and the National Resource Center on LGBT Aging at www.lgbtagingcenter.org/resources/pdfs/Post-DOMA_Medicare.pdf.

If you are uncertain whether you or your relative qualifies for Medicare, contact Social Security at 800-772-1213 or go to www.medicare.gov/eligibilitypremiumcalc/. This website also helps you calculate your premium. The Medicare Rights Center has a useful fact sheet titled "Medicare Q and A" on eligibility and the timing of enrollment at www.medicarerights.org/PartB-Enrollment-Toolkit/Part-1-QA-General.pdf.

ADDITIONAL MEDICARE ELIGIBILITY

Medicare also covers younger people with end-stage kidney disease or amyotrophic lateral sclerosis (ALS), as well as people with other disabilities who have received Social Security Disability Insurance (SSDI) benefits for a total of 24 months from the Social Security Administration or the U.S. Railroad Retirement Board. The months you wait for your application to be approved are counted in meeting this 24-month requirement.

If you or your spouse's work history does not reach the required threshold but you meet the citizenship or residency requirements, you can still enroll in Medicare Part A (hospital coverage) and pay a monthly premium, as well as in optional Part B (outpatient coverage), for which everyone pays a monthly premium. It is a good idea to do this because if you enroll later, you risk paying permanent late penalties. But if you are covered by a group health-insurance plan provided by an employer for whom you or your spouse still works, you can delay enrolling in Part B without a penalty until your employment ends.

What's included in Original Medicare

Original Medicare includes Parts A, B, and D benefits. (Part C applies only to Medicare Advantage and is just another way of packaging Parts A, B, and D benefits. See the next section for details on Medicare Advantage plans.)

Parts A, B, and D

Here is a breakdown of Parts A, B, and D:

>> **Part A:** Medicare Part A covers inpatient care in a hospital, rehabilitation services in a skilled nursing facility or rehabilitation hospital, hospice care, home healthcare (under certain conditions), and inpatient care in a religious nonmedical healthcare institution (a place for Christian Scientists who need assistance but have religious objections to conventional medicine). Medicare Part A does not require additional premiums for eligible beneficiaries; if you do not have enough working quarters to qualify, you can enroll and pay a monthly premium. There is a deductible (amount you pay before Medicare starts paying) if you are hospitalized; in 2018 this is set at $1,340 for each benefit period of 60 days. After 60 days, there is a coinsurance fee of $335 a day, and after 90 days this goes up to $670 a day until you reach the "lifetime reserve," at which point you pay all costs.

Reaching the lifetime reserve is certainly worrisome but is unlikely to occur, because hospital stays these days are generally very short, and patients who require further care are frequently transferred to a rehabilitation program in a skilled nursing facility (SNF). If this happens to you or your parent, it does not mean that you have been placed permanently in a nursing home. Although the Medicare benefit period in a rehab setting ends at 100 days, you may be discharged much earlier, perhaps within two to three weeks. You don't have to pay any fees for the first 20 days of each benefit period. For days 21 through 100, you pay a coinsurance amount per day of $167, and if you stay past day 100, you pay all costs for each day, unless you have additional insurance that covers these costs.

WARNING

To be eligible for Medicare coverage of a rehabilitation program in a skilled nursing facility, you must have been hospitalized as an inpatient for three days prior to the transfer. Some hospitals have been classifying patients as being in *observation status* — that is, not formally admitted to the hospital, even though they may be in a bed on a hospital unit getting the same treatment as an officially admitted patient. This has financial implications; their stay is not covered under Medicare Part A, which has a one-time deductible for the stay, but under Part B, which bills for every service separately as if the hospital were an outpatient setting. Moreover, days spent in observation do not count as inpatient days toward the three-day nursing facility requirement, so the patient is responsible for the entire cost of the rehab stay. This policy is being contested and may change, but for now it is worth asking at every hospital stay whether the patient is admitted or under observation. You should receive a notice that you are in observation status called a MOON (Medicare Outpatient Observation Notice). Although there is a process by which you can appeal a discharge that you feel is premature or not safe, there is no comparable process to appeal a decision that you are in observation status. Discussions with hospital administration and staff may help, but there is no guarantee that they will agree to change the designation from being on observation to being admitted. For more information, see the Center for Medicare Advocacy's website at www.medicareadvocacy.org/medicare-info/observation-status/.

>> **Part B:** Medicare Part B is an optional component that helps cover medically necessary services like doctor's visits, outpatient care, durable medical equipment, and many preventive services like flu shots. You pay a monthly premium to be enrolled to obtain coverage for these Medicare services. But Part B is heavily subsidized, so unless you have very good private insurance, it almost always makes sense to choose this option.

REMEMBER

Original Medicare Part B does not cover routine vision or dental visits or products like hearing aids.

>> **Part D:** Medicare Part D, which covers prescription drugs, is also optional but strongly advised. You pay a monthly premium, which changes every year. If you receive Social Security benefits, your Medicare premium for both Parts B and D are deducted from the check.

TIP

Unlike Part A, premiums for Parts B and D are set at a higher level for people with higher incomes. The higher premiums in 2018 start at $85,000 per year for an individual and $170,000 for a couple. For more information, see www.ssa.gov/pubs/EN-05-10536.pdf from the Social Security Administration.

What Medicare doesn't pay for

REMEMBER

Medicare doesn't pay for everything. Even if it does cover a service, you generally pay the following fees:

>> A deductible (a certain amount of actual medical costs you incur before insurance starts to pay)

>> Coinsurance (your share of these costs after the deductible has been reached, typically 20 percent)

>> Copayments (the fixed amount you pay, for example, at a doctor visit)

Many people purchase Medicare Supplemental Insurance (Medigap) to help pay for these additional expenses. These policies are offered by private insurance companies and must meet federal and state requirements. Medicare has information on how to find Medigap policies in your state at www.medicare.gov/supplement-other-insurance/medigap/whats-medigap.html.

WARNING

Current Medigap policies don't include prescription drug coverage, but if you have a policy purchased before 2006, it may still cover drugs. If you or your parent has an old policy labeled H, I, or J, you can still use it, but its drug coverage part is not nearly as good as Medicare Part D. These policies have become more expensive as fewer and fewer people use them. On the other hand, if you switch to Part D now, you must pay late penalties in addition to the plan's premiums.

What you get with Medicare Advantage plans

Medicare Part C offers an alternative to Original Medicare called the *Medicare Advantage program*, a collection of health plans (such as Health Maintenance Organizations and Preferred Provider Organizations) that combine Parts A and B services (usually with Part D prescription drug coverage) in their benefit packages. The plans are offered by private companies with Medicare approval. They must cover all the services in Original Medicare but may also offer extra coverage, such as vision, dental, hearing, and health and wellness programs. Medicare Advantage plans set their own fee schedules and choose their own network of providers and facilities; this is important information to consider when you're choosing a plan.

TIP

The 2018 Chronic Care Act passed by Congress as part of the Bipartisan Budget Act of 2018 includes a provision that gives Medicare Advantage plans more flexibility in covering nonmedical products and services, such as bathroom grab bars and wheelchair ramps. It also expands telehealth services so that people who are unable to get to a doctor's office can communicate by web-based services. For more information, go to www.thescanfoundation.org/chronic-care-act-2018-advancing-care-adults-complex-needs. There is no requirement that Medicare Advantage plans offer these add-ons and no special funding for them, so each plan will make its own choices.

REMEMBER

In Original Medicare — a fee-for-service arrangement — you go to a doctor who participates in the program and pay a copay, and the doctor bills Medicare for the visit and any tests or procedures that were performed. Medicare Advantage plans receive a set amount every month for each person enrolled in the plan, whether they use many services or just a few. The plan can charge different copays and have different rules about whether you need a referral to see a specialist, for example, or whether you can go only to doctors or hospitals that belong to the plan. There are several different kinds of Medicare Advantage plans, and their rules, costs, and benefits differ and can change each year. You can change plans once every year and at other times in certain circumstances.

WARNING

If you enroll in a Medicare Advantage plan, you can't buy a Medigap policy. This kind of insurance can be used only with Original Medicare and can't be used for any expenses under a Medicare Advantage plan. However, if you drop your Medigap policy to join a Medicare Advantage plan and then decide to go back to Original Medicare, you may not be able to get the Medigap policy reinstated.

For more information about Medicare Advantage plans, go to the Medicare Plan Finder at www.medicare.gov/find-a-plan.

Prescription drug coverage

Medicare Part D covers prescription drugs, which is often an expensive part of medical care. Following are the two main ways to get prescription drug coverage:

>> Part D plans, which add drug coverage to Original Medicare

>> Medicare Advantage plans, which include Part D prescription drug coverage (MA-PDs).

If you're choosing among Part D plans, you need to consider a few variables:

>> Are the drugs you take on the plan's formulary (list of drugs)?

>> Is the pharmacy you generally use in the plan's network?

>> Does the plan require you to use generic rather than brand-name drugs, or to give certain drugs a trial before it will approve more expensive ones?

>> Do you have to pay a deductible or copayment for drugs?

>> Are financial-assistance plans available?

REMEMBER

Most Medicare Part D plans have a so-called *doughnut hole,* a gap in coverage that begins after you and your drug plan have spent a certain amount for covered drugs. In 2018 that amount is $3,750. After you're in the doughnut hole, in 2018 you pay 35 percent of the plan's costs for covered brand-name drugs and 79 percent of the plan's costs for covered generic drugs. What you've paid from the beginning of the year — deductibles, coinsurance, and copays (but not the drug plan premiums) — counts toward getting out of the coverage gap, as do any discounts for brand-name drugs that you get in the gap. After you reach $4,550, catastrophic coverage takes over and pays 95 percent of Part D drug costs. To estimate how much you'll have to spend in the doughnut hole, see www.medicare.gov/part-d/costs/coverage-gap/part-d-coverage-gap.html. Under the Affordable Care Act, the doughnut hole was supposed to shrink every year until it disappeared in 2020, but as part of the Bipartisan Budget Act of 2018, it will now end in 2019.

Even with Medicare Part D, prescription drugs can be very expensive. Financial assistance may be available from Medicare, your state, pharmaceutical companies, or charities. Here are some resources for financial assistance:

» **Extra Help:** Medicare's Extra Help program provides low-cost Part D coverage for people with incomes and assets under a certain level. Income limits are higher if you have dependents living with you or if you live in Alaska or Hawaii. Assets include money in savings or checking accounts, stocks, bonds, and other investments, but not your home, car, or household items. If you qualify and join a Medicare drug plan, you get help paying for your monthly premium, yearly deductible, coinsurance, and copayments. If you have Medicaid and live in a nursing home, this drug coverage is free. To apply for Extra Help, go to www.socialsecurity.gov/i1020 or call 800-772-1213.

» **State Pharmacy Assistance Programs:** Many states have State Pharmacy Assistance Programs (SPAPs) that help some people pay for prescription drugs based on financial need, age, or medical conditions. To find out what is available in your state, contact your State Health Insurance Assistance Program (SHIP). Find your state SHIP at www.medicare.gov/contacts/organization-search-criteria.aspx.

» **Pharmaceutical assistance programs:** Many major pharmaceutical companies help people who are taking their drugs but can't pay the full price. There is a list of drugs and potential pharmaceutical or patient assistance programs at www.medicare.gov/pharmaceutical-assistance-program/. Even if the drug is not on the list, try calling the company to see what help you can get. The formal request must be made by a doctor.

» **Charity programs:** Charity programs include organizations that help people with low incomes pay for prescription drugs. These organizations often serve people with a particular disease, such as cancer or neurological conditions. The Medicare Rights Center lists some of these charities at www.medicarerights.org/pdf/copay_charities.pdf.

Private insurance (such as retiree benefits) in addition to Medicare may help with prescription drug coverage. Check with your plan to see how it coordinates benefits. Medigap supplemental insurance, however, doesn't cover drug expenses.

TIP

The Medicare Rights Center has a comprehensive guide to financial assistance for prescription drugs with information by state. You can access the guide at www. medicareinteractive.org/pdf/SPAP-Chart.pdf.

Durable medical equipment coverage

Medicare Part B covers durable medical equipment (DME), which includes devices like canes (except white canes for blind people), walkers, wheelchairs, hospital beds, commodes, and other aids that a person with a disability or a chronically ill person needs at home. (*Home* can be a house, an assisted-living facility, or wherever the person lives.) A walker, for example, that you need only to take a walk down the street would not be covered.

DME can be used over and over, distinguishing these items from disposable supplies like adult diapers, bandages, and sterile gloves that can be used only once. Disposable items like these are not covered by Medicare. However, non-reusable diabetic supplies like test strips and lancets are covered, as are oxygen supplies.

TIP

In July 2013 Medicare started a National Mail-Order Program for diabetic testing supplies. You need to use a Medicare national mail-order contract supplier if you want to have these items delivered at home. You can still purchase them at your regular pharmacy or other supplier. The costs are the same and include a 20 percent coinsurance payment.

WARNING

Phone or mail offers to supply DME at extremely low costs are likely to be scams. Make sure that you're alert to these phony offers and buy only from suppliers that Medicare has approved.

REMEMBER

DME is one of the most confusing parts of Medicare, and the rules keep changing. However, here are some points to remember:

>> Medicare covers DME only when ordered by a physician.

>> The equipment must be ordered from companies that have an agreement with Original Medicare or with a Medicare Advantage plan.

>> Some areas of the country are included in Medicare's Competitive Bidding Program, which is designed to prevent overcharging to Medicare. It applies only to Original Medicare and may mean that you have to change suppliers for certain items. For more information, go to www.medicare.gov/what-medicare-covers/part-b/competitive-bidding-program.html.

>> If you are in Original Medicare, you are responsible for a 20 percent coinsurance payment of the Medicare-approved amount (which may not be the full price).

>> Some items can be rented rather than purchased. There are special rules for renting oxygen equipment.

>> Medicare pays only for the basic model. If you or your parent needs a customized wheelchair or a special bed, you must pay the extra charge.

>> Medicare covers repairs and maintenance to keep equipment in good working order, but the rules are different depending on whether you own or rent the equipment. Delays in getting DME repaired are unfortunately common.

>> If your claim for DME that a doctor has ordered is denied by Medicare's contractor in your region (a private insurance company that reviews Medicare claims), you have the right to appeal that decision.

Home healthcare services

Help at home is probably the most-often-needed service for an older adult, and it's the area where Medicare coverage is weakest and private costs are highest. Medicare does pay for some home healthcare services, however, under these conditions:

>> A doctor confirms in writing that he or she has examined the person within 30 days and that the patient needs skilled nursing care, such as care provided by a registered nurse or physical therapist. Without this signed paper, the home healthcare agency cannot "open the case" (begin treating the person). The doctor can be a hospitalist or an emergency department doctor (employed by the hospital) or a community-based doctor. The visit must be face-to-face, not a phone conversation or a report from a nurse.

>> If there is a documented need for skilled care, the person may also receive some home care aide services, although usually for a few hours a day or a few days a week.

>> The person is homebound (meaning that leaving the house is hard).

>> The person needs only short-term or part-time skilled services.

>> The services are provided by a Medicare-approved home health agency (HHA). The HHA may have its own home health aides or contract with licensed agencies to provide these workers, but Medicare will not pay for services provided only by licensed agencies or companion agencies. (See Chapter 15 for a description of the various types of home care agencies.)

TIP

The so-called "improvement standard" (denial of physical or occupational therapy because the Medicare beneficiary is no longer making improvements) no longer exists (it was never a regulation even though it was commonly used). As a result of a lawsuit (*Jimmo v. Sebelius*) filed by the Medicare Advocacy Center, CMS has officially ended this practice. See the agency's statement at www.cms.gov/Center/Special-Topic/Jimmo-Center.html. The cap on reimbursement for these services has also been lifted, although providers are subject to a review of their fees if they reach a threshold of $3,000. For more information on this case, go to www.medicareadvocacy.org/medicare-info/improvement-standard/.

I cover more home care issues in Chapter 15. You can also find more information from Medicare at www.medicare.gov/homehealthcompare/search.html.

Medicaid Ground Rules

Medicaid, a publicly funded healthcare program for low-income families and individuals, is a shared responsibility of the federal and state governments. While eligibility for Medicare is generally based on the applicant's age, eligibility for Medicaid is generally based on the applicant's income and assets. Medicaid pays for more than 60 percent of people living in nursing homes. Nearly a quarter of people enrolled in Medicaid are older adults or people with disabilities, but they account for more than 60 percent of all Medicaid spending because they need more and often more expensive healthcare.

The federal government sets basic rules about what benefits must be included in state Medicaid plans and shares the costs. The federal government matches state Medicaid funding on at least a 50 percent basis, but the match may be higher in states with low per-capita income. States set their own eligibility requirements and have considerable flexibility in designing their benefit packages.

REMEMBER

Medicaid is changing as eligibility rules under the ACA are expanded or revised depending on the state. Some states are adding work requirements under demonstration programs negotiated with the federal government, but these are being challenged in courts. Other states have received approval to charge higher premiums for Medicaid coverage than those normally allowed under federal rules, with disenrollment and lockout periods for nonpayment. In general, these changes do not affect people applying for long-term care services and supports in their homes or communities or in nursing homes. At a minimum, if you or your parent are already on Medicaid, make sure you read any notices you get about changes in coverage.

TIP

States call their Medicaid programs by different names: Medi-Cal in California, TennCare in Tennessee, and MassHealth in Massachusetts, for example. Some states seem to go out of their way to avoid using Medicaid in their program name. For the name and program offices in your state, go to www.medicaid.gov/medicaid/by-state/by-state.html and follow the link to your state's website.

Are you eligible for Medicaid?

To receive federal funding, state Medicaid programs are required to cover certain populations, such as children in low-income families and pregnant women. Older adults with low incomes and persons with disabilities who receive cash assistance through the Supplemental Security Income program (SSI) are eligible in the states that use SSI criteria. (Nine states continue to use more restrictive 1972 welfare eligibility standards.) Eligibility requirements differ considerably from state to state. Some people who are not now eligible for Medicaid may become eligible as the ACA is implemented in those states that have opted to accept the Medicaid expansion program. This website gives you some basic information on eligibility requirements in your state: www.healthcare.gov/do-i-qualify-for-medicaid.

In the past several years, Medicaid programs have been under pressure to control costs, and one way they have done this is to tighten the eligibility requirements. In some places the entry process is very time-consuming and difficult. On the other hand, some states are streamlining the process by making it easier to enroll online or without a face-to-face interview.

REMEMBER

Unlike Medicare, where there are clear federal eligibility standards, Medicaid varies by state. However, there are certain basic approaches:

>> According to federal rules, Medicaid must cover certain populations (such as children in low-income families, pregnant women, and people with disabilities receiving SSI).

>> States set their own, typically stringent, levels for income, often some percentage of the federal poverty level.

>> For adults over age 65 and people with disabilities, all states (except Arizona) limit the amount of assets a person can retain to be eligible for Medicaid; this is usually a small amount, although eligibility may be delayed for individuals transferring larger assets within a "look-back" period prior to applying. (Under the ACA, nondisabled children and nondisabled adults under age 65 are no longer subject to asset limits.)

Medicaid is intended as a safety net, and states take that goal seriously.

Medically needy programs

In addition to income and asset limits, 33 state Medicaid programs have *medically needy* programs that assist people who have high medical expenses but whose income exceeds the maximum threshold for Medicaid eligibility. Older people living in nursing homes and children and adults with disabilities comprise a significant fraction of the 3.2 million people enrolled in these programs.

Eligible participants can subtract their healthcare expenses from their income. States vary in their rules for eligibility and the way they determine the number of months a person must pay these expenses privately before Medicaid kicks in. Some of these people may become eligible for Medicaid directly through the ACA. See the report from the Kaiser Commission on Medicaid and the Uninsured for state-by-state information at www.kff.org/other/state-indicator/medicaid-eligibility-through-the-medically-needy-pathway/.

Exchanges

Starting in October 2013, all states were required to have a new Health Insurance Marketplace or exchange. These are websites where various health plans can offer their policies to prospective consumers. The Marketplace offers information about a range of selected private health plans as well as Medicaid. People with certain income levels can receive subsidies, and the goal is to benefit everyone because of the large risk pool. For more information about your state, go to www.healthcare.gov or see the state profiles at the Kaiser Family Foundation website, www.kff.org/state-health-exchange-profiles.

You may want to ask a family member or friend to help you access the information you need. The ACA also offers funding to local nonprofit organizations, or "navigators," that may assist individuals with enrollment in the exchange. To find navigators in your area, go to localhelp.healthcare.gov.

REMEMBER

As of January 2014, the federal government established new methods of calculating eligibility for health insurance and subsidies under the ACA, including Medicaid. Access to health insurance was expanded to new groups, and the income eligibility level was increased to 138 percent of the Federal Poverty Level (FPL), which varies by the number of people in the household. There is also a new method of calculating income based on IRS tax records, called MAGI (modified adjusted gross income). People who do not fit these new categories are called non-MAGI applicants. The goal is to have a standard and streamlined process of application and choice of health insurance. Many states have established navigator assistance sites to help people figure out whether they fit into the MAGI or non-MAGI groups, so check your state Medicaid office for assistance.

Estate recovery

WARNING

Becoming eligible for Medicaid is one challenge; what happens after death can be another. The 1993 federal estate recovery rules require state Medicaid programs to recover from the estate of an individual over the age of 55 certain benefits paid on behalf of a Medicaid enrollee. They may be payments to a nursing home, home- and community-based services, or hospital and prescription drug services. There are limits, however. States cannot recover money from the estate of a Medicaid enrollee who is survived by a spouse, a child under the age of 21, or a disabled child of any age. States vary in how aggressively they pursue estate recovery. It is important to understand the provisions of your state's estate-recovery program. Although the amount recovered for the state is usually very small, it can present hardships for the surviving family members. However, states are required to establish procedures for waiving estate recovery if heirs would experience undue hardship. For more information, see AARP's report on varying estate recovery practices at assets.aarp.org/rgcenter/il/inb137_medicaid.pdf.

TECHNICAL STUFF

Estate-recovery laws are different from filial responsibility laws, which exist in 30 states and generally require adult children to provide support to their indigent parents, with some exceptions. These laws have seldom been enforced, but in 2012 a Pennsylvania court upheld a decision requiring a son to pay a nursing home $92,000 for his mother's care while she applied for Medicaid. She left the county before Medicaid determined that she was not eligible. In cases like this, the nursing homes are the party seeking payment, not the government recovering its expenses. Some states are moving to repeal these laws. Here's a link to a blog on state laws by a law professor: lawprofessors.typepad.com/elder_law/2013/08/filial-support-laws-news-from-montana-new-hampshire.html.

What services Medicaid offers

Federal rules require states to provide a basic set of services to Medicaid recipients, including hospital stays, doctor visits, preventive care, laboratory and X-ray services, transportation to medical care, home health services, and nursing-facility care. States have the option of adding, among other things, physical and other kinds of therapy, personal care, hospice, and case management. Prescription drug coverage is optional, as are dental and vision services. Many Medicaid services are designed for children and pregnant women.

Unlike Medicare, Medicaid covers long-term care in nursing homes and in the community through home- and community-based waivers (permission from the federal government to spend money that would have gone to nursing homes or community-based services instead) and other approaches.

States can determine the criteria for nursing home care and home- and community-based services, so a person eligible in one state may not be eligible in a neighboring state. Usually some level of functional limitations is required, like being unable to take care of personal basic needs like bathing, dressing, or going to the toilet. Many nursing-home residents have cognitive problems like dementia, which limits their ability to function independently.

How Medicaid works with home- and community-based programs

Because nursing-home care is so expensive, states have moved toward caring for these individuals in the community. Someone with functional limitations can receive care at home that may include personal care, homemaking services, case management, transportation, and other long-term services and supports. Even with these services, which may be limited by funding or workforce shortages, family members often provide some or most of the care.

Most states have a variety of Medicaid services that operate under different waiver programs from the federal government (for example, programs that include a package of services targeted for people with specific disabilities, such as traumatic brain injury or HIV/AIDS). A waiver means that the federal government allows a state to use some of its Medicaid funding for specific services that keep people in the community. However, it can be confusing to sort out which services a person may be eligible for and whether there are waiting lists and other barriers such as limits on the duration and types of services.

TIP

Some states use Medicaid waivers to allow recipients to enroll in assisted-living facilities. There may be restrictions, however — for example, requiring the recipient to pay for room and board with their own resources, or covering only certain services — and not all assisted-living facilities accept Medicaid. In January 2014 the Centers for Medicare & Medicaid Services issued a rule that strengthened community-living options for people on Medicaid by affirming that states can include assisted-living facilities as part of their home- and community-based services. The rule provides a transition period for states to ensure that standards are met. Most assisted-living facilities aren't set up to provide extensive medical services. You can check for your state's program at www.payingforseniorcare. com/medicaid-waivers/assisted-living.html.

The availability and quality of these services varies considerably by location. Some states have robust home- and community-based programs and strong leadership; others do not. Variations also result from the state's population and income characteristics, the types of providers in the state, and the state's spending priorities. Many states have waiting lists for waiver programs.

Aging and Disability Resource Centers (ADRCs) can help with referrals to appropriate programs. Operated by the U.S. Administration for Community Living, they are intended to be one-stop shopping for referrals to long-term care services. For the ADRC in your area, contact Eldercare Locator at 1-800-677-1186 or go to https://eldercare.acl.gov/Public/Index.aspx.

Medicaid managed long-term care

Many states are now setting up managed long-term care programs to provide better coordination of services, more efficient program administration, better monitoring of quality, and (it is hoped) reduced costs. These programs are run by private companies under contract to the state that typically receive a per-member, per-month fee for care. In some states, some groups of people who have been receiving long-term services and supports are being moved into managed long-term care programs, and newly eligible individuals will start out in this kind of plan. Some states offer a choice of managed-care plans, while others do not.

These programs are evolving, and their characteristics vary by the length of time the program has been in operation, the population included, the types of services provided, program oversight, and the number of plans allowed within a state. Proponents claim that managed long-term care programs provide better integration of physical and behavioral health. Critics worry that managed long-term care plans will avoid enrolling the sickest and most vulnerable people or will fail to provide the extensive and costly care they need. Vigilant monitoring is needed to ensure that plans meet their obligations to all clients.

Depending on the competition among plans within an area, people eligible for Medicaid long-term care services can choose from several plans. Here are some questions to ask whether you are the person choosing a plan or a family member:

>> Will someone come to the home to assess the person's needs?

>> Will the person and family be able to participate in the development of the care plan and raise concerns?

>> If a family member is involved in care, will that person's needs for training and support be evaluated?

>> Will the same aide who has been caring for the person be allowed to stay on?

>> Is there a number to call when problems arise?

>> How are complaints or grievances resolved?

>> How does the person change plans?

In 2016, federal regulations added several Medicaid managed-care requirements and protections, including new rules applying to managed long-term care. These rules required states to establish enrollee support systems to provide independent counseling and information; standards for identifying individuals needing long-term care and developing their service plans; and network adequacy standards for plans' long-term care providers. More information is available here: files.kff.org/attachment/CMSs-Final-Rule-on-Medicaid-Managed-Care.

TIP

To keep informed about Medicaid managed-care plans in your community, contact the state's Medicaid office, the state's long-term care ombudsman (who investigates complaints), or a legal-aid organization that advocates for low-income people. Some states have set up special ombudsmen for Medicaid managed long-term care. You can find the ombudsman office in your state on the map at theconsumervoice.org/get_help.

Coordinating Benefits

According to www.medicaid.gov, about 8.3 million people qualify for both Medicare and Medicaid. Although they are a diverse group, many are heavy users of acute medical care (hospitalization) as well as long-term services and supports. Depending on income level and assets, a dually eligible person may get the full range of Medicaid services and assistance with Medicare premiums, deductibles, and cost-sharing (full dual) or just financial assistance in paying Medicare premiums and fees (partial dual).

With some combinations of payers, squabbles can occur about who pays for what and who pays first — the arcane world of *CoB*, or *coordination of benefits.* If the payers are Medicare and Medicaid, however, the rules are clear. Medicare is the primary payer for covered services. To simplify the process, the ACA created a new office in the Centers for Medicare & Medicaid (CMS) to coordinate benefits for people who are dually eligible: www.cms.gov/Medicare-Medicaid-Coordination/Medicare-and-Medicaid-Coordination/Medicare-Medicaid-Coordination-Office/index.html. Although you aren't likely to interact directly with this office, it is a good resource.

TIP

People who have Medicare and are eligible for the full Medicaid benefit package are automatically qualified for Medicare's Extra Help program of financial assistance for prescription drugs. See the earlier section "Prescription drug coverage" for more about Extra Help.

PACE programs

Another program worth investigating is the Program of All-Inclusive Care for the Elderly (PACE). Although supported by both Medicare and Medicaid, participants do not have to be dually eligible for both programs. However, according to the National PACE Association, more than 90 percent of participants are dually eligible.

PACE programs have been in operation since the 1970s. The first program was created in San Francisco's Chinatown. The original program, called On Lok (Cantonese for "peaceful, happy abode"), served families whose elderly relatives had immigrated from China, Italy, and the Philippines. In 1990, the first programs received Medicare and Medicaid waivers to support their efforts. As of 2018, 124 PACE nonprofit programs operated 255 centers and were operating in 31 states. For a listing, go to www.npaonline.org/pace-you/find-pace-program-your-neighborhood.

PACE programs serve individuals who are 55 or older (and eligible for Medicare based on disability, ALS, or end-stage renal disease), are certified by their state to be eligible for nursing-home care, can live safely in the community at the time of enrollment, and live in a PACE service area. Because the PACE programs offer comprehensive services, a PACE participant may not be enrolled in any other Medicare Advantage plan, Medicare prescription drug plan, Medicaid prepayment plan, or optional benefit, such as a 1915c Home and Community Based services waiver. It is important to note that PACE participants are also not eligible for the Medicare hospice benefit.

See www.medicare.gov/your-medicare-costs/help-paying-costs/pace/pace.html for a list of services provided in the PACE program. When needed, PACE (with funding from Medicare and Medicaid) pays for hospital or home care, prescription drugs, and other medical services. Services in the adult daycare setting include physical and occupational therapy, recreation therapy, nutritional counseling, transportation, and social-work counseling. Adult daycare also includes meals, social work, and personal care. All prescription drugs are provided.

People who have Medicare but not Medicaid can pay a monthly premium for the long-term care portion of the PACE benefit. There is no deductible or copayment for any drugs or services that the PACE healthcare team approves.

TECHNICAL STUFF

Why aren't there more PACE programs? The business model is difficult to sustain as aging clients need more extensive services. Participation of a multidisciplinary team is essential but may be difficult to organize in some locations. And in some locations, there may not be a sufficient population of eligible older adults to support the program over time. Some policymakers have suggested lowering or removing the entry age to allow for a larger pool of clients.

Coordination with other health insurance

As if figuring out Medicare and Medicaid weren't complicated enough, some people also have other kinds of insurance such as retirement insurance, government employee insurance (Federal Employee Health Benefits Program or FEHB), COBRA (continuing insurance after employment ends), or TRICARE (insurance for military personnel and their families).

If you aren't employed, Medicare is your basic healthcare coverage after you reach the age of 65. But if you retire before then, the most common type of insurance that figures into long-term care planning has been retirement healthcare insurance. However, this kind of insurance may be phased out like pension plans, with individuals left to figure out their own health-insurance strategies before Medicare begins. The healthcare insurance exchanges created under the Affordable Care Act offer another possibility and by law cannot require medical underwriting, which can be used to refuse coverage to people with preexisting conditions. This provision is being challenged, and its outcome should be watched.

REMEMBER

Be sure to check with your employer or union to find out what coverage is available. Employers aren't required to provide retiree coverage and can change benefits or premiums at will. Also find out who else may be covered under the retirement plan (a spouse or dependent child, for example) and what happens to the plan when you are eligible for Medicare. Your employer's benefits administrator can explain the process.

Chapter **12**

Paying for Care: Long-Term Care Insurance and Other Options

I t's a fact of life: No form of healthcare coverage or insurance is free. The costs may be direct (as in private healthcare and Medicare premiums, coinsurance, and copays) or indirect (as in using up your own assets before you qualify for Medicaid). Planning to cover the costs of future care is important but challenging. The marketplace is changing, and options that seemed adequate 10 or 20 years ago are now not so attractive. At the same time, new options are coming to market that offer more flexibility and may better meet your needs. Costs for all kinds of assistance are increasing, and the benefits of long-term care insurance and other sources of additional income can be important assets. While there are many cautions in this chapter, they should not outweigh the benefits of planning for financial security.

In this chapter, I review the main insurance options: traditional long-term care insurance, employer-based long-term care insurance, and new hybrid offerings linked to life insurance or annuities. I also offer suggestions for questions to ask yourself, your parent, or the agent who is selling the product.

In addition to long-term care insurance, I introduce other options that can provide financial help: annuities, disability insurance, life settlements, and reverse mortgages.

REMEMBER

If there is one Golden Rule in this field, it is that these are decisions that you should discuss with professionals, especially an elder-law attorney or a financial adviser who doesn't stand to gain by your choices. This chapter aims to help you find what insurance and income streams work best for you.

Reviewing the Ups and Downs of Long-Term Care Insurance

Long-term care insurance was designed to fill a big gap in paying for care as you age. In a nutshell, long-term care insurance is a policy you purchase when you're healthy and at an age when you can afford the premiums, with the expectation that when you reach the stage of life when you need assistance at home or in a skilled nursing facility, the benefits will be available to help pay for the types of care you need. While many more options for community-based care are available and welcome, the costs can be challenging unless you're prepared. Long-term care insurance is one option to help you with financing. (For a review of the basic features of long-term care insurance, see AARP's report at www.aarp.org/health/health-insurance/info-06-2012/understanding-long-term-care-insurance.html.)

To decide whether long-term care insurance is right for you, you have many points to consider. First, consider your future expenses. Medicare and private healthcare insurance won't cover all your needs, and long-term care insurance was created to help fill that gap. As a start, here are the most significant items that Medicare Parts A and B and private insurance do not cover:

>> **Nursing-home care** (except for short-term rehabilitation stays after a hospital stay): In 2017, the median annual rate for a semiprivate nursing-home room was $85,776, and it was $97,452 for a private room, according to the Genworth Cost of Care Survey available at newsroom.genworth.com/2017-09-26-Genworth-2017-Annual-Cost-of-Care-Survey-Costs-Continue-to-Rise-Across-All-Care-Settings. All the cost estimates are increases over the previous year.

>> **Assisted-living facilities:** The median cost is $45,000 per year, but costs vary depending on location and services provided.

>> **Adult daycare:** Non-24-hour care goes for a median daily rate of $70.

>> **Home healthcare aides** (except in limited, short-term circumstances): The private pay median rate charged by a licensed home healthcare agency is $21.50 an hour.

>> **Customized durable medical equipment such as electric wheelchairs or special mattresses for hospital beds:** The cost can range from a few hundred dollars to many thousands, not counting the ongoing costs of maintenance or repairs.

>> **Disposable supplies** (with a few exceptions, such as diabetes supplies): This category includes adult diapers, lotions, bed pads, wipes, and a variety of other products. For adult diapers, the cost varies by the type of product and the supply needed but may cost $50 to $100 a month. While most of the other disposables are relatively inexpensive per item, the overall cost adds up.

>> **Deductibles, coinsurance, and copayments:** Insurance policies vary in their requirements for deductibles, coinsurance, and copays; for Medicare beneficiaries, these fees differ for Parts A, B, D, or Medicare Advantage plans. For Part B (outpatient care), there is a 20 percent coinsurance charge. See www.medicare.gov/your-medicare-costs/costs-at-a-glance/costs-at-glance.html for details.

>> **Some prescription drug costs:** Medicare Part D covers these costs but with a doughnut hole that requires you to pay until you reach the designated cap (see Chapter 11).

>> **Home or vehicle modifications:** Adapting the home can be relatively inexpensive (installing a ramp or grab bars), but major renovations are costly. The same is true of vehicle modifications. See Chapters 5 and 10.

>> **Special diets:** Special diets may require gluten-free or low-sodium products; these are often higher-priced than regular foods. If the special diet includes foods that can be purchased only in health-food stores or specialty shops, the costs will be higher. If you live in an area with limited access to fresh fruits and vegetables, transportation to markets may be an extra cost.

Of course, these costs vary across the country, but wherever you live, they add up quickly and are not going to get cheaper. If you need these items or services for years, they can overwhelm a family budget. According to the U.S. Centers for Disease Control and Prevention (CDC), in 2016 total out-of-pocket spending (which includes all direct consumer payments such as copayments, deductibles, coinsurance, and spending for noncovered services) increased 3.9 percent — the fastest rate of growth since 2007. Out-of-pocket spending accounts for 11 percent of all healthcare spending. The U.S. Department of Health and Human Services estimates that one in four people now age 65 will face over $50,000 during their remaining years in out-of-pocket care expenditures, and many will have to pay much more.

Depending on the policy, long-term care insurance will help fill some but not all these gaps. For example, nursing-home care and home healthcare aides are generally included, but home and vehicle modifications are not.

REMEMBER

In calculating your need for additional coverage for the costs of long-term care, consider all your assets: savings, IRAs, pensions, 401(k) plans, Social Security income, and other resources. If you're still working, make sure you're contributing to your retirement fund the maximum amounts allowable. You can use this figure to compare to the costs of different types of care.

You need to consider the following general questions in determining whether long-term care insurance is right for you:

>> Given my health, age, and assets, should I consider buying long-term care insurance?

>> If I already have an existing policy and the premiums are increasing, should I drop the policy or take one of the options to reduce both payments and benefits?

>> How can I ensure that the benefits I expect to receive are delivered?

The following sections will help answer these questions — and more.

Traditional long-term care insurance

Most people who buy traditional long-term care insurance are in their 50s and 60s, although some companies sell policies to people in their 70s. Once you're older, the policies are usually prohibitively expensive or unavailable because of your health status. Long-term care insurance is *medically underwritten*, meaning that people with preexisting conditions that are likely to get worse are priced out of the market or may not be offered coverage.

The costs of long-term care insurance vary by company, and even within companies by segment of the market they are hoping to attract. Generally, the cost for a single person age 55 is about $2,000 a year, based on a daily benefit rate of $150 and a three-year benefit period. But that's just an example, not a rule. In comparing companies, you may find higher or lower premium rates. The cost for a couple may double or be a better deal than for a single person.

REMEMBER

Beyond your age and health status, the decision to buy long-term care insurance depends on other factors, such as other savings or assets that can be used to pay for long-term care and other financial responsibilities such as tuition for college-age children. I would add an emotional factor: your tolerance for risk and uncertainty. If you'll feel more secure with a long-term care insurance policy, you can afford the premiums, and you determine that premium cost is worth the payout you may receive over time, then your task is to investigate the options and choose a company that you can trust.

Group and employer-based long-term care insurance

Many states now have long-term care group insurance partnership programs that don't require medical underwriting. Purchasing the policy as part of a group may — but is not guaranteed to — offer some protection against steep premium increases, which have become common, even among large group policies. You may be eligible for some limited federal tax credits for qualified long-term care insurance policies, and some states have tax credits too.

Some employers offer group long-term care insurance to their employees. You should certainly consider this possibility, especially if you have a medical condition that would make you ineligible for coverage as an individual. If you're in good health, you should compare the cost of the employer-based option with what you would pay as an individual. You may find that individual coverage is cheaper. Remember too that your employer may not continue the offer or can change insurance carriers, which would have financial implications for you. See the SCAN Foundation's policy brief on employer-based long-term care insurance at www.thescanfoundation.org/sites/default/files/TSF_CLASS_TA_No_14_ Employer_LTCi_Participation_FINAL.pdf.

TIP

Current or former federal employees, active and retired members of the uniformed services, and their qualified relatives can apply for coverage under the Federal Long-Term Care Insurance Program. You can apply anytime during the year. There are exclusions for certain medical conditions or combinations of conditions described in the application at www.ltcfeds.com/epAssets/documents/full_ underwriting_app.pdf. You can get more information at www.ltcfeds.com/ eligibility/index.html or by calling 1-800-582-3337.

Hybrid long-term care insurance

In the past few years, new products have come on the market to meet the needs of people who want some protection against the costs of long-term care but do not want to get locked into a long-term care insurance policy. The new policies are called *hybrid* or *linked* policies because they combine a life-insurance policy or annuity with long-term care benefits. You may need to provide only basic medical information and not undergo a medical exam. (I provide more information on annuities later in this chapter.)

For policies linked to life insurance, this is how it works: You purchase a life-insurance policy for, say, $200,000, and pay for it with a single premium — maybe $50,000 to $75,000. This money goes into an account for long-term care benefits if and when you need them. The death benefit, minus any money spent on your long-term care, goes to your beneficiary.

This option may be good for you if

>> You have a reason to buy life insurance in the first place — for example, if a spouse or dependent child relies on you for financial support.

>> You have enough money put away to pay for the premium without creating any hardship for you or your family.

The process is similar for annuities: You can purchase a fixed deferred annuity with a long-term-care rider attached. That's a one-time cost. The annuity may pay out for a specific number of years or for life.

On the other hand, you may gain more by investing this substantial amount of money with the help of a financial adviser. So far, these policies aren't widely available. They are niche products, and if you fit into the niche, they may well be something to investigate.

Short duration long-term care insurance

Short duration long-term care insurance policies (also known as recovery care or limited long-term care insurance) have come on the market in the past few years. They are designed to meet the needs of people who, for a variety of reasons, are not eligible for or can't afford traditional long-term care insurance but need some level of short-term coverage. Unlike traditional long-term care insurance policies, they can have no waiting period for coverage to begin. Policies offer different coverage levels but generally include home healthcare, assisted-living costs, and skilled nursing facility stays. Short duration policies provide insurance coverage for up to a year.

Because these policies are new, there are still regulatory issues to resolve. The National Association of Insurance Commissioners is currently drafting a new model act and model regulation to guide states in addressing these policies. The American Association for Long-Term Care Insurance recently created the National Advisory Center for Short-Term Care, which has helpful information at www.shorttermcareinsurance.org/short-term-care-insurance/. Click on the STC Learning Center hyperlinks. Also see www.aaltci.org/short-term-care-insurance/. Experience with these policies is limited so far; as always, it is prudent to check with a trusted financial adviser.

Asking questions when considering any type of long-term care insurance

When you consider long–term care insurance, ask insurers the following:

>> **Are there coverage exclusions for some conditions, such as mental-health problems or substance abuse?**

>> **Are there waiting periods for some preexisting conditions?** Long-term care insurance policies usually define a *preexisting condition* as one for which you received medical advice or treatment within a defined period — for example, within the past six months or a year. Some companies look further back in time than others. The policy may include a provision that it will not pay for costs related to that condition for a specific period, such as six months or longer after the policy goes into effect.

>> **Is there an elimination or waiting period before benefits start, and if so, how long is it?** This is different from the waiting period for preexisting conditions. The waiting period in this instance is like a deductible. Short duration long-term care insurance products can have no waiting period. For traditional stand-alone policies, you must pay a certain amount of your own money after you are eligible for a benefit before the policy kicks in. Some people decide to pay for the first 30, 60, or 90 days of their care, so their policies don't begin paying benefits until the waiting period has expired.

Some companies sell policies with a specific dollar amount as the policy deductible instead of a waiting period. Some companies count only the days you receive paid care against the waiting period; others count every day from the first day you become eligible for and receive care. Some companies require you to meet this waiting period once in your lifetime; others require you to meet it each time you qualify for benefits and need long-term care assistance.

>> **What does the policy pay for?** Does it cover services provided at a range of facilities, including at home and in assisted living, adult daycare, and nursing homes? Do these facilities have to be licensed?

>> **Does the policy have restrictions on who can provide the services?** Does the home healthcare aide have to be licensed or supervised by a home health agency, or can you hire a family member, friend, or neighbor? Are there restrictions on the services the home healthcare aide can provide, such as administering medications?

>> **How are claims made?** What documentation is required? This process may not be simple and may involve requirements you were not aware of.

>> **How is eligibility for services defined?** Usually there is some threshold of activities of daily living (ADLs), which include bathing, dressing, and going to the toilet. A good policy should include the need for supervision due to cognitive problems, such as wandering or memory loss, as a trigger for paying for services.

>> **How much does the policy pay?** It may be a fixed amount per day, per month, or a percentage of the costs.

>> **Who decides what is covered and what is not?** You may disagree with the company about whether a service is needed.

>> **How long will coverage last?** If you choose a shorter period, say three years instead of ten, the premiums will be less.

>> **What is the payment schedule?** Some policies pay a daily or monthly amount. Others have what has often been called a *pool of money,* and if you don't use your full benefit in one month, it will roll over and extend the life of your policy.

>> **Can the premiums be locked in at a current rate?** Large rate increases have been a major problem for many current policyholders.

REMEMBER

After you gather all this information, you can evaluate whether a policy provides the coverage you may need in the future. Then ask yourself one important question: Can you afford the premiums? If you purchase a policy in your 50s or 60s, you are likely to pay premiums for 20 to 30 years or longer before you need the benefits. And you should expect your premiums to increase over time.

REMEMBER

Long-term care insurance does not replace Medicare. It is intended to cover some of the services that Medicare does not.

Continuing to pay rising premiums

Many people approaching retirement are now finding that the long-term care insurance policy they counted on is on shaky ground. Five of the ten largest sellers of long-term care insurance, including giants like MetLife and Prudential, have sharply reduced or discontinued sales. As the insurance market is shrinking, premiums are rising — from modest increases to a stunning 77 percent. Women, who on average live longer than men, are likely to be charged higher premiums when they apply for individual policies. The policies now in force are likely to be honored, but they may be transferred to another company. And because some companies are no longer writing new policies and therefore not adding as many payers into the system, premiums for new buyers are likely to increase as more policyholders die.

As part of its Model Regulation on Long-Term Care Insurance, the National Association of Insurance Commissioners mandates that insurers offer a nonforfeiture benefit if the policyholder stops paying premiums. This means that if you agree to shorten the benefit period or give up part of an inflation-protection provision, your premiums won't be raised quite so much. Some states have mandated a nonforfeiture benefit provision for all long-term care insurance policies, but others require insurers to offer at least one of a list of options, including a shortened benefit period or giving up an inflation-protection clause.

How you decide to handle this situation, should it arise, depends on how much you have already contributed to the policy and what sacrifices you would have to make to keep it active. You can also appeal the increases to the company and make a hardship case for keeping the premiums affordable. Some states may have options for assistance in these cases, such as a shortened benefit period. The American Association for Long-Term Care Insurance has a list of state offices that you can contact at www.aaltci.org/long-term-care-insurance/learning-center/state-insurance-guaranty.php.

Getting your claims paid for

When it comes to submitting claims, you can minimize the red tape by keeping careful records, understanding the benefits and limitations of the policy, and seeking assistance from your state office of insurance regulation. Even if you have an active policy, have paid all your premiums, and believe the services you've paid for are eligible under your policy, you're not in the clear.

You still have to submit claims and documentation that the services you're receiving are indeed covered by the policy. Companies can deny claims for many different reasons or no specific reason at all. The paperwork to justify what seem to be clear-cut needs and services can seem daunting.

These are the primary reasons for claims denials:

>> **Deductibles:** During the waiting period of 30, 60, 90, or 100 days, depending on your policy, the costs of care can run to thousands of dollars. The company may calculate the waiting period so that it lasts much longer if the person is receiving home care only a few days a week as opposed to 24/7.

>> **Ineligibility:** The company may decide that the person's functional limitation doesn't qualify for assistance.

>> **Unlicensed caregivers:** Some plans require the policyholder to hire a licensed caregiver and won't pay for anyone else. Other policies, called cash plans, have fewer restrictions.

>> **Assisted living:** Some plans, written before assisted living became popular, pay only for nursing-home care. In some cases, a 24-hour nurse on-site is required for assisted living to be approved, but many assisted-living facilities do not provide this level of nursing care.

>> **Inadequate documentation:** Home healthcare aides hired through an agency may be required to keep "notes," including hours spent and tasks provided, but the company may not accept these without medical documentation of the need for personal care or household tasks.

TIP

For more information about long-term care insurance and what to look for in policies, and how to get the most out of an existing policy, see the National Association of Insurance Commissioners Shopper's Guide to Long-Term Care Insurance at `www.naic.org/documents/prod_serv_consumer_ltc_lp.pdf`. This guide has a useful glossary and worksheets to compare information from different insurance companies.

Receiving Money through Annuities

Annuities are investments that guarantee a steady income for a certain length of time that is specified in the contract. For retirement, this is usually as long as the annuitant (the person holding the annuity) lives. However, it is also possible to buy an annuity that also pays income to the annuitant's beneficiary after the initial owner dies. Several different types of annuities are available:

>> **Immediate annuities** pay a monthly sum in exchange for a one-time (or more than one-time) premium.

>> **Deferred annuities** begin to pay benefits at a certain date in the future. In recent years, deferred annuities that would begin to pay income for life beginning at a set age, such as 80 or 85, can be purchased using a certain percentage of money from a 401(k)-like account or an IRA without being considered a taxable withdrawal.

>> **Variable annuities** are more like investment products and are suitable for knowledgeable investors.

The main advantage of annuities is that you can receive a series of guaranteed payouts, usually for life, that can supplement your Social Security benefits. No additional payments are required once you purchase the contract. The annuities market is rapidly changing, with new products and features appearing regularly. Some of these features, such as inflation protection, are very attractive and potentially valuable, but they may come at a high cost.

The main disadvantages — other than the stipulation that you have a bundle of cash such as your retirement savings just sitting around with which to purchase the annuity — are the commissions that you pay the broker (as much as 10 percent), high annual fees for managing your money, and the high surrender charges (some as high as 20 percent) if you take out your money within the first several years. In addition, there is no FDIC insurance with an annuity as there is in a bank account.

Meeting the guaranteed returns promised on some annuities has proved costly for some companies. As a result, these companies are trying to persuade holders of variable annuities (in which contracts allow changes in investments) to take buyouts or move their investments into ones with lower returns. It is important to review all communications about an annuity, because some of these changes to the contract or rider may not be apparent.

If you have a deferred annuity, when you do take out your money (preferably after the age of 59½ to avoid taxes), you have several payout options:

>> **Lifetime payments, with no survivor benefits:** This option is less expensive because payouts end with the annuitant's death. The payout period may be long or short but depends solely on the person's remaining years.

>> **Income for life with guaranteed period-certain benefits:** You receive a guaranteed payout for life that includes a certain benefit period. If you die during that period, your beneficiary continues to receive the payout for the remainder of the period.

>> **Income for a guaranteed period, say 5 or 20 years:** If you die before the end of the period, your beneficiary receives the remainder of the payments for the guaranteed period.

>> **Joint and survivor annuity:** Your beneficiary continues to receive payouts for the rest of his or her life. In certain situations, a married person must choose this option unless the spouse agrees in writing to a different withdrawal method.

Some financial advisers believe that annuities should be considered only after you have reached the limit on other investments with tax advantages like 401(k) plans or IRAs. At that point, the tax-free growth rate may be attractive, especially to people in high income-tax brackets.

Some options for more flexible annuities, such as taking part of a pension as an annuity, may make this option more affordable and attractive to employees.

The appeal of a guaranteed retirement income is understandable and powerful, but it is also important to know all the costs and risks. For all major financial decisions, consult a knowledgeable adviser and investigate all the details.

Using Disability Insurance

Most people don't consider disability insurance as part of long-term care if they think about it at all. Disability insurance pays for a portion of lost income if you become disabled and unable to work because of an accident or illness. Most disability insurance is provided by employers, not purchased by individuals. If you become disabled and have this type of insurance, you don't lose all your income, so you don't have to use up savings or other assets to pay for care that isn't covered by health insurance. Usually you have a 90-day waiting period for benefits to begin, and they last for about three years, when most people can go back to work. But some disability claims last much longer. Although disability insurance doesn't pay for long-term care directly, it is an income source at a time when a person isn't receiving salary. Consider it an additional resource, not a substitute for basic coverage.

You can use the money to pay bills, for home care, or for anything else. There are no requirements for submitting claims as there are in long-term care insurance.

TIP

The decision to buy disability insurance or to add to an employer's coverage is a personal one, influenced largely by your assessment of the risk of an event that is low probability but high impact. The Council for Disability Awareness, an insurance-supported organization, has a calculator called "What's My Disability Quotient?" You can figure out your own risk at www.whatsmypdq.org. Again, your tolerance for risk may have little to do with the probabilities of an accident or illness.

Selling Your Policy: Life Settlements

Life settlements — which essentially means selling existing life-insurance policies at a steep discount — are being marketed as a way to get cash for long-term care. The appeal for older adults is easy to understand, especially if keeping up the premiums on the policy is a financial strain.

TECHNICAL STUFF

The practice of selling life-insurance policies recalls the so-called *viatical settlements* that arose at the height of the HIV/AIDS epidemic in the 1980s and 1990s, when many young men were dying quickly and did not have either money to pay for their care or families for whom they were responsible financially. Investors bought up policies in the expectation that the policyholders would die quickly, and many unethical practices resulted. But unlike the viatical-settlements industry, the life-settlement industry focuses on individuals with a longer life expectancy or existing needs for long-term care.

Some states are authorizing older residents to use their existing life-insurance policies to pay for long-term care. This practice gives the residents money to pay for care and helps the state avoid costly Medicaid bills. In Texas, for example, people applying for Medicaid can now sell their life-insurance policies to a third party at a discount — more than the cash value of the policy but significantly less than its death benefit. For example, an 87-year-old female with a $65,000 policy would qualify for a monthly benefit of $1,115 for 15 months and a funeral benefit of $3,250, for a total of $16,725. The money goes into a special account for the policyholder's long-term care, and the person may still be eligible for Medicaid when that money runs out. Similar bills have been introduced in other state legislatures.

Caution is always a good first step when considering any insurance arrangement. Here are some things to consider about life-settlement policies:

>> The financial institution that buys your policy gets the death benefit. In exchange for money now, the beneficiary named in the policy gets nothing from the life-insurance policy. If your spouse or a dependent child will need financial support in the future, a life settlement removes that option.

>> Older people with serious health conditions who are unlikely to live long are a prime target for unscrupulous brokers trying to get you to sell your life insurance. Be wary of hard sell pitches.

>> Life settlements have high transaction costs. Commissions paid by life-settlement companies to brokers and other consultants can be as high as 40 percent.

>> The lump sum you receive is likely to be taxable; check with your tax adviser. Depending on state law, it may also make a person ineligible for Medicaid.

>> If you change your mind and want to purchase another life-insurance policy, you may be unable to find one that will accept you because of your age or health, and the premium will certainly be higher.

>> One alternative that offers a tax benefit is a 1035 exchange, so called because it stands for Section 1035 of the Internal Revenue Code. This provision allows you to exchange an insurance policy you own for a new one insuring the same person without paying tax on the investment gains on your original contract. This is a complex area of tax law, so you should consult an attorney or tax accountant to determine whether this would be a potential choice.

For more information on life settlements and 1035 exchanges, see "Seniors Beware: What You Should Know About Life Settlements" at www.finra.org/sites/default/files/InvestorDocument/p125848.pdf. This was produced by the Financial Industry Regulatory Authority, an independent regulatory organization empowered by the federal government to protect investors.

Check your state's insurance laws regarding life settlements for information that must be provided to the owners of the policy and the insured person. For an example, see New York State's comprehensive list of items: `law.onecle.com/new-york/insurance/ISC07811_7811.html`. You can search online for your own state's rules on life settlements or contact your state insurance department.

WARNING

Beware of STOLIs (stranger-originated life insurance). STOLI transactions usually involve an older person being approached by a life-insurance agent or another party to obtain new life insurance, with the policy being controlled from the start and paid for by a third party. Some older individuals are offered compensation for their participation as the insured. If they participate, they can be considered participants in a fraud on the insurance company.

State laws generally prohibit someone from initiating or facilitating the issuance of an insurance policy for the intended benefit of a person who, at the time the policy is issued, has no "insurable interest" in the life of the person being insured. Someone with an insurable interest is a family member or someone who has a substantial economic interest in the continued well-being of the person (a business partner, for example). The purpose of these laws is to ensure that the person seeking the policy is not the victim of a scam.

Considering a Reverse Mortgage

Many older adults are house-rich and cash-poor. The equity built up over years of reducing a mortgage is a tempting resource. Reverse mortgages, also known as *home-equity conversion mortgages* (HECMs, pronounced *heck*-ums), are designed to take advantage of this asset without requiring the home to be sold. Be sure to consult your financial adviser before proceeding with a reverse mortgage.

Reverse mortgages are different from home equity loans, which you may have used to remodel a kitchen or make other improvements. In a home equity loan, a bank loans you a certain amount of money, which you repay, with interest, in monthly installments. In a reverse mortgage, you receive a line of credit, a lump sum, or monthly payments, which you don't need to repay until you sell the home, move permanently into a nursing home, or die.

You can use the money for medical or other bills, and the proceeds are tax-free. However, reverse mortgage proceeds may affect eligibility for means-tested public benefits such as Medicaid, Supplemental Security Income (SSI), and food and nutritional benefits. Consult a public benefit expert to determine whether a reverse mortgage will affect your eligibility.

As you may expect, you need to meet certain qualifications and be prepared for some financial requirements. Here are the basics you need to know:

REMEMBER

>> The homeowner must be 62 years old or older to qualify.

>> Very important: You are responsible for payment of property taxes, homeowner's insurance, homeowner's association dues and assessments, maintenance, and all the other responsibilities of home ownership. Reverse mortgages can go into foreclosure if the homeowner fails to pay these bills. You are also responsible for utilities, although nonpayment will not result in foreclosure.

>> You will have to pay a large origination fee and closing costs as in a standard mortgage.

>> Your total debt increases over time based on the amount borrowed, accrued interest, and ongoing mortgage insurance premiums, which compound monthly and are added to the loan balance.

>> A reverse mortgage is available on a home in which the existing mortgage has been paid off or where there is a large amount of home equity. Reverse mortgages can also be used to finance the purchase of a new home.

There are three types of reverse mortgages:

>> **Single-purpose reverse mortgages** are offered by some state and local government agencies and nonprofit organizations. These are the least expensive option, and the proceeds can be used only for the specified purpose (not long-term care). This option may be useful for paying for home modifications or repairs or property taxes. Most low- or moderate-income homeowners can qualify.

>> **Federally insured reverse mortgages,** known as home-equity conversion mortgages, are insured by the Federal Housing Administration (FHA), an arm of the U.S. Department of Housing and Urban Development (HUD). Before applying for a HECM, you must meet with a HUD-certified counselor from a government-approved housing counseling agency, who explains the loan's terms, costs, and other possible alternatives. You can choose from among several payment options. These loans are widely available and can be used for any purpose. You can find out more at www.hud.gov/program_offices/housing/sfh/hecm/hecmhome.

HECM requirements have changed a lot over the past few years. Borrowers have access to less money than in the past, upfront mortgage insurance premiums have increased for most borrowers, and the FHA now requires prospective borrowers to undergo a financial assessment to ensure that they have the capacity and willingness to meet their obligations to pay property taxes, homeowner's insurance, and other monthly expenses. Based on the results of the financial assessment, the lender may be required to set aside enough money from the loan proceeds to pay for property taxes and insurance for the expected life of the loan. There are also limits on the amount of the loan proceeds that can be taken out in the first year.

>> **Proprietary reverse mortgages** are private loans made by lenders and are not insured. Proprietary loans are available for high-value homes that exceed the loan limit of the HECM program. Often, these loans lack important consumer protections that are required for HECM borrowers, such as housing counseling.

TIP

Many people ask: I own a co-op (or condo); can I get a reverse mortgage? The answer for co-op owners is no; for condo owners, the answer is maybe.

>> Co-op owners hold shares in a company, not real property like a house. At present co-op owners are not eligible for reverse mortgages, although there have been efforts to changes the rules.

>> Condo owners, however, do own the physical property and so may be eligible for a reverse mortgage under certain very specific circumstances. Consult an expert.

The National Council on Aging has a booklet on reverse mortgages, billed as the "official reverse mortgage consumer booklet approved by the Department of Housing and Urban Development"; go to www.ncoa.org/resources/use-your-home-to-stay-at-home/. You can also check out AARP's booklet "Home Made Money: A Consumer's Guide to Reverse Mortgages" at assets.aarp.org/www.aarp.org_/articles/revmort/homeMadeMoney.pdf. While last revised in 2006, this booklet has useful basic information.

WARNING

Beware that scammers see a vulnerable target in older people who have equity in their homes but may be having financial difficulties.

Chapter **13**

Financial Matters: Money Management, Wills, Trusts, and More

I n many families, money is a taboo topic. Talking about bank accounts or wills happens only when a crisis occurs. All too often, when a person dies, he doesn't even leave a will to guide the heirs. "Why make a will," some people reason, "when it will be expensive and complicated? My family will know what I want." And predictably, conflict and confusion ensue.

REMEMBER

Wills are only one of the legal and financial instruments that should be discussed, created, and periodically reviewed as part of a future care plan. Knowing how to deal with an older person's funds is essential for handling home care or assisted-living expenses. This chapter reviews general reasons for the primary legal documents and suggests some points to consider. However, it doesn't substitute for the advice of an experienced attorney or financial adviser (or both).

Managing Money

Understanding how to manage money is one of the most important skills we can acquire and pass on to our children. Yet it's one of the least-taught skills. Some people never think about money, and some people think about nothing else. But most of us get some basic introduction to financial management that serves well enough in ordinary times. Illness or aging, however, can create special situations that challenge our usual routines. This chapter describes some of those challenges. One is loss of control over one's money (or fear of that happening). For others, it is the daunting responsibility of taking charge of someone's financial affairs when they were shielded from money problems as they grew up.

Giving up control of money matters is often difficult for an older person, just as it is hard to give up driving. You may view losing any control over your finances as the beginning of the end of your independence. Because financial matters are so vital to aging comfortably and can be so difficult to manage, however, passing part of the control over to a trusted person not only makes sense but is also imperative in certain situations.

Right now, before a crisis, talk to your children or trusted adviser about the options for managing money should illness occur. Two basic options allow for shared control: a joint bank account or a financial power of attorney. The two options can be combined. I delve into the logistics of each option in the following sections.

Opening joint bank accounts

When you or your parent are no longer able to control spending or keep track of money coming in and out, it may be in everyone's best interest to have a shared bank account with a trusted family member responsible for managing it. But many older people have had their own bank accounts for decades, possibly a joint account shared with a spouse, and giving up some or all control to a child or other relative can be hard. If you're thinking of opening a new joint bank account, there are pros and cons to consider. As with other financial and legal matters, check with a professional.

>> In most joint bank accounts, with a right of survivorship, there is no "my money" and "your money." Two people have access to the account in its entirety, no matter which one earned or deposited the money. One person can withdraw the entire amount for any purpose without notifying the other owner.

>> Most joint accounts are set up so that if one person on the joint account dies, the entire account passes to the second person. But in certain states, this presumption can be challenged. The joint amount of money in the account is not included in the person's estate to be divided among the heirs. If the amount in the account is substantial, other family members may object. Even if the amount is small, other heirs may see this uneven distribution of assets as unfair. There may be income and inheritance tax implications as well.

>> An alternative but little-used option for a bank account is a *multiparty account without a right of survivorship,* sometimes called a *convenience account.* The account is held by a primary person, with a cosigner. In this type of account, the cosigner has the authority to make deposits and withdrawals, but if the primary person dies, the remainder of the account goes into the estate and does not pass to the cosigner. Although banking laws permit these accounts, many banks do not encourage their use, possibly because they require extra training of staff and monitoring. Still, if this seems a good option, talk to a banker about it.

WARNING

Adding another person to a bank account can have implications for future Medicaid eligibility. The account can be considered a transfer of assets at less than fair market value. If this transfer happens within five years of an application to Medicaid, the primary account holder will be penalized according to Medicaid look-back rules.

WARNING

Obviously, setting up a joint bank account should be done only with someone you trust completely. Even so, it may be prudent to keep only the minimum amount necessary to pay bills and avoid bank fees that may apply to a minimum balance. A large amount of cash sitting in a bank account can turn out to be an "attractive nuisance." This term is more commonly used to describe something on a property, like an open pipe, that a child may find both dangerous and appealing. If the joint owner of the account takes out money for personal use, even with all the best intentions of repaying the money, there's always the possibility that he or she won't be able to fulfill that promise. The annals of elder abuse are filled with stories of relatives, household help, and new "friends" who have taken advantage of a trusting older adult to enrich themselves or to pay themselves for taking care of an older person when that was never part of the agreement. Best not to put temptation into the picture.

REMEMBER

A key concept when someone has access to another's money is *fiduciary duty*, which occurs when one person depends on another to act in his or her best interest. The responsible person has a duty of loyalty to act only for the other person's benefit, to act with good faith in furthering the other person's interests, and to disclose all relevant information. Anyone taking on the responsibility of a joint bank account should be reminded about these ethical and legal requirements.

TIP

Consider drawing up an agreement that states the sources of money to be deposited into the account (such as Social Security, pension, and family contributions), how it will be spent (such as rent or mortgage, household expenses, medical bills, and household help), and what should happen to the balance if one party dies. This document is not legally binding but makes clear to both people (and to the rest of the family) how the joint account is intended to be used. The agreement may need to be changed if circumstances change.

Granting financial powers of attorney

If you need to step in to help take care of an older person's finances, an alternative to holding a joint bank account is receiving financial power of attorney. Two types of financial power of attorney are available: conventional and durable.

Conventional financial power of attorney

Conventional financial power of attorney is granted by a document, signed by one person, giving another person permission to take care of different kinds of financial affairs, such as signing checks, paying a contractor for home repairs, handling bank accounts, and taking care of other tasks. The power of attorney may be limited to specific tasks, such as paying monthly bills, or it may be general and all-encompassing (allowing everything including selling property and assets like stocks, filing taxes, and managing a retirement account).

Depending on state laws, some powers can't be assigned to another person. Those include the power to make, amend, or revoke a will or change insurance beneficiaries.

The person signing the document is known as the *principal,* and the person who is designated to act in the principal's name is called the *agent* or *attorney-in-fact.* Unless specifically stated, a power of attorney goes into effect right away. But the principal can set it to expire on a certain date, and the principal can revoke the power of attorney at any time. Furthermore, conventional power of attorney ends if the principal becomes legally incapacitated, which means he or she is unable to understand choices and make decisions.

To avoid personal liability, agents should sign a check or any document, for example, as John Brown (your name), attorney-in-fact for Mary Brown (your mother).

Durable financial power of attorney

An alternative to a conventional financial power of attorney, which ends when the principal (the person who signed away some powers) becomes legally incompetent, is a *durable financial power of attorney,* which continues even if the person becomes incapacitated. Therefore, durable power of attorney lets the agent remain in control of certain financial and legal matters even if the principal is no longer able to understand the decision to be made or its implications. For example, a person with advanced dementia would be considered incapacitated, as would someone in a coma. All states recognize some form of durable power of attorney, but the specifics vary.

A version of durable power of attorney is called a *springing durable power of attorney.* It sets conditions under which the durable power of attorney "springs," or goes, into effect — for example, when a doctor certifies that the person has become incapacitated. The springing durable power of attorney may be more acceptable to an older person and avoids the lengthy, costly, and emotionally difficult process of guardianship, an alternative that I discuss later in this chapter. However, the springing durable power of attorney must be very clear about what counts as the springing event so that the principal, agent, and other third parties who need to rely on the power of attorney can easily determine when the principal intended the agent to take over. Without clarity, a court may have to decide. This would negate one of the benefits of having a power of attorney, which is that financial and legal matters can be handled without going to court.

Even if you have a durable power of attorney in a form approved by your state, your bank or other financial institution may require its own form. Even the Social Security Administration requires its own version of a power of attorney. Be sure to ask your financial institutions whether they honor the standard form or require their own.

The fiduciary duty applies to durable power of attorney as it does to joint bank accounts (discussed earlier in this chapter). Agents are required to act in the person's best interests, maintain accurate records, and avoid any conflict of interest. Most people are not well versed in the fiduciary responsibilities that accompany being named an agent in a durable power of attorney. The same temptations that can occur in a joint bank account are present with a durable power of attorney, and here the stakes may be even higher. Therefore, all financial actions taken on behalf of the person who is incapacitated must be transparent, and all family members involved in the care of the older person must be apprised of significant outlays. Disagreements may arise, but better to have them resolved early rather than cascade into serious trouble.

A financial power of attorney does not extend to making healthcare decisions. That requires a separate document, which can be called by different names but is usually termed a *healthcare proxy* or a *durable power of attorney for healthcare.* It's discussed in Chapter 17.

Where There's a Will . . .

If you have any money, property, family heirlooms, or just personal treasures, or if you have children or other dependents who will need a new guardian after your death, you need a will. (In some cases, a trust is an appropriate way to distribute property instead, and I discuss that type of document later in this chapter.) A will ensures, as much as possible, that your wishes are followed. One way to convince a resistant older person of the importance of creating a will is to make one yourself or to remind the person that you went through the process, and although it wasn't easy, it was a relief to have completed it.

Many people believe that if you die without a will, your family will automatically divide up your property. Not exactly. A person who dies without a will is legally *intestate* (defined, simply, as not having a will). In that case, state law operating through a probate court determines how the property will be divided, often leading to outcomes that the person would never have wanted. Blood relatives will likely be favored over domestic partners. Children will be treated equally, even if one of them has been estranged from the parent for years. Stepchildren may not be included, even though they are well loved. Such unwanted outcomes can be avoided through the creation of a valid will.

Many people overestimate the monetary value of their possessions but underestimate their sentimental value to family members. An older person may say, "That old painting? Who would want that?" The answer may be, "A lot of your children or grandchildren who remember it hanging on your wall when they came to visit." Or that item may be promised to more than one person. Your parent may say,

"When I'm gone, that painting is going to be yours. It's worth a lot of money." Whether the painting has financial value or not, promising it to several people is bound to create conflict.

TIP

"Who Gets Grandma's Yellow Pie Plate?" is an online resource that has advice about distributing items that are laden with family history and thus have great potential for conflict. For example, a widowed father who remarries should consider his biological children's wishes about their mother's belongings. The website has many cautionary stories. Check it out at www.extension.umn.edu/family/personal-finance/decision-making/who-gets-grandmas-yellow-pie-plate/.

REMEMBER

Instructions about burial or cremation and funeral or memorial service plans should not be put in a will. A will is generally read several days or weeks after death, when it is too late to honor the person's wishes. Specific directions about those logistics should be put in a separate document and shared openly with close family or, if not, opened at death. It is best to alert family members about this document to avoid conflicts. AARP has helpful guidance on planning funerals at www.aarp.org/home-family/friends-family/info-2017/funeral-planning-tips-fd.html.

Preparing a will is very important, and it will be a valued document when an older person passes. Look at the following sections to find out how to get started and what types of wills are available.

TIP

As early as possible, consult an attorney who can guide you through the process of taking inventory of your assets, determining what kind of will best suits your situation, choosing the executor, considering provisions to include, and finalizing the will.

Taking inventory of your assets

In considering a will (and for estate planning in general), start by making a list of assets to be distributed and indicating whether they are jointly held or have a designated beneficiary, including:

>> Liquid assets (things that can quickly be turned into cash), such as bank accounts (checking and savings), certificates of deposit, savings bonds, and money market funds.

>> Fixed assets, such as a home or other real estate.

>> Certificates of deposit that are payable to a named person on death.

>> Retirement accounts, such as 401(k) plans, IRAs, Keogh accounts, and pensions. These accounts should be included in the inventory whether or not they have a designated beneficiary. If there is no beneficiary, they go into the probate estate. If there is a designated beneficiary, they are not distributed by the will or the probate estate.

>> Stock or investment accounts.

>> Transfer-on-death stock accounts, which are payable to a named beneficiary.

>> Valuable personal items such as jewelry, antiques, and artwork (items with only sentimental value can be kept in a separate list).

TIP

Community property is the law in nine states (Arizona, California, Idaho, Louisiana, Nevada, New Mexico, Texas, Washington, and Wisconsin). Alaska recognizes community property if both spouses agree to divide their assets in this way. This means that property acquired during a marriage is shared equally by a married couple regardless of who purchased the property or earned the money. Only the share owned by one person can be distributed in a will. This may call for some Solomonic decisions, but it can be addressed in a will by a spouse giving his or her half of the community property to the surviving spouse.

Considering types of wills

According to the American Bar Association, there are several types of wills:

>> For an uncomplicated estate, a *simple will* provides for the outright distribution of assets.

>> A *pour-over will* assigns some assets to a trust that has already been established.

>> A *holographic will* is handwritten but not witnessed. About half the states recognize this kind of will, but it's not a preferred option.

>> An *oral will* is spoken but not written down. Very few states recognize this kind of will, and then only in cases of final illness. It, too, is not a good option.

Choosing the executor

Choosing the executor — the person responsible for making sure that the instructions in the will are followed — is an important step. Being named as an executor is not an honorary title; it involves a considerable amount of time-consuming work. The executor must create an accurate accounting of assets to be distributed, find all debts that need to be paid, and resolve tax questions. Consultants such as accountants and attorneys may need to be hired. Unhappy relatives may need to be placated. The ideal executor is a person who is adept at understanding finances, detail-oriented, and even-tempered.

If this job description fits someone in the family, then that person would be a good choice. If not, then look outside the family for a trusted friend or professional.

A professional will expect to be paid, and fees may be a flat amount or a percentage of the estate.

The person named as executor should be willing to take on that job, because if the person declines, a court will name another executor and it may be someone you would not choose. You should name an alternate in the will in case your first choice to be executor cannot serve.

Taking the final steps

After you've made these decisions about the will, the American Bar Association says there are several more steps to take:

1. Execute the will.

This step means having witnesses present as you sign the will. All states require at least two witnesses as proof that the will is valid — that is, the person signing the will knew what he or she was doing. Witnesses' signatures must be notarized. The witnesses should not be the executor or people named in the will to receive any gifts (even of modest value). Usually the witnesses are employees in an attorney's office, who do this every day.

2. Decide where to keep the will.

You should have only one signed original that you keep in a safe place. The attorney who drafts the will may or may not take the responsibility of storing it for you. Family members who need to know about its contents can be given unsigned copies and told where the original is stored.

WARNING

Putting the original will in a safe deposit box is not a good idea, because upon death, some banks restrict access to safe deposit boxes until there is a court order that it can be opened, which may not happen quickly.

3. Review the will at regular intervals.

Creating a will is important for all adults. But people who create a will at one stage of their lives (for example, when they have young children) may forget about the will as the children grow up and have children of their own. In that case, almost everything has changed in their lives, but the same will exists. Any major life-changing event — divorce, death of a family member named in the will, remarriage, birth or adoption of a child, sale of a business, moving to a new state, onset of a life-threatening illness — is a reason to review a will and make appropriate changes. In the case of moving to a new state, you need to make sure that the new location will honor your will executed in another state, or you may need to draw up a new will. Your priorities may be the same or they may be different. In either event, the will should be kept up-to-date.

Settling the Estate with Probate

Probate is a word that is often preceded in advice columns by the word *avoiding*. What exactly is probate and why do so many people want you to avoid it?

Probate is the process of settling an estate. It is also the name of the state court that handles wills and estates, among other responsibilities. The probate court determines the validity of the will, reviews the executor's inventory of assets and list of creditors, and determines what debts should be paid and what taxes are owed. After all these obligations are taken care of, the remainder of the estate is distributed according to the terms of the will. Failing to write a will is not a good way to avoid probate, because a court will be involved in settling your estate anyway.

REMEMBER

Probate addresses only certain assets in an estate, mainly assets that are not designated to go to a named beneficiary. Probate assets typically include a home, other property owned solely by the person, artwork and other personal items, and bank accounts held only in the person's name. Assets that normally don't pass through probate include joint bank accounts, pay-on-death accounts, life-insurance policies, retirement accounts, and other assets with a named beneficiary. Property held in trusts does not normally pass through probate.

Why are people so eager to avoid probate?

>> **It can be costly.** It involves court fees, attorney fees, and other fees, which can add up. Some costs are set; others may depend on a percentage of the value of the estate.

>> **It can take time.** Heirs eager to have closure or get their share of the estate may be frustrated by the slow but steady process of probate. Time has to be allowed for creditors to be notified and to come forward, ownership of assets to be determined, and all the other details that must be resolved and can complicate settling an estate. It can take 9 to 12 months to close a larger or complicated estate.

Many states have streamlined the probate process, allowing spouses and minor children to get the money they need to live on without waiting for the entire estate to be settled. Other states have a simple probate process for smaller estates that can be closed in weeks at reduced costs.

There are different kinds of probate, depending on state law:

>> **Small-estate:** The simplest form of probate that can be used (but not in every state), for estates ranging in value from $1,000 to $10,000, depending on state law.

>> **Unsupervised or independent:** A reasonably simple and less expensive form of probate used when the estate is more than the value of a "small estate" but doesn't require a lot of court supervision. It can be requested when all the beneficiaries agree (and consent, if the will requires consent).

>> **Supervised:** Typically applied to large estates and wills with complicated provisions, with the court playing a major role in approving every action. Supervised probate is used if the will is contested, someone named in the will requests it, or the court is concerned about the executor's abilities.

REMEMBER

If the will involves property in more than one state, the probate court in each state will be involved, adding to the costs.

One of the best ways to avoid the costs and delays of probate is to have a good estate plan in place. If the will is up-to-date and properly prepared, all the provisions are made in clear simple language, and the beneficiaries are advised about what they can expect (and won't be getting), chances are that the will can be probated at minimum cost and with minimum delays. The more money that is involved and the more people who will stand to gain (or lose) from the will, the more likely it is that there will be complications. Even so, planning can reduce some of the potential problems.

Reviewing the Rules on Estate Taxes

"In this world nothing can be said to be certain, except death and taxes." So said Benjamin Franklin in 1789. And in the administration of estates after a person's death, the two are inextricably linked. To add to the complexity, the Internal Revenue Service itself says, "The laws on Estate and Gift Taxes are considered to be some of the most complicated in the Internal Revenue Code." Among its many publications is a guide to estate taxes, available at www.irs.gov/pub/irs-pdf/p950.pdf.

Part of the executor's responsibilities in overseeing the provisions of the will is to ensure that all taxes have been paid, including income taxes and estate taxes.

In 2017 the basic amount an individual can exclude from estate taxes was $5.25 million, doubled for a married couple. At that level, according to the Tax Policy Center, a nonprofit arm of the Urban Institute and the Brookings Institution, just 3,800 estates were expected to be big enough to owe any federal taxes. All that changed with the Trump administration's tax reform bill, enacted in 2018. The estate tax exclusion doubled so the base for exclusion became $10 million for tax years 2018–2025. Because the exemption is adjusted for inflation, an individual can shelter $11.2 million in assets. Another federal estate law provision called *portability* lets couples who do proper planning double that exemption. So, a couple can exclude $22.4 million for 2018. But in all likelihood, individuals who have this much money already have tax accountant numbers on their speed dials.

The law is designed to "sunset," or end, in 2025. If Congress does not renew it, the exemption amount will revert to the $5 million base, again adjusted for inflation.

With regard to making gifts to family members or others, the amounts that someone can give to each of these individuals as a gift tax-free each year increased from $14,000 in 2014 to $15,000 in 2018. States have their own estate or inheritance taxes, so be sure to investigate the rules in your state. State taxes are typically lower than federal taxes but still can affect the distribution of assets — and the tax man gets paid before the family.

REMEMBER

Consulting a very experienced tax attorney or accountant is recommended. There may be some ways to reduce a tax bill, but unless the estate is worth many millions of dollars, estate taxes may not be an issue for you.

Establishing a Trust

If, after reviewing information about wills and probate, you realize that the estate will probably qualify for a simplified probate process, will not have a big tax bite taken out after death, and will not involve complicated financial arrangements to distribute your assets, then setting up a trust will probably not get you much but will be costly and cumbersome. Even so, many people are attracted to the idea of a living trust (maybe it's the word *living*, which sounds like it moves planning out of the realm of death).

A *trust* sets aside certain assets or an amount of money for another person. It allows money to be disbursed over time rather than as a lump sum both before and after the grantor's death. A trust is a good option to consider for people with beneficiaries who aren't able to manage money well. These beneficiaries may be minors, have intellectual disabilities or cognitive impairments, or just be unreliable with money. Sometimes trusts are used to transfer property, such as a vacation home, that is not easy to divide evenly among several beneficiaries. If that vacation home is in another state, putting it into a trust avoids having to go through the probate process in a second state. Trusts are also often used by people with very substantial assets because they can help reduce estate taxes. Probably the most common reason people set up trusts is that they want to control the disposition of the property more readily than they can in a will.

You can set up a trust so that the beneficiary receives the proceeds of the trust after your death or upon reaching a certain age. For instance, you can set up a testamentary trust in which you put some assets with conditions on their use, such as for a grandchild's education or when the child reaches the age of 25.

REMEMBER

If you choose to prepare a trust, you still need to have a will. The will provides a safety net if for some reason some of the trust property can't be transferred. A will may include specific provisions about the distribution of assets that are not in the trust. A trust can hold money, real estate, stocks and bonds — anything of monetary value. You need to pick which assets you want held in trust and which ones you want to be distributed by your will. The trustee is a person or institution that you select to manage the trust property. The trustee has a fiduciary duty (that term again!) to use the property as the grantor has indicated. The property stays in the same place, but legal ownership is transferred to the trust.

A living trust is often touted both as a way to retain control of assets and to avoid probate. This is how a living trust works: While you are alive and not disabled, you set up a trust that you own and control as both the trustee and the beneficiary. You also name the successor trustee who will manage the trust after your disability or death, and you name successor beneficiaries who will get the assets in the trust after your death. You can name someone else as trustee while you are alive and able, if you choose, and you can revoke that decision later.

Read on for a list of advantages and disadvantages with living trusts and information on other kinds of trusts.

Pros and cons of living trusts

Living trusts have the following advantages:

>> If you have an accident or illness that makes you unable to manage the trust and you have named someone as a successor trustee, the trust provides a way to manage the assets placed in the trust while you are still living.

>> A trust is a private document and does not become public as does a will. Anyone who wants a copy of a will can request it from the court, so trusts have more privacy protections.

>> A trust is easy to change. A will is easy to change too but may involve costs.

>> Assets in the trust do not go through the probate process.

WARNING

There are, however, some potential problems:

>> You must transfer legal title to the assets you want to be held by the trust and add new assets as you acquire them.

>> Just like a will, you should remember to update the living trust in case of a life-changing event. For example, the person named as beneficiary may now be an ex-spouse.

>> Having a trust can affect your eligibility for Medicaid or other benefits. Your state may count assets in a trust in determining eligibility.

>> Because the management of a living trust is outside a court's jurisdiction, there is no oversight, which means no probate court costs but also no supervision in case of disagreements. You can go to all the trouble of creating a living trust and still have your estate wind up in litigation.

WARNING

Be wary of salespeople who pitch kits that promise to include everything you need for a living trust — at a cost of several thousand dollars. They take the money and run, or give you a document that does not fit your circumstances and may not even be valid in your state. The "free lunch" session on how to avoid probate with a living will kit is going to cost you. Several states have filed consumer fraud actions against these con artists. If you or a parent is really a good candidate for a living trust, you need competent legal advice from an experienced lawyer in your community.

Special-needs trusts

There are many kinds of trusts — such as charitable trusts to give money to favorite organizations, generation-skipping trusts, spendthrift trusts, and others — but one additional type deserves attention because it applies to a lot of people. A *special-needs trust* is an instrument that allows a parent or other person to set aside money for the care and needs of a person with disabilities. This money does not count in the determination of the person's eligibility for Medicaid or other government benefits, an important consideration. It can be spent on items and services that improve the person's quality of life. The trustee may be a parent or other relative who manages the trust in the disabled person's best interests.

Special-needs trusts are valuable protections for people with disabilities and help assure that they get appropriate care. The Special Needs Trusts Fairness Act, which allows individuals to set up their own special-needs trusts so they do not have to rely on family or courts, was included in the 21st Century Cures Act, which became law in 2016. For more information, see `https://attorney.elderlawanswers.com/snt-fairness-act-becomes-law-15906`.

Considering Guardianship

While many people see the value of living trusts, online wills, and other financial instruments, guardianship has few advocates because it is a costly and often demeaning process for the person, whose frailty and inabilities to manage have to be presented in court. Court-appointed guardianship (or conservatorship) does have a role in protecting the property and interests of older adults who are unable to make decisions themselves and do not have natural advocates such as a trusted family member with authority to make decisions. Generally, guardianship is used as a last resort for people who have failed to plan for their disability and now need the help of someone else to make important decisions about their care and finances. Having a stranger appointed as guardian introduces another element into an already difficult situation. Some court-appointed guardians have failed to follow their fiduciary duties and have made decisions that benefit themselves rather than the person for whom they are legally responsible.

REMEMBER

Even if the court-appointed guardian is a family member, the responsibilities of being a guardian are more onerous than simply being a caring child, niece, or nephew. You will be required to report periodically to the court about how you're spending the money and how you're caring for the incapacitated person. You have a fiduciary duty to properly manage the resources for the benefit of the family member.

Following are the two kinds of guardianship:

>> **Guardianship of the estate:** Having authority to manage money and other assets; this is called *conservatorship* in some states

>> **Guardianship of the person:** Having the responsibility to make healthcare and other decisions that affect the well-being of the person

Guardianship situations usually arise when a person is mentally ill, has an intellectual disability, advanced dementia, or otherwise lacks capacity. Courts determine capacity in different ways, depending on state law, but it generally involves a legal finding that a person cannot make certain kinds of decisions. Capacity is specific to the task or decision. Someone may have capacity to make healthcare decisions but not to manage money.

If there is conflict among siblings, for example, over whether a parent's assets should be used to hire home care workers or to place the parent in a nursing home, one sibling may file a guardianship petition to be able to make the decision. The court may appoint one person or co-guardians.

If no family member or friend seems to be an appropriate guardian or the family situation appears irrevocably torn, the court may appoint a person outside the family to take on this role. It can be a private professional guardian, public guardian, volunteer, or attorney.

WARNING

Although the guardian is required to act in the person's best interests or expressed interests, sometimes courts do not fully investigate the background of the guardians they appoint, and their shortcomings are realized only after they have committed fraud or abused or neglected their wards.

REMEMBER

Money matters and legal issues are complicated. Don't make any decisions without consulting an experienced attorney or accountant.

4

Managing Your Healthcare

Find the best doctor for you, whether it's a geriatrician, an internal medicine doctor, or a family-practice doctor.

Cut through the confusion surrounding home care with a discussion of the many varieties of services, who provides them, and who pays. I also offer tips on working with home health aides, who are the mainstay of paid home care.

Discover how to choose a high-quality, person-centered skilled nursing facility.

See why advance care planning is important to ensure that you get the care you want and avoid the care you don't want. Think about two options for advanced illness: palliative care and hospice.

IN THIS CHAPTER

» **Understanding special medical needs you may have**

» **Finding the right doctors**

» **Making your way around hospitals**

» **Managing medications**

Chapter **14**

Choosing Good Medical Care

The good news is that Americans are living longer, and many older adults are in good or excellent health. How can you get the best medical care to stay healthy? How do you manage prescription and over-the-counter medications? And what should you do if you require a hospital stay? This chapter covers all those topics.

I also discuss geriatric care. The term covers a wide spectrum of necessary services, but most often it refers to managing the medical side of aging — from doctors to hospitals to medications.

One question commonly asked is this: "Who is in charge of managing the medical side of care?" That answer used to be simple: "The doctor who has treated my family for years." In today's complex and constantly evolving healthcare system, the answer is more likely to be your primary care provider or perhaps a specialist, such as your cardiologist. But sometimes it may seem that nobody is in charge — and having someone in charge is important. In this chapter, I help you find the right medical quarterback.

REMEMBER

The information in this chapter is intended to provide general information and does not substitute for advice from a qualified physician or other healthcare professional.

Checking on the Special Medical Needs of Older Adults

Many factors contribute to length of life, but in general women live longer than men do. According to the U.S. Centers for Disease Control and Prevention (CDC), life expectancy at age 65 for both women and men is on average 19.3 years. For men, it's a little less — 18 years — and for women, a little longer — 20.5 years. Of course, these ages are averages, and everyone knows 90- and 100-year-old men who are doing fine and women who have died at much younger ages.

Increased longevity has increased the burden of chronic disease. In earlier days, people died from acute (rapid onset) conditions like pneumonia, bacterial infections, or accidents. Although these causes of death still exist, the more common conditions are chronic — that is, they last a long time and can be treated but typically can't be cured.

Identifying common chronic conditions

According to the CDC, in 2012 about half of all adults — 117 million people — had one or more chronic health conditions. Chronic diseases and conditions — such as heart disease, stroke, cancer, type 2 diabetes, obesity, and arthritis — are among the most common, costly, and preventable of all health problems.

Seven of the top 10 causes of death in 2014 were chronic diseases. Two of these chronic diseases — heart disease and cancer — together accounted for nearly 46 percent of all deaths. Arthritis is the most common cause of disability. Of the 54 million adults with doctor-diagnosed arthritis, more than 23 million say that arthritis causes trouble with their usual activities. Diabetes is the leading cause of kidney failure, lower-limb amputations other than those caused by injury, and new cases of blindness among adults.

Alzheimer's disease is the fifth leading cause of death for people over the age of 65. This statistic may be an underestimate because the immediate cause of death may be recorded as some other condition. More than 5 million people have this disease or another dementia. It is probably the most feared chronic disease, more so than cancer.

Among other chronic conditions are:

>> **Hypertension:** Hypertension (high blood pressure) is the most prevalent condition among older adults, affecting 71 percent of people over 65. Untreated or poorly controlled hypertension can lead to strokes.

>> **Dyslipidemia:** Too much LDL (low-density lipoprotein) or "bad" cholesterol, a condition known as *dyslipidemia*, affects 45 percent of older adults and is associated with blood clots and heart disease.

>> **Lung disease:** Lung conditions, such as chronic obstructive pulmonary disease (COPD), emphysema, or chronic bronchitis, affect 14 percent of older women and 11 percent of older men. Not surprisingly, COPD is three times higher among current smokers compared with those who have never smoked.

>> **Osteoporosis:** Osteoporosis (thinning of bones) is more common among older women (26 percent) than men (4 percent). Osteoporosis increases the risk of fractures after a fall.

>> **Vision problems:** Cataracts are the most common vision problem among older adults, affecting 41 percent. People with diabetes are more likely to have cataracts and glaucoma than nondiabetics.

>> **Incontinence:** Over a third of older adults experience urinary incontinence, and the prevalence is higher among women (47 percent) than men (18 percent).

>> **Mental health problems:** Mental health problems — depression, anxiety, obsessive compulsive disorder (OCD, which manifests in hoarding), and others — add to the burden of physical conditions.

TIP

Many of the chronic conditions that older adults experience are accompanied by pain. Chronic pain limits function and well-being. But overprescription and over-use of pain medications can lead to serious side effects and dependence. Talk to your doctor about ways to manage pain that are less risky than opioids such as fentanyl and morphine and many brand-name drugs. If you're using these drugs, be sure to keep them securely stored, away from children and others who may be tempted to use or sell them. The American Geriatrics Society's Health in Aging website has helpful information about non-narcotic ways to manage pain. Go to `www.healthinaging.org/aging-and-health-a-to-z/topic:pain-management/info:care-and-treatment/`.

Dealing with multiple ailments

Approximately one in four Americans has at least two chronic conditions, but the burden of chronic disease is even higher in older adults. Among Original Medicare beneficiaries, over two-thirds have two or more chronic conditions. About one in seven have six or more, and this group accounts for almost half of total Medicare spending. Older adults with several chronic conditions are known in medical jargon as *multimorbid*.

Chronic conditions are not only difficult to manage on their own; they also frequently lead to loss of function. A person with two arthritic knees or hips has a hard time just getting around without pain, and immobility leads to other problems. Strokes can affect speech and movement. Heart disease and COPD may limit activity. And memory and behavior problems associated with Alzheimer's disease and other dementias that worsen over time create difficult situations in which the older person's personality, judgment, and ability to communicate undergo major changes.

REMEMBER

Preventive measures, such as those to reduce the risk of falls, can help maintain good health. These measures are discussed in Chapter 5. The benefits of good nutrition, exercise, social activity, and moderation in alcohol use are well known. Genetics, we are finding out, plays a part as well, although how genes interact with other factors is still unclear.

REMEMBER

Whatever the combination of factors that apply to a specific person, it is essential to have good medical care — that is, care that considers the way aging affects the body and the difference in medication absorption and side effects between older adults and the younger populations on which most drugs were tested. When looking for a doctor, consider technical competence as well as the professional's ability to focus on the whole person, not just body parts and disease. I give more guidance on finding a good doctor in the following section.

Finding the Right Specialist to Manage Care

As you age, you may stay with your current doctor. Or you may seek a geriatrician or gerontologist — someone who specializes in aging. What is the difference between a geriatrician and a gerontologist?

>> *Geriatrics* is a medical subspecialty. *Geriatricians* are physicians, primarily internal medicine doctors, who have taken additional training that focuses on the diseases of aging and their treatments. They have been certified by the American Board of Internal Medicine to practice geriatric medicine.

>> *Gerontology* is a multidisciplinary study of the mental, physical, environmental, and social aspects of aging. *Gerontologists* do research, teach aging in universities, participate in organizational planning and policy, and contribute to the broad knowledge about the impact of aging on individuals and society.

Perhaps the simplest distinction is this: While both geriatricians and gerontologists are called *doctor*, a geriatrician is an M.D. or a D.O. (doctor of osteopathy) and a gerontologist is usually a Ph.D. An M.D. can prescribe medications; a gerontologist can't. Geriatricians see patients individually, while gerontologists generally do not, although they may work in settings like nursing homes or government agencies to advise on practice and policies.

TECHNICAL STUFF

Within geriatric medicine, there are even more specialists: geriatric psychiatrists, cardiologists, pulmonologists, and others. Some nurses and social workers also become specialists in this field.

Considering the need for a geriatrician

Is it essential for an older adult to be treated by a geriatrician? No. Many internists (internal medicine doctors) and family physicians provide excellent primary care for older adults. Although they may not have advanced training, they have the benefit of experience. Among their patients are undoubtedly many older adults, and experienced doctors have learned that older adults may need more time during office visits and react differently to medications than their younger patients.

The American Geriatrics Society recommends that a geriatrician should be consulted in the following circumstances:

>> An older person's condition causes considerable impairment and frailty. These patients tend to be over the age of 75 and coping with several diseases and disabilities, including cognitive (mental) problems.

>> Family members and friends are feeling considerable stress and strain as caregivers.

Many older people want to stick with a doctor they have known for years. (But the doctor, of course, is aging too, which may be something to consider.) If you or your parent or other relative have a good relationship with a doctor and the care needed is not highly specialized, then you have no reason to make a change.

REMEMBER

Be sure to be particularly observant about symptoms that may indicate a change in your or your relative's condition, or a medication side effect that may be related to a person's age. If your regular doctor doesn't take questions or observations about memory or behavior changes seriously, this may be a sign that it's time for a change. Family members and sometimes older people themselves are often the best reporters of changes that may indicate something serious. Maybe it's a side effect of a medication (even one that has been taken for a long time) or a urinary tract infection. Maybe it's a sign of depression. Maybe it's a sign of early dementia. Geriatricians can do comprehensive evaluations of these worrisome but often nonspecific reports and can recommend further testing if necessary.

TIP

If your regular doctor refers you to a specialist, ask specifically about that person's experience and qualifications for treating older adults.

Finding a geriatrician

If, for whatever reason, you are looking for a new doctor, I recommend finding a qualified geriatrician. But it's not as easy as it sounds, because there's a shortage of geriatricians (see the nearby sidebar "The shortage of geriatric specialists"). Some established geriatricians aren't taking new patients, or there may be a long wait for an initial visit. Many geriatricians see patients only part of their time because they are involved in training programs.

Here are some suggestions for finding a geriatrician:

WARNING

>> **Check online.** Members of the American Geriatrics Society (geriatricians, geriatric nurse practitioners, and geriatric physician assistants) who want to participate in its referral program are listed at www.healthinaging.org/ find-a-geriatrics-healthcare-professional. The society does not endorse individual providers, but all the physicians listed are either Board Certified in Geriatric Medicine (internists) or have a Certificate of Added Qualifications in Geriatric Medicine (family physicians).

Some commercial websites also offer to help you find a geriatrician. These lists can be useful, but they are not comprehensive, and the doctors have probably paid to be listed.

>> **Contact a hospital.** Contact a hospital or academic medical center in your area. Its "Find a Physician" lists provide names and qualifications.

>> **Use Medicare resources.** If you or your parent is a member of a Medicare Advantage plan, look at the list of providers in the plan to find geriatricians.

>> **Ask around.** Use the old-fashioned method of asking friends and family. Ask specific questions about how efficiently the office is run, whether the doctor has good communication skills with older adults, whether he or she has emergency backup if needed, and any other questions that may apply to you or your parent. Is the office easily accessible, even for a wheelchair? Are the staff pleasant and responsive to older people? If you have to be admitted to a hospital, which one will it be? Does the doctor make hospital and home visits?

THE SHORTAGE OF GERIATRIC SPECIALISTS

According to the American Geriatrics Society, currently about 7,300 certified geriatricians work in the United States. Given projections about the increase in the 65-and-older population, approximately 20,000 geriatricians are needed now to take care of 14 million people (30 percent of the population over 65). In addition, there are only 2,000 geriatric psychiatrists, and less than 1 percent of registered nurses, pharmacists, and physician assistants and 2.6 percent of advanced practice nurses are certified in geriatrics. The situation is no better in other professionals that routinely see older adults; about 3 percent of psychologists devote most of their practice to older adults, and 4 percent of social workers specialize in geriatrics.

The future does not look promising, as very few medical school graduates are pursuing advanced training in geriatrics. The lack of interest may be because geriatrics is not a high-income specialty, work schedules are less predictable than in other specialties, and working with older people may not be considered as stimulating or challenging as other fields. Yet older adults account for a disproportionate share of all healthcare services, from 26 percent of all physician office visits and 35 percent of all hospital stays to 90 percent of all nursing-home care.

Navigating Hospitals

Nobody likes having to go to the hospital, but it is a necessary factor in some medical equations. When a hospital stay truly is necessary, keep in mind certain points to help the experience go more smoothly. The next sections discuss these areas.

Where to go for emergencies and non-emergencies

Emergency departments (EDs) are often the first stage of a hospital stay. Most people still call them *ERs* for emergency room, but the formal term is ED. Whatever the title, they are usually busy, chaotic, and difficult environments for anyone, but particularly for an older person. Yet all too often they are the default solution for a problem instead of a well-considered decision.

Emergency departments

EDs are designed to treat real emergencies — difficulty breathing, choking, loss of consciousness, severe pain — not for problems that can be treated at home or at an urgent care center and followed up with a doctor visit in the next day or two. Of course, no one wants to make a mistake by discounting the seriousness of a medical complaint, but calling the doctor's office or your health plan's nurse hotline to get a professional opinion about the urgency of the complaint can help you avoid unnecessary trips to the ED.

WARNING

If the person answering the phone at the doctor's office doesn't ask questions or offer any suggestions but just says, "Take your mother to the emergency room," it is likely a bad sign about the care being provided. And if the default recording on evenings and weekends is "If this is an emergency, hang up and call 911," ask the doctor at a regular visit what counts as an emergency. Or suggest a different way to handle these calls.

TIP

Some hospitals have created special EDs for older adults who are not sick enough to be admitted to the hospital but are not ready to go home. These special units are quieter, staffed by nurses and others used to working with older adults, and more comfortable than the typical ED. Patients can stay in these settings while tests are run, medications are given, they're observed for side effects, and until someone can provide a safe ride home. Ask whether your local hospital has this kind of special ED.

Urgent care centers

An alternative to an ED visit is an urgent care center. Urgent care centers are walk-in sites appropriate for situations such as a fever, a sore throat, or a persistent bad cold. Staff (often ED-trained doctors) can evaluate the problem, take X-rays, and prescribe medications. If they feel that an ED visit is required, they can call an ambulance. If you do go to an urgent care center, make sure to inform the regular doctor about what happened and what was recommended.

Urgent care centers can be a very convenient and useful option. The number of urgent care centers in many parts of the country has been increasing. They are often less expensive than an ED and may be located nearer to you. The waiting time is also usually shorter than in an ED, and these centers take most insurance plans. Your health plan may not consider an urgent care center near you as part of its network, so it's a good idea to find out now just in case you need one later.

Another option is a full-service ED that offers more than an urgent care center but is not located at the hospital, although it may be part of a health system network. This may be an option if there is one in your area. They can provide a wide range of services and arrange transportation to a hospital should that be necessary. Finding out whether your insurance will cover these visits is important here too.

Being admitted to the hospital

A hospital stay, especially a long one or one that involves being in an intensive care unit (ICU), is certainly upsetting for everyone, and infection is an ever-present risk. You can become disoriented by the noise, lights, constant questioning, and different people coming in and out of the room. Long waits in cold corridors for X-rays and other tests add to the misery.

Patients may not get enough to eat, especially if doctors order them to fast before procedures. Getting a full night's sleep is next to impossible. Patients are often prescribed painkillers or other medications that can leave them confused or even delirious, especially in the unfamiliar surroundings of a hospital. Extended bed rest can weaken patients' muscles and bones. Even with kind and caring staff explaining what is happening (not always the case), a hospital stay is almost guaranteed to be unpleasant at best and debilitating at worst.

TIP

Some hospitals have special units for older people called Acute Care for Elders (ACE) units. They are staffed by a specially trained interdisciplinary team, which can include geriatricians, advanced practice nurses, social workers, pharmacists, and physical therapists. The team assesses patients daily, and nurses are given an increased level of independence and accountability. These units have been shown to shorten length of stay and result in lower cost while maintaining patients' functional abilities. If hospitalization is necessary, ask whether your hospital has an ACE.

WARNING

If you or your parent have been given a bed on a regular hospital floor, make sure that you have formally been admitted as an inpatient. If the doctor or nurse isn't sure, ask the admitting office. The hospital may claim that you were under observation, even though you received the same services as everyone else. Because you haven't been formally admitted, Medicare will not consider this stay as a Part A (hospital) benefit, for which you pay only an inpatient deductible, but as a Part B (outpatient) benefit. Your portion of the bill may be higher and will include costs for lab tests, X-rays, medications, and other things that would typically be covered under Part A. And if you go to a rehab program in a nursing facility after this stay, you will have to pay privately since you will technically not have had the required three-day inpatient hospital stay required by Medicare. Legislation has been proposed to change Medicare rules on observation stays, but the outcome is pending. For now, make sure you ask whether you are admitted or on observation. You're supposed to receive a notice called a MOON (Medicare Outpatient Observation Notice), but that may not happen. There is no way to appeal the hospital's decision to place you on observation, but you can register a complaint with the hospital administration and with Medicare. The Center for Medicare Advocacy has advice at www.medicareadvocacy. org/medicare-hospital-outpatient-observation-status-toolkit/.

TIP

Your primary doctor, whether a geriatrician or not, may or may not visit you in the hospital. It would be good to ask at a regular visit whether your primary doctor visits patients when they are hospitalized and which hospitals they visit. Increasingly, hospital care is managed by specialists called *hospitalists.* These doctors are trained in critical care medicine and are skilled at handling medical crises that happen to seriously ill patients. They generally work in teams so that someone from the team is available at all hours of the day and night and on weekends. This also means that patients may not see the same staff every day. Hospitalists are employed by the hospital or belong to a group practice that is under contract to the hospital. They do not generally see patients after discharge, although some groups do have physicians who work both in the hospital and in the community. For more information, see the United Hospital Fund's Next Step in Care guide to hospitalists at www.nextstepincare.org/Caregiver_Home/Hospitalist.

Planning for a hospital stay

Hospitalization for an elective (planned) surgery for an older adult is in theory easier than an admission through the ED because you have time to get ready. But there's a lot to think about, no matter the reason for the surgery.

REMEMBER

All surgery has risks, and you want to be sure that the potential benefits are worth the risks. Someone's age alone should not be a reason to decide against surgery, but a very frail person in poor health and perhaps with moderate or advanced dementia is probably not a good candidate for surgery. Be sure to ask about and consider alternatives.

The surgeon is generally a specialist recommended by the geriatrician or the primary care physician. An orthopedic surgeon replaces hips and knees, a cardiac surgeon replaces valves and inserts pacemakers and stents, and a renal surgeon takes care of kidney problems. They are experts in their specific area, but you need someone to look after the whole person, and that is the geriatrician or primary care doctor.

REMEMBER

It is important that these doctors talk to each other, not just in the initial referral but also as the surgery is approaching and definitely afterward. The time spent in the hospital may be very short, which is a good thing, but it also means that the recovery time needed at home is longer, and care must be taken to avoid complications. Older people react differently to anesthesia, may experience more pain, and take longer to recover than younger people undergoing similar surgery.

TIP

Many hospitals will inform primary care doctors when one of their patients is admitted, but this doesn't always happen. If you're the patient, ask a family member to call your regular doctor's office to give that information and the name and contact information of the hospital doctor in charge of your care. And ask the hospital doctor — probably a hospitalist — to contact your regular doctor to discuss your diagnosis and treatment. This is especially important as you get ready to be discharged because you will need follow-up at home. Both hospital and primary care doctors are busy and may need some reminders about making sure they both know the specifics of your care.

REMEMBER

Because so many older adults are undergoing surgery, the American Geriatrics Society and the American College of Surgeons worked together to create a series of guidelines for surgical teams. These "best practice" guidelines are intended for surgeons, but they are also useful for the person undergoing surgery and family members. Here are some of the key points:

>> Talk to the surgeon about what to expect from the surgery:

- What are the treatment goals? Will the surgery fix the problem, or will there still be limitations?

- What kind of anesthesia will be used? Are there common side effects?

- How long will the surgery last? How long will the person be in the recovery room?

- How will pain be treated? Ask about alternatives to morphine and other opioid drugs to lessen the risk of dependence on them. But don't suffer in silence. Pain is debilitating and should be treated.

- Will there be physical limitations such as being able to climb stairs, get in and out of bed, and use the toilet? Even a generally successful surgery like hip replacement Is always followed by a period of restrictions on mobility. Can the person follow instructions so that the surgery is not undone by a fall or other accident?

>> Ask where you or your parent will go after surgery. You may expect and want to go home, but the surgeon may recommend a short stay of a few weeks in a rehabilitation program, probably in a nursing-home rehab unit. There you can recover more fully and get therapy to restore and improve function. Even that new hip takes time to get used to, especially if you have been in pain and not walking properly for some time before the surgery.

Some health plans have specific rehab programs in their network and going out of network will be costly. Even if you feel you have no choice, it is important to investigate the sites to see which ones best suit your needs. Location is important, of course, but quality matters too, so try to find out as much as you can about whether other patients with similar conditions have had good outcomes. The government website Nursing Home Compare at www.medicare.gov/nursinghomecompare/search.html has information on long-stay residents but not much on short-term rehab.

>> Ask about costs. Medicare or other insurance will cover some or all the surgeon's fees (but there will be a copayment) and the hospital fee. But the anesthesiologist will submit a separate bill. Review Medicare's policies at www.medicare.gov if you are in Original (fee-for-service) Medicare, and if you are a member of a Medicare Advantage plan, ask the plan for details about costs. For Medicaid and other insurances, ask the case manager, usually a nurse in charge of planning your care after discharge.

>> Ask ahead about eligibility for some skilled nursing visits and possibly physical therapy at home after discharge from the hospital or rehab program. It will take some time to get used to being at home, and everyone can benefit from some extra help.

>> Make sure the surgeon is aware of any special problems, like depression or alcohol use that may affect responses to surgery or recovery. For a comprehensive list of the guidelines, go to www.nextstepincare.org/ Caregiver_Home/Elective_Surgery.

TIP

A new law called the CARE Act (Caregiver Advise, Record, Enable) has been enacted in 42 states and territories. This law, which AARP supports, is designed to ensure that family caregivers (as identified by the patient) are included in discussions about the post-discharge care plan, informed about the day of discharge, and given instructions about all medical tasks that need to be done at home, such as managing medications or caring for surgical wounds. If you're the patient, you should know that you will be asked to identify someone who can help you at home until you can manage on your own. And if you're the family caregiver, you should know that you do not have to agree to perform all the necessary tasks but that you can get help from the hospital staff to learn what needs to be done. Go to this video to see how the CARE Act works: http://videos.aarp.org/detail/video/ 5793819744001/how-the-care-act-works-%E2%80%94-aarp. A map of states with CARE Act legislation as of 2017 is at www.aarp.org/content/dam/aarp/ caregiving/2017/11/care-act-map-11-2017-aarp.pdf?intcmp=AE-CAR-LRS-IL, and a report from the AARP Public Policy Institute on the implementation of the legislation is at blog.aarp.org/2017/08/29/154354/.

Polypharmacy: Too Many Drugs?

More and more people take a lot of medications and vitamins, dietary supplements, herbal preparations, and other drugstore items that don't require a doctor's prescription. It's called *polypharmacy*. Advertisements persuade people that a certain drug must be good for you. If it's new, it must be better. If it's sold without a prescription, it must be safe. If it's "natural," it must be better than something created from chemicals. If it's been around for years, like aspirin, it can't hurt you. For all these beliefs, the reality is this: Not exactly. Taking aspirin, for example, is sometimes used jokingly, as in "Take two aspirin and call me in the morning." But overdoses of aspirin can kill, and even nonlethal doses can cause stomach bleeding and other problems. Always check with your doctor.

With all these drug-promoting ideas in the culture, it may seem as though everyone follows the directions from the doctor, pharmacy, or package label very carefully. Not at all. People get into trouble when they take too many of the wrong medications or skip some that they should be taking and generally adopt a casual attitude about these powerful concoctions. According to the CDC, more than 700,000 ED visits every year are related to adverse drug events. And a growing epidemic of addiction to prescription medications is taking a toll on all ages across the United States.

People often don't tell doctors about everything they are taking and not taking. When the doctor asks, "Are you taking your medicines?" the answer is likely to be "Yes" when the reality is "Not so much." And the doctor may not ask whether you're taking any other medications. Even if the question is asked, people may answer with what they consider a truthful "No," because they don't realize that all the over-the-counter items are in fact medications, not harmless concoctions.

It's easy to get confused about medications. They come in brand names (the advertised versions) and generic preparations, which are cheaper but have harder names to remember. Hospitals have their own formularies (list of drugs they use), which may not be the same as the drugs used at home.

Using caution with certain drugs

Recognizing that certain drugs are potentially risky for older adults, the American Geriatrics Society periodically updates a list called the Beers Criteria for Potentially Inappropriate Medication Use in Older Adults. This list contains medications and types of medications that are "potentially inappropriate" for older people and can be replaced with safer or more effective medications or nondrug remedies. Some drugs are listed to be used only with caution. The Beers list updated in 2015 is available at onlinelibrary.wiley.com/doi/pdf/10.1111/jgs.13702.

HealthinAging.org, an educational arm of the American Geriatrics Society, has prepared a list, viewable at www.healthinaging.org/files/documents/tipsheets/meds_to_avoid.pdf, of ten medications older adults should avoid or use with caution. For example, long-lasting nonsteroidal anti-inflammatory drugs (NSAIDS) used to reduce pain and inflammation can increase the risk of indigestion, ulcers, and bleeding, as well as increasing blood pressure, and make heart failure worse. Shorter-acting NSAIDs like ibuprofen are better choices.

Other medications on the list are certain diabetes drugs as well as medications used for anxiety and insomnia.

REMEMBER

The Beers List and other similar lists are not the final word on whether a particular drug is right for you or your parent. The drugs on the list have been approved by the Federal Drug Administration, so they are marketed legally. But if you're taking one of these drugs or your doctor prescribes a new one, you need to review the choices and any alternatives. One of the drugs that the list says to avoid or use only with caution may in fact be the best choice for your specific condition. But unless you ask, you won't know why the doctor has recommended this drug rather than another one that seems to be less risky.

Getting medications right

REMEMBER

You can do many things to make sure that you're taking the right medications at the right time in the right dose:

>> Keep an updated list of all your medications, prescription and OTC, and show it to every doctor at every appointment. Review the list at least once a year and certainly after a hospital stay.

>> Whenever a new drug is prescribed, ask why you should be taking it, what side effects to look out for, whether it interacts with any of the other drugs you're taking, and what to do if you miss a dose.

>> Read the label on the bottle. If the type is too small or the language too dense, ask the pharmacist for an easy-to-read version.

>> Follow the directions, and if you don't understand them, ask the doctor or the pharmacist. Sometimes medical professionals think that directions are clear ("Take this on an empty stomach") when they are not (what constitutes an empty stomach — two hours after eating? first thing in the morning?). Take the drug for as long as you've been told — not for a longer or shorter time.

>> Report any changes in your medical condition, which may be related to a new drug. If the reactions are serious, such as an extensive rash, difficulty breathing, or swelling in your throat, they count as emergencies. Call 911 or go the nearest ED.

>> Throw out any unused medications. Don't give them to anyone else, and don't take medications that were not prescribed for you.

>> Be especially careful to keep pain medications where they don't create an "attractive nuisance" for a child who may want to taste or drink them and where they aren't easily accessible to adults in the family, workers, or visitors.

Insurance may cover certain drugs and not others. Even with insurance coverage, drugs can be expensive. If you have financial problems and need help paying for prescriptions, see the resources listed in Chapter 11.

Other risks and questions

Given the well-known and serious risks of polypharmacy in older adults, it is not surprising that among the American Geriatrics Society's "Five Things Physicians and Patients Should Question," medications accounted for four of the five items. This list is part of the "Choosing Wisely" Initiative of the American Board of Internal Medicine Foundation, in which various medical specialties came up with their own list of common but questionable practices in their field.

REMEMBER

Four of the five recommendations concern medications, and the first is a common medical procedure:

>> **Don't recommend percutaneous (tube) feeding tubes in patients with advanced dementia; instead, offer oral assisted feeding.** Tube feeding is associated with agitation, increased use of physical and chemical restraints, and worsening pressure ulcers. Careful hand-feeding for people with severe dementia is at least as good as tube feeding in terms of the outcomes of death, aspiration pneumonia, functional status, and comfort.

Tube feeding is a procedure that has emotional and ethical as well as medical implications; the American Geriatrics Society's recommendation focuses on the medical risks and benefits. It is particularly important for nursing-home practice where tube feeding is sometimes a method of convenience, not a medical or ethical choice.

>> **Don't use antipsychotics as a first choice to treat behavioral and psychological symptoms of dementia.** These drugs provide limited benefit and can cause serious harm, including stroke and premature death. Identifying and addressing causes of behavior change can make drug treatment unnecessary.

>> **Avoid using medications to achieve hemoglobin A1c < 7.5 percent in most adults age 65 and older; moderate control is generally better.** The A1C test, which has other names, is a common blood test used to diagnose type 1 and type 2 diabetes and then to gauge how well you're managing your diabetes. The A1C test result reflects your average blood sugar level for the past two to three months. Specifically, the A1C test measures what percentage of your hemoglobin — a protein in red blood cells that carries oxygen — is coated with sugar (glycated). Some studies have shown that efforts to reduce the A1c levels to less than 7 percent have resulted in higher mortality.

>> **Don't use benzodiazepines or other sedative-hypnotics in older adults as a first choice for insomnia, agitation, or delirium.** Large-scale studies have consistently shown rates of motor vehicle accidents, falls, and hip fractures leading to hospitalization and death can more than double in older adults taking these drugs. Their use should be limited to alcohol withdrawal or severe anxiety disorder unresponsive to other therapies.

>> **Don't use antimicrobials to treat bacteriuria (the presence of bacteria in the urine) in older adults unless specific urinary tract symptoms are present.** Urinary tract infection is diagnosed with specific clinical symptoms.

REMEMBER

Good medical care can enhance your quality of life and sense of well-being, but it requires a partnership between you and your healthcare team. It's worth the effort.

IN THIS CHAPTER

» **Understanding types of home care**

» **Choosing a home care agency or finding your own workers**

» **Working with home care aides**

» **Considering family or friends for home care**

» **Discovering doctor home visits**

Chapter **15**

Demystifying Home Care

As we age, having the right kind of help at home can make a significant difference in our quality of life and ability to remain in familiar surroundings. But the right kind of help is different for each person and is often hard to find. And for a person who values independence, accepting that help can be difficult, even when it's clearly needed.

Studies show that families provide an estimated 80 to 90 percent of care at home. But when family care isn't available or sufficient, you have the options of different types of services, different agencies that provide them, and different health and long-term care insurance coverage. You may pay privately for workers you hire on your own. Some public programs allow family members or friends to be paid to provide care. This chapter gives you basic information to get started on your search.

Examining Varieties of Home Care

Home care sounds simple. Many people think of home care as having an all-purpose assistant/homemaker/nurse/aide who spends the whole day (and maybe stays overnight) helping with personal care, doing household chores, and reminding you or your parent to take your medications — basically, doing whatever needs to be done. This description can be accurate, but only for some people, and even then, mostly for those who can pay out-of-pocket.

Home care services can range from relatively straightforward tasks such as helping someone get dressed and preparing meals to a level of care that involves operating and monitoring complex medical equipment, caring for wounds, and managing and giving medications, injections, or infusions. Where you or your parent fit on this spectrum of need determines what kinds of services you may be eligible for, who will provide them, and who will pay.

Home care services can be provided by

>> Physicians

>> Registered nurses

>> Licensed practical nurses

>> Physical, occupational, respiratory, and speech therapists

>> Social workers

>> Home healthcare aides

>> Personal care aides or attendants

>> Equipment vendors who supply durable medical equipment (DME) such as wheelchairs and hospital beds

Each of these people can play an important role in home care, but often you or a family member must coordinate the different visits and services. This can be a major responsibility involving a significant and ongoing commitment of time.

REMEMBER

According to the U.S. Bureau of Labor Statistics, "Home health aides and personal care aides help people with disabilities, chronic illness, or cognitive impairment by assisting in their daily living activities. They often help older adults who need assistance." Home health aides may be allowed to give a client medication or check the client's vital signs under the direction of a nurse or other healthcare practitioner. Personal care aides — sometimes called personal attendants — are not permitted to do these tasks. These rules apply to workers hired by home care agencies, not workers you hire and pay yourself.

This chapter first looks at home healthcare services provided by professionals through agencies, which are sometimes covered by insurance. I then turn to the options of hiring a home care worker independently and paying family or friends to help. The final section looks at physician home visits.

TIP

The AARP Caregiving Resource Center has a lot of information about home care and access to experts who can answer your questions. Go to www.aarp.org/caregiving/home-care/?intcmp=AE-CAR-R1-C3 or use the call-in number (877-333-5885; for Spanish-speaking callers, the number is 888-971-2013) 7 a.m. to 11 p.m. Eastern time Monday through Friday. You can also use the Long-Term Care Calculator (at www.aarp.org/relationships/caregiving-resource-center/LTCC) to estimate home care costs in your area.

Surveying Services from a Home Healthcare Agency

Policymakers and researchers often distinguish between formal and informal services. In policy-speak, *formal* services are services provided through an agency and paid for by insurance or privately; *informal* services are those provided by unpaid family members or friends. (No data are available on the numbers of people who do not use an agency but who instead hire and pay home care workers directly. Even though these workers are paid, they would probably be considered informal help since they are not supervised by a home healthcare agency or public entity.)

For Medicare and most private insurance, the threshold for eligibility for formal home healthcare services is the need for skilled care. *Skilled care* is defined not by what it is but by who provides it. In other words, skilled care is provided by a nurse or a physical therapist or other medical professional. Some examples of skilled nursing care are giving IV injections and tube feedings, and caring for wounds. Physical therapists who work with you to improve mobility, balance, and strength also provide skilled care.

REMEMBER

The opposite of skilled care is not unskilled care. Home care aides provide care that is sometimes called "unskilled," but that is an erroneous label. A home care aide does personal care like bathing and dressing, helps people move from bed to chair, and generally helps them do the things they used to be able to do but can no longer do on their own. Care provided by home care aides, especially if the person has dementia or cognitive deficits, is immobilized, or is uncooperative or verbally abusive, requires a high level of skill, not to mention patience and tolerance. The language of home care policies and practice, however, recognizes only what professionals do as *skilled*. And even when you or a family member learn to do the same tasks as a nurse, the task is no longer considered skilled care.

Defining different kinds of home care agencies

The definition of services provided by home care agencies is mirrored in the different types of home care agencies:

>> **Medicare-certified home health agencies (HHAs):** These are agencies approved by the Centers for Medicare & Medicaid Services (CMS) and licensed by the state to provide skilled services — primarily nurse visits, but also physical therapy or social-work visits, among others. Medicare will pay only for skilled services provided through an HHA. If there is a skilled need, HHAs may also provide aide services through their own aides or through another agency, usually a licensed agency, with which they have a contract. Medicare does not pay for aide services at home unless there is a skilled need.

TIP

You can compare Medicare-certified home health agencies in your area at `www.medicare.gov/homehealthcompare/search.html`. This site can give you some general information such as type of ownership and the results of quality measures such as the number of falls or rehospitalizations, but it can't tell you about important aspects of care such as how reliable and friendly an agency's workers are. Your state Department of Health may have comparable information online.

>> **Licensed home care agency:** Most but not all states license home care agencies to provide some nursing services and aides who do personal care. Some are contracted through Medicaid to provide long-term personal care. The Genworth 2017 Cost of Care Survey reported a national median hourly rate through licensed agencies of homemaker or companion services to be $21 and of personal care services to be $19. Rates vary by geographic area.

>> **Nonmedical or companion agency:** These rapidly growing agencies are not usually licensed by state health departments or regulated by state or federal government, and their services are not covered under Medicare or private health insurance because they are deemed nonmedical. Companion services include reading, conversation, assisting with clothing selection, organizing the mail, and picking up prescriptions from the pharmacy. Workers have varying levels of experience and training. Frequently companion agencies are locally run businesses that are franchises of large, brand-name companies. The rates for these services can range from $15 to $25 an hour.

WARNING

Companion agencies may list medication management among the nonmedical tasks within their range of expertise, but you should verify exactly what they're qualified to do. Companions may be limited to reminding the person to take the pills that have already been set up in a pillbox. You may not want a companion who lacks the necessary training to assist with multiple medications or those that should be taken in specific doses or by injection.

>> **Employment or registry agencies:** These agencies provide names of nurses and aides available to provide home care. You contact and pay them directly. Your state may also maintain a registry through the Department of Health. PHI National, an organization devoted to issues affecting home care workers, has a map showing which states have this service at `phinational.org/policy/resources/phi-matching-services-project`. Some states limit access to publicly funded (Medicaid) clients; others are more flexible.

REMEMBER

Medicare pays only for home healthcare services provided by a certified home health agency, and both Medicare Advantage plans and private insurance may require you to use an HHA in their network. If you pay privately, you can choose any agency.

Choosing a home care agency

Many people don't investigate home care agencies until they have a crisis. Often the crisis involves a hospitalization. The hospital discharge plan may include a referral to home care, and you may get a list of agencies that accept your insurance. In such a situation, you don't have a lot of time to investigate the options. But even so, you should ask questions about the agency before you sign an **agreement**. Be especially careful to find out how the agency screens, trains, and supervises home care workers. If you aren't in crisis mode, you have more time and should do a thorough search.

TIP

A hospital discharge planner may not refer you to home care services. If you need these services, ask the discharge planner or your doctor for a referral.

Although there are federal guidelines for training home health aides, each state has its own system of education and certifications. According to PHI International, fewer than one-third of states require more than the minimum federal standard of 75 hours of training. Only six states meet the higher standard of 120 hours recommended by the National Academy of Medicine. Some programs offer advanced training for home care aides on caring for someone with dementia or administering medications. Note, however, that some people prefer to train their aides directly and may not care about governmental requirements.

REMEMBER

Here are some questions to ask the agency, whether you're paying privately or expect insurance to cover the services:

>> What types of services do you provide? Ask about special kinds of care you may need, such as ventilator assistance or wound care. Some agencies contract these services to specialized agencies.

>> Do you provide backup help if the assigned worker is not available?

» Do your aides have special training to deal with medical conditions like dementia, paralysis, or stroke?

» What kind of supervision do your aides receive? Does a nurse review the case regularly and ask for their observations about the person's care?

» Do you screen aides before you hire them? Do you do a criminal background check, and if so, what does it include? Is the criminal background check for your state only, or is it nationwide?

» What is your hourly rate? How do you invoice clients? What kind of documentation do you require?

» Can your agency arrange for medical equipment when needed?

» How do you handle complaints?

» Do you provide 24-hour access by phone in case there is an emergency?

If your family member does not speak English, has cognitive problems, or follows certain religious or cultural routines, you should inform the agency.

TIP

Medicare has a useful list of ten ways to evaluate the quality of a home care agency's services at www.medicare.gov/what-medicare-covers/home-health-care/10-signs-quality-home-health-agency.html. The list includes items such as protecting your privacy, treating you and your family with respect, and explaining what to do in an emergency.

Paying for Home Care

Medicare home healthcare services are largely home healthcare visits, whereas Medicaid's may be both home healthcare visits and personal care visits. Because Medicaid home care varies by state, I start this discussion with Medicare. For people who are eligible for both programs (in policy-speak, called *duals*), Medicare is the first payer.

Looking at Medicare's rules for eligibility for home healthcare services

Medicare's eligibility rules for home healthcare services are quite stringent:

» The person must be under a doctor's care, and the doctor must have established a plan of care that she reviews regularly. The doctor must have examined you within the previous 30 days. In Medicare terminology, this is called a "face-to-face" visit.

>> The doctor must certify that you need one or more of the following skilled services:

- Intermittent (part-time) skilled nursing care (fewer than eight hours a day over a period of 21 days or fewer than seven days a week)

- Physical therapy

- Speech language-pathology services

- Continued occupational therapy (although OT, which involves therapy to restore function for everyday tasks, is not a skilled service that makes you eligible for home care on its own)

These therapy services must be specific, safe, and effective for your condition and performed only by qualified therapists, and the amount, frequency, and duration of the services must be "reasonable."

>> The doctor must certify that you are homebound, which means that

- It is not recommended that you leave the home because of your condition.

- You need help (such as using a wheelchair, walker, or special transportation) or someone else's assistance to move around.

- Leaving home requires a considerable and taxing effort.

- You can leave home only for medical treatment; for short, occasional absences for nonmedical reasons; and for adult daycare. The home care services, however, have to be provided in your home, not in another facility.

>> Medical social services to help with social and emotional concerns related to illness are covered. However, many Medicare-certified home care agencies have limited social-work staff.

>> Some medical supplies, like wound dressings, are covered when they are ordered as part of your care. Durable medical equipment is covered separately.

>> Finally, as noted earlier in this chapter, these services must be provided by a Medicare-certified Home Health Agency (HHA).

If you qualify for Medicare home healthcare services, you may also be eligible for some home health aide services. This bears repeating: Medicare does not cover aide services unless you are also getting skilled care services. Aides provide personal care and some tasks like making lunch and taking care of the individual's laundry (not the family's lunch or laundry).

TIP

For more details, see Medicare's guide to home care at www.medicare.gov/coverage/home-health-services.html or call Medicare at 1-800-633-4227. You can also call the Medicare Rights Center, which has trained volunteers to answer questions by phone (800-333-4114). If you or your relative belongs to a Medicare Advantage plan (a private company that contracts with Medicare to provide benefits), check with the plan.

The duration of home healthcare services under Medicare

You probably want to know how long Medicare will continue to pay for home healthcare, but that question isn't easy to answer. Under Medicare, home health agencies receive payment based on a 60-day episode of care. Some cases require the full 60 days of expensive care; other cases are closed in a shorter period and require mostly routine care. Under this prospective payment system, agencies have an incentive to close cases rather than keep them open.

REMEMBER

If your doctor refers you or your parent for home healthcare services, a nurse from the agency will come to the home to assess your needs. An agency does not have to accept the case if it can't offer the needed services, the home is not safe, or for other reasons. The agency, however, cannot discriminate based on race, religion, or other personal characteristics.

Based on the evaluation, the nurse determines where you or your parent fit into one of 153 home health resource groups (HHRGs). (If the nurse estimates that fewer than five home care visits will be necessary, the case is not included in these groups, or categories.) Where you fit in this complicated scheme plays a part in how long the episode of care lasts. The HHRGs range from groups of relatively uncomplicated cases to those involving people who have severe medical conditions or functional limitations and need extensive therapy. If an episode of care involves an unusually large number or costly mix of visits, the HHA may be eligible for an *outlier payment* — an extra fee based on the more-intensive-than-average services.

On average, Medicare home healthcare clients have two episodes of care per year (not necessarily consecutive and not necessarily lasting 60 days). Each episode of care involves an average of 17 visits, 80 percent of them by a nurse or therapist. Home health aide visits account for only about 15 percent of visits.

What does this mean in practice? As an example, the nurse who does the assessment may recommend a schedule of services, including a nurse visit two to three times a week, a physical therapist twice a week, and a home health aide for four visits a week of two to three hours each. This schedule will be reviewed and may be changed weekly. If the number of visits starts to decline, or the physical therapy visits stop, ask the agency how much longer the service will continue.

Some home healthcare services can go on for a longer period — for example, for treating chronic obstructive pulmonary disease (COPD) or continuing occupational therapy. A doctor can recertify a person for home care services, although the continuing need for skilled services will have to be documented.

Appealing Medicare decisions on home care

Home health agencies are required to give you a Home Health Advance Beneficiary Notice in the following situations:

>> When you will be receiving medical services and supplies that Medicare doesn't pay for. You will have to agree to pay for these services on your own.

>> When you're required to make a 20 percent copayment of the Medicare-approved amount for medical equipment, such as wheelchairs, walkers, and oxygen equipment. The Medicare-approved amount may not be the same as the supplier's bill.

>> When the HHA reduces or stops providing you with some services or supplies because the doctor has changed the orders.

>> When the home health agency plans to give you a home health service or supplies that Medicare probably won't pay for. (The determination that Medicare won't pay is made not by Medicare itself but by contractors — insurance companies under contract to Medicare to review claims.)

TIP

Claims for continuing rehabilitation services can no longer be denied by an assertion that the patient is not improving. The Medicare standard is whether a skilled service such as physical therapy is needed to prevent or delay deterioration, not whether the person is going to get better. Go to the Center for Medicare Advocacy's website for more information on the lawsuit, *Jimmo v. Sebelius,* that led to a federal court ruling on this question: www.medicareadvocacy.org/toolkit-medicare-home-health-coverage-jimmo-v-sebelius/. The Centers for Medicare & Medicaid Services followed up with a statement on its policies; see www.cms.gov/Center/Special-Topic/Jimmo-Center.html. Although this has been law for a few years, the old practice of denying claims based on "lack of improvement" is reported to persist. If this happens to you, you may need to advocate for continued services.

The home health agency is supposed to give you a written document called a Notice of Medicare Provider Non-Coverage at least two days before all covered services end. The notice should tell you the date all your covered services will end and how to ask for a fast appeal through the regional Beneficiary and Family-Centered Care Quality Improvement Organization (BFCC-QIO). The BFCC-QIO will generally give you an answer within two days. If the agency decides coverage should end, you must pay for any services you received while the appeal was being considered. You can find information on how to file a complaint with the BFCC-QIO in your state at qioprogram.org/file-complaint.

REMEMBER

Not all home health agencies provide the required notices in a written form or even in advance. The nurse or aide may simply tell you one day, "This is my last visit." If this happens, you can complain to the BFCC-QIO. But try to keep on top of the situation by asking the agency to give you an estimate of how long services will last. In general, services last weeks, not months.

Understanding Medicaid home care

Medicaid provides long-term services and supports (LTSS) for low-income older adults and people with disabilities. Since the beginning of Medicaid in 1965, most of these services have been provided in institutional settings, but over the past decade a greater emphasis has been placed on "rebalancing" the system and keeping people in the least restrictive setting, which means the individual's home or in the community of the individual's choosing. To accomplish this, many states are providing more home- and community-based services so that people don't have to go into nursing homes or other facilities, which are generally costly and not the individual's preference.

Medicaid's rules vary by state, and each state sets its own financial threshold for eligibility, which are typically very low income and few or no assets. Federal regulations require all Medicaid programs to provide home health services. Optional services include personal care and even private duty nursing. States can choose which optional services they want to provide.

In addition, states can apply for a variety of waivers from the federal government that allow them to provide a much broader range of medical and nonmedical service. Benefits can include case management, home care aide services, personal care, adult day healthcare, and respite care, as well as other services that states were previously not permitted to offer, such as home modification assistance. The goal of all these programs is to keep people safe and cared-for at home. These waiver programs, plus state funds, come under the general heading of home- and community-based services.

States facing severe budget shortages may decide to eliminate optional services or opt out of waiver programs altogether. Agencies may restrict access through their practices of establishing eligibility for Medicaid itself or for specific waiver services. Not all states have agreed to participate in the Affordable Care Act's expansion of Medicaid, which includes financial incentives to expand the Medicaid ranks to include people who were formerly uninsured. See Chapter 11 for more information.

Although the range of home- and community-based services may seem impressive (and in some states actually is), many states have waiting lists. You also may have difficulty finding out about these programs and whether you're eligible for them, and if so, whether there are any limits on the services. It is at best a patchwork quilt, without strong seams holding the pieces together.

Many states are changing the way they manage Medicaid by turning to Medicaid Managed Long-Term Care plans. Managed care organizations run these plans and are paid to coordinate services and supports. Although considerable potential exists for better integrated care and improved outcomes as well as higher utilization of community-based service options, these plans are still evolving. See the report by AARP's Public Policy Institute on promising state practices at www.aarp. org/health/medicare-insurance/info-08-2013/consumer-choices-and-continuity-of-care-AARP-ppi-ltc.html.

Whether you receive services under the traditional Medicaid system or under a managed Medicaid plan, you should be given adequate notice of a decision to reduce, deny, or terminate a Medicaid service, as well as an opportunity to appeal that decision. For further assistance with a Medicaid appeal, you can contact your local Legal Services Organization (www.lsc.gov/what-legal-aid/find-legal-aid) or the state's Protection and Advocacy (P&A) agency at www.ndrn.org/en/ndrn-member-agencies.html.

Other kinds of insurance

Long-term care insurance policies usually include some home care services for which you qualify after certain eligibility thresholds have been reached. The criteria vary by policy but generally include some level of functional problems, such as needing assistance with at least two activities of daily living (ADLs). The policy may also include waiting periods during which you pay privately for care as well as restrictions on who can be hired. It is important to check the policy and ask your insurance agent to explain the process. (See Chapter 12 for more information.)

You may also be eligible for home care services from the Veterans Administration (see Chapter 19 for details), a retirement health insurance policy, or other resource. It may take some investigation to see how and if these policies work together. A family member or adviser may be able to help you.

Hiring home care workers on your own dime

After formal home care services end, or even before, many people turn to hiring home care workers themselves and paying them privately. The benefits include overseeing the care, deciding how and when certain tasks are performed, and in theory at least, having continuity of workers. People usually do better when they have the same aide or team over time. Some Medicaid programs permit qualified enrollees to hire and fire their own workers, with fiscal oversight. Spouses are often excluded from being paid under these programs.

Workers paid privately may charge less than an agency, depending on where you live, and of course get to keep more of the pay. A downside of hiring privately may be the lack of backup. If the regular worker isn't available, you must find a substitute on your own. You also must juggle additional responsibilities for financial management and supervision. You can hire someone to manage the payroll and Social Security tax, but this adds to the cost. Yet this investment can make the difference between your family member's willingness to accept the help (not a foregone conclusion!) and your comfort with the quality of care being provided. Someone who is reluctant to have help at home may feel more comfortable with a person who lives in the community or is someone personally recommended, not sent by an agency.

TIP

Agencies must pay home care workers minimum wage and overtime, according to the U.S. Department of Labor. If you hire home care workers directly, you must follow the U.S. Department of Labor rules implementing the Fair Labor Standards Act. For more information, go to www.dol.gov/whd/homecare/homecare_guide.pdf. This guide covers when home care workers must be paid minimum wage and overtime as well as exemptions for workers who provide only "companionship."

In interviewing potential aides, describe the aspects of care that are particularly important to you and ask how well the person can meet those needs. If you need night or weekend help, ask whether the person will be available for those times. If you want the aide to take you to the doctor, you need to ask about a driver's license and any limitations on the license.

You should get several recent references from people who have been cared for by this person. Ask previous employers about the person's work habits, attitude, and reliability. Check with the state Department of Health's registry to see whether any past complaints of abuse or neglect have been filed against the worker.

TIP

You may want to have a trial period before hiring a worker. Sometimes what looks like a good match turns out not to be one, and you'll be better off acknowledging that early on. Establishing a set of house rules that respect both your family member's privacy and your own as well as the home care worker's needs will help create a good working relationship.

Working with Home Care Aides

When you go to a doctor's office, an outpatient clinic, or a hospital, you enter someone else's space and give up some control. Your home, however, is your private space, and the strangers who come in and out to help are essentially your guests. Still, it's a different kind of relationship because the person comes to provide a service, not to chat. Bringing someone into your home or your relative's home can ease your responsibilities, but it shouldn't add stress to your life.

Compared to nurses or physical therapists, aides typically will spend more time with you or your parent or other relative. To help make the arrangement more comfortable, plan to spend some time on the aide's first visit just getting to know each other and the physical space in which she (and it's almost always a woman) will be working.

REMEMBER

The United Hospital Fund's guide "Working with Home Health Aides" offers some suggestions on establishing a good working relationship that can make your situation more comfortable. Here are some key points (and you can find the full guide at www.nextstepincare.org/Caregiver_Home/Home_Health_Aides):

>> Be clear about what services you expect. Write them down in a simple agreement. Clarify what the aide cannot do, whether because of regulations, competence, or willingness.

>> Include in your agreement the terms of employment: the hours and pay you have agreed on, documentation required, if meals and travel costs are included, and the vacation time you offer. Also indicate limits on visitors, texting, phone calls, and other potential distractions from the job. Putting this on paper will help prevent misunderstandings later on.

>> Have a backup plan in case the aide can't arrive in time or cancels.

>> Discuss how to handle emergencies. Leave a list of emergency phone numbers, including the doctor's office. Develop an emergency plan, and make sure the aide knows what it is.

>> Talk about whether and when to call 911. If you or your parent has an in-home DNR (do not resuscitate) order, signed by a doctor, then the aide should not call 911 in an emergency. You should discuss with the aide what you mean by "emergency" and whom to call if it is not 911.

Respect and tolerance for individual and cultural differences is essential for both you and the aide. Ask the aide whether she prefers to be called by her first name or full name. And make sure she knows how you or your parent prefers to be addressed. Some older adults don't like to be called by their first name or "sweetie" or other nicknames that are not meant to be offensive but may seem so.

Food and religious differences are areas in which conflict can arise. If you or your parent follows certain religious practices that are new to the aide, explain what they are and why they are important. Just as important are the aide's food preferences and religious practices. Aides should feel that they can observe their personal choices, but they should not impose them on others.

Paying Family or Friends to Provide Care

After trying to navigate the maze of home care services and insurance requirements, some people say, "Why can't I just get paid for taking care of my parent?" And in fact some options to do that exist, but they are very limited. As you consider having yourself or a friend or family member provide paid care versus hiring an aide or personal attendant, here are a few general points to remember:

>> Wages will be low. Think rates for home care aides, not nurses.

>> Consider how this will fit into your own life and affect your relationship with the person you're caring for.

>> There are no benefits in the sense of paid vacations, health insurance, or pension.

>> Where you live matters. State programs differ significantly.

The following sections provide some more information on who may be paid to provide routine, ongoing care.

State programs

Most states have programs that help pay for in-home care called variously *consumer-directed, participant-directed, cash and counseling,* or other titles. These programs differ by state in terms of funding, eligibility, option of paying family members, exclusion of certain people such as spouses or legal guardians, limits on the number of hours, wage scales, and more. Even within the same state, different programs may have different rules about whether family members can be paid. Waiting lists are common. As states cut their budgets, these programs may be further limited.

Most, but not all, programs require the person receiving care to be eligible for Medicaid. He or she also must meet the requirements for the consumer-directed option. If you or your parent meet these requirements, a counselor will work out a monthly budget. Some states limit the budget to an amount that is not greater than the state would pay for home care agency services. With final approval, you or your parent can now hire and fire whomever you choose. Or you can use the money for other approved uses. States generally offer the services of a fiscal agent to manage the budget and file necessary reports.

TIP

For more information, follow up with your state's Medicaid or aging services department. It may take time to find the right person to help you.

Long-term care insurance

Some long-term care policies make payments to family members who are providing home care. However, a policy may exclude people who live in the same household. Ask the insurance agent to explain this benefit and its conditions.

Caregiver contracts

You or your parent may be willing to pay a family member directly through a caregiver contract. Consult an elder-care lawyer to make sure that the contract meets tax requirements, deals with inheritances, and is approved by all other interested parties (your siblings, for example). Be mindful of the emotional pitfalls in this arrangement. The pay should be reasonable and in line with what you would pay if you hired an aide.

WARNING

Courts haven't looked favorably on caregiver contracts that seemed to be ways to transfer assets — for example, by paying very high salaries — to become eligible for Medicaid or avoid estate taxes rather than pay for care. Avoid these situations by getting good legal advice.

Is There a Doctor in the House?

A doctor making a home visit? That may sound like a scene from a 1940s movie, but in fact the number of doctors who see patients in their own homes has recently increased. Usually doctors visit people who would have difficulty getting to an office or who are homebound for other reasons. Often doctors making home visits work in teams, so you get the added benefit of a nurse or physician's assistant and perhaps a social worker. Home-visit programs may be organized by a hospital, by a large physician practice in the community, or by a health plan. These organizations want to keep people out of the hospital, where care is costlier and debilitating for people.

Medicare is conducting a three-year demonstration project called Independence at Home to test whether home-based care by teams of doctors, nurses, and other clinicians can reduce hospitalization and costs. The results so far have been encouraging, with patients having fewer rehospitalizations and Emergency Department visits.

Insurance coverage varies, but some doctors' home visits can be covered under Original Medicare. If you belong to a Medicare Advantage plan or have private insurance, check the plan. Physician visits are covered by Medicaid, but usually these visits are in a clinic or office. Some home-visit programs may accept Medicaid.

TIP

Here are some ways to identify a physician who makes home visits or a program in your area:

>> Check local hospitals, academic medical centers, and healthcare systems for doctor visiting programs and doctors-in-training who participate in home visits.

>> Visit the website of the American Academy of Home Care Physicians, founded in 1984. It maintains a list by state and zip code of physicians, physician assistants, and nurse practitioners who make home visits. The academy doesn't endorse any of these practitioners, so it's up to you to check out qualifications and fees. You can find the list at www.aahcm.org/?Locate_A_Provider.

>> Beyond home visits, physicians participate in home care by referring people to home care agencies for services, certifying their need for skilled care, and approving a plan of care.

Chapter **16**

Understanding the Different Roles of Nursing Homes

D on't skip this chapter because you've always said, "I'll never put my mother in a nursing home!" or because you don't want to even think about this option for yourself. There is no denying that moving permanently to a nursing home is at the bottom of most people's want list.

Just to be clear: A nursing home is a long-term care facility that offers 24-hour room and board and healthcare services, including nursing care, rehabilitation therapies, and a range of other treatments and programs. Nursing homes increasingly have two types of services: short-term rehabilitation programs and long-stay units.

You may never need a nursing home. As I point out in other chapters, many people have other options for care at home and in the community. Still, you may need a nursing home for rehab programs, which can ease the transition from hospital to home. And for some people, particularly those with advanced dementia or complex medical needs, family care and home- and community-based services may be insufficient.

In this chapter, I discuss both short- and long-term stays in nursing homes, with the emphasis on long stays. I offer steps for selecting a nursing home. I also describe some new models that stress "person-centeredness" and home-like settings. (If you or your relative is in a continuing-care retirement community with a nursing-home unit, you have already made an initial choice. See Chapter 8.) Finally, I provide information about residents' rights that are important after you've moved in.

Beginning with Nursing Home Basics

By choosing a nursing home for a long stay, rest assured that you aren't abandoning your parent or other relative. You'll need to remain involved at many levels to ensure that the person receives the most appropriate care, is respected as an individual, and is able to maintain the highest level of function possible and enjoys a good quality of life. Starting with that premise, here are some basic facts about nursing homes today.

Defining nursing homes

Nursing homes are, in bureaucratic language, *skilled nursing facilities* (abbreviated as SNFs and pronounced *sniffs*). Nursing homes, unlike assisted-living or other community settings, offer skilled care by professionals such as nurses, doctors, and therapists. For instance, nurses administer intravenous (IV) injections and physical therapists help residents regain or maintain function. The facility may have a medical director on-site, or a doctor may be on call.

REMEMBER

Nevertheless, the amount of time these professionals spend with patients is limited. Most nursing-home services are provided by aides (called certified nursing assistants or CNAs) who do personal care and assist with activities of daily living (ADLs), such as bathing and dressing. Federal law requires CNAs to have a minimum of 75 hours of training, although some states require more training. CNAs are the people with whom residents have the most contact. Getting to know them as individuals is important.

Nursing homes vary by type of ownership:

>> Voluntary homes are run by nonprofit organizations, which may be sponsored by religious, fraternal, or community organizations.

>> Public or municipal homes are owned and operated by local governments.

>> Proprietary homes are run by for-profit corporations, which may have only a few facilities or be national in scope. This sector now constitutes 69 percent of all nursing homes.

The type of ownership of a nursing home provides no guarantee of quality, which should be assessed individually. There is some evidence to suggest that nonprofit nursing homes offer better-quality care.

Some nursing homes are large, and some are very small. Most nursing homes have between 50 and 200 residents, according to the CMS Nursing Home Data Compendium of 2012. (*CMS* is the Centers for Medicare & Medicaid Services.) But again, size isn't the key determinant of quality. Small homes may offer a more intimate environment, but large homes may have more specialized staff and more activities.

Moving from a hospital to short-term rehab

More than 60 percent of nursing-home admissions come directly from hospitals, so it's not surprising that most people face the decision about entering a nursing home in a crisis or just after one. The crisis may be a stroke, a bad fall, or a worsening of a chronic condition. Going home from the hospital may be the preferred choice, but the family may not be able to provide the needed care, even with the home healthcare and rehabilitation therapy that Medicare and other insurance coverage provides (see Chapter 15). A short stay in a skilled nursing facility rehabilitation program is one option that can give the person and family time to adjust to the new requirements and be better prepared to manage at home.

TIP

Don't panic if the hospital nurse or social worker says, "We're sending you to a nursing home tomorrow." Although this information shouldn't come at the last minute, it often does. It usually means that you're being referred to a short-term rehabilitation program at a nursing home, not being sent to a nursing home permanently.

In these situations, you'll be asked to make a quick decision about which nursing-home rehab program to choose, and the choices may be limited. The discharge planner at the hospital may hand you a list of three or four nursing homes in the area and say, in effect, "You choose." The discharge planner will then see what is available right now. Your choices may be limited by the facilities' bed capacity, their ability to provide the kind and level of care needed, location, whether they are part of your health plan's network, and other factors. Frequently the list includes only those nursing homes with which the discharge planner works frequently; it may not include the full range available and appropriate. Some hospitals are creating post-acute networks of SNFs to facilitate transfers.

If you're interested in nursing homes not on the list, you can ask that specific nursing homes be added, but the hospital won't keep your parent until a bed in your preferred nursing home becomes available. You can try to push the hospital to delay discharge for a few days, and you can file a formal appeal to postpone it. (If you lose the appeal, however, you'll have to pay the costs of the additional hospital days.)

The push to move patients quickly from hospitals to nursing homes is in hospitals' and nursing homes' economic interests. Hospitals want to ensure that they can discharge their patients quickly, and nursing homes want to maintain that source of new income.

Medicare pays for the initial episode of nursing-home rehabilitation services if the person has been discharged after a minimum three-day hospital admission, but patients don't always get to stay for three days. Original Medicare pays for the first 20 days of each benefit period; you pay a coinsurance of $167.50 per day for days 21–100 (in 2018), and you pay all the costs for each day after day 100. You must be hospitalized for three days to start a new benefit period. If you have a Medicare Advantage plan or private insurance, check with the plan.

WARNING

To be eligible for Medicare coverage for short-term rehabilitation services, you must have been formally admitted as a hospital inpatient for three days. After an observation stay, no matter how long the stay lasted, Medicare will not pay. Check to make sure your family member has actually been admitted to the hospital. You can complain to the hospital if you aren't given accurate or timely information. If you're on observation (not formally admitted), you should receive a Medicare Outpatient Observations Notice (MOON) that describes how this status affects your bill.

There are steps you can take without the pressure of an imminent hospital discharge or a rapidly deteriorating situation at home. The first step is to look broadly at the options in your area. Then you can be more focused on specific nursing homes and how to evaluate them.

TIP

Sometimes a person admitted for a short-stay rehab program is unable to return home as hoped, and then another decision point is reached: to stay in the same nursing home as a long-stay resident or move to another facility. There may be interim steps to prepare for going home — for example, home modifications or hiring extra help. For advice on how to handle that transition, see the United Hospital Fund's Next Step in Care guide "When Short-Term Rehab Turns into a Long-Term Stay" at www.nextstepincare.org/Caregiver_Home/When_Short_Term_Turns_into_Long_Term/.

Comparing nursing homes for a long stay

Nursing Home Compare is an online Medicare tool that includes information on health inspections and complaints, staffing (hours of care provided by nurses and nursing assistants per resident), and quality measures such as incidence of pressure sores. CMS maintains the database that compares more than 15,000 Medicare- and Medicaid-certified nursing homes that provide skilled services at www.medicare.gov/nursinghomecompare/?AspxAutoDetectCookieSupport=1. You can search for a nursing home by name or look for nursing homes in your zip code. Medicare also has an extensive guide at www.medicare.gov/Pubs/pdf/02174-Nursing-Home-Other-Long-Term-Services.pdf.

Nursing Home Compare ranks nursing homes based on three ratings, two of which are self-reports by the nursing homes. Only state inspections are external evaluations. These three ratings (from a low of 1 star to a high of 5 stars) are combined to calculate an overall rating. In addition, Nursing Home Compare reports penalties that have been imposed on the facility.

REMEMBER

Nursing Home Compare is a valuable tool that allows you to eliminate some of the lowest-ranking nursing homes. However, it doesn't include many important factors such as the interactions between management and staff and between staff and residents, how residents' individual needs and preferences are addressed, and the general atmosphere and style of the facility. You need to assess these factors in your visits. Given two nursing homes with similar ratings, you need to take the next step of determining which one seems to best meet your needs or those of your parent. (See the following section for help choosing a nursing home.)

WARNING

Keep in mind that Nursing Home Compare includes data from a limited period. More important, even the data coming from inspections in some states may tend to underreport deficiencies. And Medicare uses a grading curve, so exactly 10 percent of nursing homes in any one state are awarded the top ranking of five stars. This means that a lower-ranking nursing home may have just missed the cutoff on the ranking curve; on the other hand, it may mean that the curve limits the number of nursing homes that would fall into the lower categories.

In addition to Nursing Home Compare, many state departments of health have similar comparisons on their websites. Other sponsored websites offer to compare nursing homes, but they generally base their data on government websites and may include only facilities that pay to be on the list. You can also check consumer ratings on websites. These personal stories can give you insights into services and staff, but they can overstate both good and bad experiences in the facility.

Visiting Nursing Homes

A nursing-home visit is essential if you're deciding which facility is the best fit. Doctor and family recommendations are important, but nothing compares to what your own senses can tell you during a live visit.

The federal Centers for Medicare & Medicaid Services (CMS) sets minimum standards for nursing homes. States, however, are responsible for monitoring and ensuring that nursing homes provide the required level of care. Some states go beyond the federal requirement, but others aren't so diligent.

REMEMBER

Make sure you discuss the choices with your parent if possible. This may be difficult, but you can make a much better decision if you get as much information as you can about what's important to your parent: location, language spoken in the nursing home, meals, visits, activities, and so on. If your parent is unable to participate because of cognitive impairments or a medical condition, think of what you know she values as you visit facilities.

COMFORT CARE FOR DEMENTIA PATIENTS

"Encouraging Comfort Care," the Greater Illinois Alzheimer's Association's guide for families of people with dementia living in care facilities, has a checklist with many useful suggestions. Unlike many other guides, this one approaches the need for hospice care, active dying, and what happens after death forthrightly. It also addresses medical decision making around aggressive treatments and artificial nutrition and hydration, topics that are often avoided.

Particularly useful are six principles that should guide care for people with dementia. Staff members

- Anticipate the needs of people with dementia.

- Know each person so well that basic needs never become major problems.

- Embrace the philosophy of "person-centered" care.

- Use a "soft" approach (verbal and nonverbal cues to facilitate communication).

- Recognize and treat pain aggressively.

- Recognize the resident and family as true partners in care.

The guide is available at www.alzheimers-illinois.org/pti/comfort_care_guide.asp.

Checking off important points

After you've narrowed the possibilities through Nursing Home Compare, your state's Department of Health, or another source (as I explain earlier in this chapter), you can begin to focus on the most likely facilities. Medicare has a seven-page "Nursing Home Checklist" at www.medicare.gov/NursingHomeCompare/ checklist.pdf. It is meant to be filled out at each nursing-home visit and has room for your comments.

You can fill in basic information, such as whether the nursing home is Medicare- and Medicaid-certified and whether it has the level of care you need, including specialized services such as ventilator care or a special unit for persons with dementia.

WARNING

Just because a nursing home has a dementia or "memory care" unit is not a guarantee that it provides good-quality dementia care. Many residents with dementia may not even be on the special unit, and the staff may not have special training or expertise in providing person-centered care for people with dementia. If this is a priority, you need to investigate further.

A particularly important factor noted on the checklist is location. You want to be close enough so that family and friends can visit often. Their continued involvement at the nursing home is critical to residents' happiness and well-being. Getting to know the staff, participating in activities, observing different situations — all these interactions are not just nice things to do but also indications to the staff that someone cares deeply about residents and will be actively engaged in monitoring their care. Don't underestimate the importance this may have in the quality of care.

REMEMBER

Don't rush through your nursing-home visit, and make sure to visit more than once, preferably at different times and on different days of the week. Evening and weekend visits are especially important, because staffing is likely to be lowest at these times. If you're using a checklist, note that using your eyes, ears, and nose is more important than completing every item. You can find out a lot just by observing how people talk to each other, whether there are smiles and touching, or whether the atmosphere is chilly and controlled. Often the person who takes you on a tour of the facility is a salesperson who will not be part of your daily experience after admittance.

Here are some categories to review during a nursing–home visit, with a few specific examples:

>> **Resident appearance:**

- Are the residents clean and well groomed?

- Are they appropriately dressed for the time of day and season?

>> **Living spaces:**

- Is the nursing home clean, well lit, and free of offensive odors? Note the use of sprays that cover up odors.

- Is the temperature comfortable?

- Is smoking allowed? If so, is it restricted to certain areas?

- Are all common areas, resident rooms, and doorways designed for wheelchair use?

>> **Staff:**

- Does the staff appear to be polite and respectful to the residents?

- Does the staff wear name tags?

- Does the management run background checks for abuse and neglect before hiring staff? Are these state or national checks?

- Is there a licensed nurse on duty 24 hours a day and a registered nurse present at least 8 hours a day?

- How are physician services provided? Is there a full-time medical director on-site?

- Do families hire private duty nurses or aides to supplement care?

>> **Residents' rooms:**

- Can residents have personal belongings and furniture in their rooms?

- Is there adequate storage space?

- What policies and procedures are in place to protect personal belongings and recover or compensate for their loss?

- Do residents have access to a personal phone, TV, and computer? Is there access to cable TV and the Internet? What are the costs?

>> **Menus and food:**

- Do residents get a choice of food at each meal?

- Can the nursing home provide for special dietary needs (low-fat, kosher, halal)?

- Are nutritious snacks available? How are they offered? Do residents have to request them?

- How many staff are in the dining room during mealtimes to assist residents?

>> **Activities:**

- Ask to see a monthly activity calendar for three consecutive months, not including December (when holiday parties dominate).

- How are residents who are unable to leave their room able to take part in activities?

- How do staff encourage and facilitate residents' use of outdoor areas?

- Are trips to places outside the facility scheduled? What kind, how is transportation provided, and is there an additional cost?

- How are residents' views on the choice of activities solicited?

- If your family member enjoys certain activities like reading, knitting, or attending religious services, how does staff make these available?

- How does the facility provide opportunities to explore creative activities such as art, music, or writing?

>> **Care:**

- Does the nursing home ask about someone's personal routines as soon as he is admitted? For example, someone should note what time the resident gets up in the morning, what time he goes to bed, and when he prefers to take a shower or bath. In a person-centered approach, residents have more choices about their schedule, and quality of life is the focus.

- Is the same staff assigned to take care of the resident most days? Consistent assignment helps develop good relationships.

- Is there transportation for doctor appointments or other reasons? Will an aide accompany the person if you or another family member can't?

- Are there regularly scheduled care planning meetings with staff to discuss what is going well, what needs to be changed, and who will be responsible for carrying out the suggestions? If you can't attend at the scheduled time, can the meeting be rescheduled or can you participate by conference call?

>> **Safety:**

- Are exits clearly marked?

- Are there smoke detectors and sprinklers?

- Are handrails and grab bars appropriately placed?

- Do you understand the details of the required emergency evacuation plan? Make sure you get a copy. What are the plans for notifying you in case of an evacuation?

>> **Resident or family council:** The 1987 Nursing Home Reform Law gives residents and family members the right to form independent councils to discuss issues related to care, safety, activities, or whatever else is appropriate.

- What is the name of the head of the family council, and how can you contact him or her? The person leading the family council should not be a nursing home employee. Staff may attend resident or family council meetings only at the request of the council.

- How does the nursing home inform family members of council meetings? Do notices appear in newsletters, bulletin boards, or monthly billing?

- How often does the council meet?

- What issues have been raised by the council?

- How have these issues been addressed?

Noting policy details

Medicare's nursing-home checklist and other similar checklists give you basic information about the nursing home, but they may not tell you everything you want to know. Here are some important questions to ask:

>> **What is the nursing-home policy about transfer to an emergency department (ED)?** Is a family member consulted? In the past six months, how many residents were transferred to the ED and then returned to the nursing home for "care in place" — that is, providing the needed medical care at the nursing home?

WARNING

Sometimes family members request transfer to an ED when they suspect something is wrong. And sometimes they're right because they notice small changes or big problems that staff may have ignored. However, transfer to an ED is not necessarily a good move. In general, you want to avoid these transfers, which can be unnecessary and result in confusion, frustration, and even deterioration in the resident's condition.

TIP

Ongoing communication with staff will help you determine when a real emergency occurs, what can be handled at the nursing home, and when a physician needs to be called. But trust your own instinct as well. You may be seeing something new that staff have ignored. Improvements in this area have been demonstrated with the INTERACT training and interventions for reducing transfers to hospital EDs from nursing homes. More information is available at www.pathway-interact.com. Although intended for staff training, these tools can help family members recognize and report problems so that these transfers can be avoided.

>> **Does your family member have an advance directive that outlines the types of care she wants or does not want?** Does it include preferences about CPR (cardiopulmonary resuscitation)? Is this information known to all staff and easily available for ambulance and ED personnel? (See Chapter 17.)

>> **What is the nursing home's policy or practice about feeding tubes?** Sometimes feeding tubes are recommended (with accompanying risks) because feeding by hand takes too long, not because it is medically necessary. This is a complex decision that should be discussed thoroughly and not seen as routine practice.

>> **What kind of training do staff receive for specific situations?** Are they trained in dementia care? Do they receive sensitivity training about working with lesbian or gay residents or residents from different cultural or religious backgrounds?

Getting answers to these questions helps in streamlining your options and making the best choice possible.

Checking Out New Models of Nursing-Home Care

The stigma associated with nursing-home scandals in the 1970s and 1980s, which led to the 1987 federal Nursing Home Reform Law, continues to some degree to this day. Many clearly substandard nursing homes still exist, and the industry has much room to improve. So diligence is still required, of course, but someone looking at nursing homes today is less likely to find the kind of warehousing and abuses that existed years ago.

Some efforts have been devoted not just to improving existing nursing homes but also to creating new models of care. The following sections highlight three examples.

REMEMBER

All the efforts to improve nursing-home care come under the general heading of *culture change,* which means creating a person-centered environment. The Pioneer Network, a group of long-term care professionals, was formed in 1997 to move nursing-home practice from hospital-like management to a person-centered approach, which better integrates quality of life with quality of care. The Pioneer

Network has a consumer's guide to finding a nursing home involved in culture change at www.pioneernetwork.net/Consumers/Guide. The guide has many key questions, such as the following:

>> How is your nursing home involved in culture change?

>> Do you have a rehabilitation team and access to therapists such as speech pathologists, physical therapists, and occupational therapists?

>> Do you measure the turnover of your staff? If so, what is the turnover rate for your direct care workers? (Any number under 40 percent is good; the national average is 70 percent.)

Eden Alternative

The Eden Alternative was created in 1971 by Dr. William Thomas as an effort to deinstitutionalize nursing-home care. Eden Alternative does not own or operate Eden Homes; instead the organization works with facilities and individuals to create a caring community for elders (his preferred term for older adults). People live in small houses of 10 to 12 residents, and care partners — the workers involved in daily activities — are given a major role. The emphasis is on placing the person at the center of the care and doing away with the hierarchy associated with the medical model of care. Medicaid funding may be available in some states.

TIP

Read more about the Eden Alternative philosophy and principles at www.edenalt.org/about-the-eden-alternative/mission-vision-values/. Facilities implement the Eden Alternative in different ways, so it is still important to visit and observe.

Green House Project

An offshoot of the Eden Alternative, the Green House Project was also founded by Dr. Thomas. The project, funded by the Robert Wood Johnson Foundation, has more than 100 homes in 32 states, with more in design. The basic idea is a new way to create senior housing by building or converting residential homes into settings that can provide high levels of care. Some of these homes are licensed as nursing homes and others as assisted-living communities. Green Houses take advantage of technology such as adaptive devices, computers, pagers, and ceiling lifts. They also try to live up to their name: In this case *green* means living in the natural world, with plants, gardens, and access to outdoor areas.

TIP

For more information, go to www.thegreenhouseproject.org/. The site has an interactive map that shows the homes operating and in development by state.

Beatitudes

Comfort Matters (www.comfortmatters.org/) is a program started at Beatitudes Campus, a continuing-care retirement community in Phoenix, Arizona. It works with people who have dementia by creating a personalized home-like environment, anticipating the resident's needs so that discomfort (and the behaviors that are often the resident's only way of expressing discomfort) is avoided. Personal comfort is promoted at all times.

TIP

The program was started when Beatitudes partnered with Hospice of the Valley to create a model program in dementia care. The model is being implemented in three New York City nursing homes. For more information, see caringkindnyc. org/_pdf/caringkind-palliativecareguidelines.pdf.

Responding to Residents' Problems in Nursing Homes

Selecting the best nursing home is critical, but your responsibilities do not end there. Because this will be a long stay, it is important to monitor the quality of care and deal with problems that may arise. You and your family member have a right to expect good-quality care, respect, and sensitivity to any special issues.

Still, the situation that exists when your family member is admitted may change over time. Your family member's condition may deteriorate, her roommate may become agitated, and her favorite aide may leave and be replaced by a competent but not-so-friendly person. You should be familiar with residents' rights in nursing homes and be a vocal advocate for ensuring that they are enforced. At the same time, you should distinguish between situations that are unacceptable and those that can be the focus of compromise and negotiation. Of course, if the problems involve serious incidents of abuse or neglect, you should take immediate action.

If the problem does not involve abuse or neglect, is isolated, and can be resolved, your first approach should be a frank but friendly discussion with the staff person who is the source of the problem. For example, your parent doesn't like the shampoo the aide is using because it stings if it gets in his eyes. Maybe a different shampoo or technique will solve the problem.

If the problem is more serious or you see it happening to other residents, but it hasn't risen to the level of abuse or neglect, then speak to the head nurse or the director of the nursing home. Most nursing homes want satisfied residents and family members and will generally try to resolve the problem. Of course, you may encounter some defensiveness or denial.

REMEMBER

If these informal approaches fail, then your next recourse is to contact your state's *ombudsman*, a person assigned to investigate complaints in nursing homes, adult homes, and assisted-living facilities. The Long-Term Care Ombudsman Program is run by the U.S. Administration on Aging and has volunteers and staff in every state (see ltcombudsman.org/about/about-ombudsman for information, including a state map). To find your local ombudsman office, call ElderCare Locator (800-677-1116) or your State Health Department. In some areas you can call Adult Protective Services. Police should be called if the resident is in imminent danger. Be prepared to document your concerns with dates, names, and specific violations. Try to take pictures of visible violations to further support your claims.

Get familiar with the very comprehensive list of nursing-home residents' rights, which every nursing home is required by law to observe. I tell you more about this list in the nearby sidebar "Nursing-home residents' rights." If you can link the problem to a violation of patient's rights, you'll be on stronger ground.

If the problem persists, you can file a formal complaint with your State Health Department. There are other avenues such as private litigation that you may want to investigate.

TIP

Another good resource is a booklet by Eric Carlson from Justice in Aging. It presents 20 common nursing-home problems and ways to resolve them. You can find it at https://aging.idaho.gov/News%20Updates%20Articles/20Common NurseHomeProblems.pdf.

NURSING-HOME RESIDENTS' RIGHTS

The 1987 federal Nursing Home Reform Law guarantees residents' rights and places a strong emphasis on individual dignity and self-determination. A person living in a nursing home has the same civil rights as someone living in the community. The law states that all nursing homes that participate in Medicare and Medicaid are required to "provide services and activities to attain or maintain the highest practicable physical, mental, and psychosocial well-being of each resident in accordance with a written plan of care that . . . is initially prepared, with participation to the extent practicable, of the resident, the resident's family, or legal representative." Among the rights listed are the right to be fully informed of available services and charges as well as the right to receive information in a language they understand; the right to complain; the right to participate in one's own care; the right to privacy and confidentiality; the right to dignity, respect, and freedom; the right to visits; and the right to make independent choices. There are also special rights relating to transfers and discharges. For a complete list of the rights, go to http://ltcombudsman.org/uploads/files/issues/residents-rights-factsheet.pdf. There is no comparable federal statement of rights for assisted-living residents, although some states have statements of rights for these residents.

Chapter 17

Getting the Healthcare You Want (And Avoiding What You Don't Want)

O f all the difficult topics to discuss in planning for the future, the one most avoided is what you want to happen should you or your parent become seriously ill or have an accident. But all too often, the discussion of what to do if you become incapacitated and can't speak for yourself happens only in a crisis — the worst time for thoughtful and well-informed conversations.

Nothing will make these profound discussions easy. But you can lay the groundwork in ways that increase your family's chances of being prepared when decisions about treatment and level of care must be made. This chapter suggests ways to organize your thinking, create legal documents, and understand care options. This chapter covers the types of documents you can create in advance of an emergency, how to choose a healthcare proxy (someone to speak on your behalf if you're incapacitated), and the difference between palliative care and hospice. Both are potential choices in serious illness but have different goals and insurance coverage.

Talking about Future Healthcare Decisions

It's hard to think about it, but there may come a time when you may be ill and not be able to speak for yourself. Anyone at any age can be in an accident or develop a serious illness. But as people age, the likelihood of an event requiring a treatment decision increases. And a quick conversation about a friend's situation or a news report most likely will not ensure that your own or your parent's wishes are understood and followed. What everyone should do is start a series of conversations with family, doctors, clergy, or other trusted individuals. In this section, I underline the importance of the different aspects of care that you should address in advance. Another good resource is AARP's *The Other Talk: A Guide to Talking with Your Adult Children About the Rest of Your Life* by Tim Prosch (McGraw-Hill).

The Conversation Project has materials to help families talk about advance care planning. See its website at theconversationproject.org.

Realizing the importance of advance planning

No one can predict how and when the need for someone else to make a medical decision for you will arise, what the medical situation will be, and what choices will have to be made. That is why a series of discussions is more likely to convey your thinking in depth than a one-time conversation.

Although you and your family members are probably reluctant to have a serious discussion about the possibility of a serious injury or illness, keep in mind that talking about it does not make it happen. In fact, everyone will probably feel better afterward. However, wishes may change, so it is important to review any documents you have created at least every few years and more often if warranted to make sure that they still reflect your current thinking. The results of the conversations can then be incorporated in a variety of documents, which I describe in the following sections.

If you don't have a documented advance care plan, state law will determine who makes decisions for you. Most states have a priority list of family members who will be chosen to speak for you when you can't make a healthcare decision. The person you would have chosen to speak for you may be far down on the list or not on it at all. And if family members can't agree, a court may be called upon to make the decision.

Making wishes known with advance directives and living wills

An *advance directive* or *living will* is a general term for a document that tells healthcare providers the kinds of medical treatment you do or do not want. For example, you may want to refuse tube feeding or ventilators or antibiotics if, in your view, they will not provide you with sufficient benefit, even if they may prolong your life. You have a right, which is well established in law and medical ethics, to refuse any treatment for whatever reason. You can also say that you want all treatments that offer any possibility of prolonging your life, even if they will be painful or burdensome.

But you do not have a right to demand any particular treatment, because healthcare providers may not be willing to provide it for reasons of conscience or because they consider it *futile,* a vague term but one that carries some weight in medical and legal circles. If they refuse to treat you according to your documented wishes, they must refer you to another provider or go to court to challenge your wishes or your capacity to make this decision.

With advance directives, you can also name the person you want to make healthcare decisions on your behalf if you're unable to speak for yourself. The choice of your healthcare proxy (sometimes called a healthcare agent or surrogate decision maker) is especially critical, because the decision may not be clear-cut and may require interpretation of what you have expressed in the advance directive (information on choosing a healthcare proxy appears later in this chapter). Did you mean, for example, no antibiotics ever or just when they would prolong dying? Would you have agreed to a trial of a therapy to see whether it improved your condition? Talking about these questions ahead of time gives your healthcare proxy some guidance.

REMEMBER

An advance directive comes into play only when the person is unable to make healthcare decisions. If, for example, you and your parent disagree about whether surgery is advisable, and you are the healthcare proxy, you can't decide in favor of surgery without your parent's consent. Usually the healthcare proxy takes over when the patient is in a coma or unconscious, or a doctor determines that the patient is unable to make healthcare decisions.

Dealing with the Rules of Advance Directives

As with everything in medical care, paperwork is involved in making your wishes known. When you plan ahead and make your wishes clear, all parties involved will have a road map to follow and transitions will be smoother. Take a look at the following sections to put advance directives into motion.

Finding the forms for advance directives and living wills

To start putting together your advance directives, your first (but not only) option is a state-approved advance directive form that tells your doctors, either in general terms or in detail, your wishes regarding treatments. The form often includes a section where you can express your wishes on organ donation. For a state-by-state map of advance directives requirements, see `www.everplans.com/advance-directive`. If you or your parent spends a lot of time in more than one state, it's a good idea to complete each state's advance directive.

TIP

You don't need a lawyer to create an advance directive or a living will, but you do need to follow your state's requirements about signing and witnessing these documents. Many online kits provide a template for an advance directive. If you use one of these, make sure you complete it following your state's rules. If you're unsure of whether you have met your state's requirements, it is wise to consult a lawyer or other trusted professional.

Putting all your wishes down on paper

A popular form of advance directive is the *Five Wishes* document. This document, written with the help of the American Bar Association's Commission on Law and Aging, gives you the opportunity to convey your personal, emotional, and spiritual needs as well as your medical wishes. In 42 states and the District of Columbia, it substantially meets the legal requirements for an advance directive. Check `https://fivewishes.org/Home` to see whether your state is included. Even if it isn't, you can complete the Five Wishes to accompany your state's approved advance directive.

Here are the five categories of wishes:

>> The person I want to make care decisions for me when I can't

>> The kind of medical treatment I want or don't want

>> How comfortable I want to be

>> How I want people to treat me

>> What I want my loved ones to know

Each of the sections contains an extensive list of things to consider. For example, the document describes four situations — close to death, in a coma and not expected to wake up and recover, permanent and severe brain damage and not expected to recover, and in another condition in which I do not want to be kept alive — and lists the choices that may apply. You can access and fill out the Five Wishes form online at https://fivewishes.org/five-wishes.

Choosing a healthcare proxy

REMEMBER

One of the most important decisions you can make is the choice of *healthcare proxy*, surrogate, or agent: the person who will make healthcare decisions for you when you're unable to do so yourself. This person should be someone you trust to put your wishes ahead of his or her own feelings. A calm, careful approach to problem solving is an asset, as is the ability to listen to other points of view and mediate differences of opinion. The ability to absorb medical information and ask clarifying questions is a valuable skill. Disagreements often stem from poor communication about the person's medical condition, and sometimes doctors are reluctant to give bad news in a direct and nonevasive way. The proxy may have to read between the lines or ask very direct questions.

Location is another factor in choosing the person; although your healthcare proxy doesn't need to live with you or even in the same town, it's not a good idea to pick someone far away in case decisions must be made quickly.

A family member is usually the first option, but you may want to choose a friend instead. (Your doctor can't be your healthcare proxy.) If you have siblings or more than one child, think which one best meets these personal characteristics, regardless of birth order, age, or profession. It's a good idea to choose an alternate as a backup.

TIP

Make sure your healthcare proxy understands your wishes. Many people chosen as healthcare proxies may ask a doctor, "What would you do if this were your mother?" This isn't a good question because it assumes that their mother and the doctor's mother have the same history, beliefs, and wishes. The doctor's mother may have wanted something very different from what their mother expressed. Many experienced doctors deflect this question by saying, "Tell me a little more about your mother." That conversation can lead to a better understanding of the options.

REMEMBER

Before naming your healthcare proxy, be sure to discuss this responsibility with the person you think is best suited for the job and ask whether he or she is willing to take on this responsibility. It should never be a surprise to that person. Make sure you tell other involved family members about whom you have selected to make medical decisions for you. They should not be surprised, either. If you're the healthcare proxy, make sure you keep other family members informed about what is happening and what is likely to happen. Many deathbed family conflicts arise because of lack of communication, which leads to lack of trust.

Adding do not resuscitate (DNR) orders

Do not resuscitate orders are a special kind of advance directive. They tell doctors, nurses, emergency medical technicians, and others that a person has decided not to undergo CPR (cardiopulmonary resuscitation) if his heart stops beating or he stops breathing. A doctor must sign the DNR order for it to be active. In a hospital or other healthcare facility, staff will start CPR if there is no DNR in the medical record.

Why would anyone not want CPR if it can restore a heartbeat? Success rates for CPR vary, but much depends on the person's overall medical condition. CPR may not be effective for older people with serious chronic conditions. And these interventions can be quite brutal, leading to broken ribs and other injuries, especially for an older person.

Most state laws authorize a doctor to enter a special DNR order that will be honored outside the hospital. This is important because when emergency medical technicians respond to a 911 call at home, they are legally required to start CPR unless there is an out-of-hospital DNR order signed by a doctor.

TIP

Even with the proper documentation, in the heat of the moment, sometimes DNR orders are ignored. Or, as the ambulance pulls up, the paperwork can't be found. At home the DNR order should be easy to find, not something that has to be hunted down in a crisis. You can post the DNR order on the refrigerator door, for example, or on an easy-to-see bulletin board.

Because a DNR order is a doctor's order, you'll need to ask your doctor to fill out the form. If she is reluctant to do so, ask why. It may be a good way to start an important conversation about your wishes.

Keeping your advance directive accessible

A carefully completed advance directive is useless if no one knows where it is when you are seriously ill or in an accident. A safe deposit box is great for precious jewelry — but not for advance directives.

Discuss your advance directive with your doctors, and tell them the name and contact information for the person you have selected as a healthcare proxy. You should provide a copy of the document, which can then go into your medical record. In a hospital, a doctor called a hospitalist (a specialist in critical care medicine) will probably oversee your care, so it is essential to have the advance directive as part of your hospital record. When you're admitted to a hospital or other healthcare facility, you'll be asked (it's a federal requirement) whether you have an advance directive. If this is a planned admission, be sure to bring the document with you.

Your healthcare proxy should have a copy of your advance directive as well as any supporting material that documents your wishes. You should review the advance directive every few years, or more often if your health condition changes. The document should have a relatively recent date. A document created 15 years ago is likely to make someone ask, "But what if he changed his mind?"

TIP

You can register your advance directive online at www.uslivingwillregistry. com. It will then be available to all providers. Be sure to update the registry if you change the document. Another resource is the American Bar Association's toolkit on advance directives. See www.americanbar.org/groups/law_aging/resources/ health_care_decision_making/consumer_s_toolkit_for_health_care_ advance_planning.html.

Choosing Physician Orders for Life-Sustaining Treatment (POLST)

A recent development in advance directives is the Physician Order for Life-Sustaining Treatment (POLST). POLST started in Oregon but has spread to many states. In New York, it is called MOLST (Medical Orders for Life-Sustaining Treatment), and in Iowa, IPOST (Iowa Physician Orders for Scope of Treatment). Programs in other states have their own names. See polst.org/programs-in-your-state/ for a state-by-state listing of POLST Paradigm programs.

The names and forms may vary by state, but the basic idea is the same. The POLST is intended for people with serious advanced illness who may be expected to face major treatment decisions within a foreseeable time. The form lists medical interventions you can choose, ranging from comfort care to full treatment, and there is a place for additional orders. The patient (if able), the legally recognized decision maker (if there is one), and a physician must sign the form.

The POLST form is intended to be sent with the person upon transfer. For instance, an EMT can follow a POLST directive if 911 is called. If a person is transferred from hospital to nursing home, the POLST form describes to the nursing-home staff the treatment plan that should be in place.

Why would you need a POLST if you have an advance directive, a living will, and Five Wishes, as well as a healthcare proxy? Because these can be insufficient to guarantee that your wishes will be followed. Hospital, nursing-home, and other clinical staff may be wary of following anything but a physician's order, even though your paperwork is signed and legal. A medical order signed by a physician helps ensure your wishes are followed.

But a POLST isn't intended to take the place of more traditional advance directives. Although the POLST program addresses a common problem of medical staff failing to follow a person's wishes even when documented in an advance directive, it doesn't take into account the fuller range of choices recognized in, for example, a living will or Five Wishes.

In the most common situations in which POLST is used, the discussion preceding the physician's signing of the order is brief and limited to the items on the checklist. And hospital staff may not have training or experience in discussing the options with the patient, healthcare proxy, and family. POLST addresses a serious shortcoming in medical practice, but be sure to have more traditional advance directives in place as well.

Understanding Care Options for Serious Illness: Palliative Care and Hospice

"There is nothing more we can do" is one of those phrases that should be erased from the medical vocabulary. Perhaps there is nothing to be done to cure a patient. But something can always be done to keep a person's pain and symptoms under control and to support the emotional and spiritual needs of a person with advanced illness and the family that experiences distress and loss.

Two options that stress holistic management of serious, life-threatening illness are palliative care and hospice. They are different but related. Both suffer from misperceptions that choosing either means "giving up," as if serious illness were something that can be cured by willpower or yet another last-ditch effort. Some people do not want to die in full battle mode but are urged on by doctors and family to try one more round of chemotherapy or a drug that is still being tested and has nasty side effects. Hospice and palliative care provide other, more peaceful options.

Both palliative care and hospice are voluntary choices. No one can force you or your parent to accept this type of care if you don't want it.

Palliative care

Palliative care is a relatively new medical subspecialty practiced by specially trained physicians, nurses, physician assistants, social workers, clergy, and others. Most palliative care is delivered by hospital teams, but home-based services are increasingly available. Palliative care offers services that improve how individuals function in everyday life, even as they undergo active treatment for a serious illness. Care focuses on pain relief, symptom control, and improving quality of life. Palliative care can be time-limited or ongoing. The ill person and family members are considered part of the palliative care team.

Palliative care can be provided along with treatments intended to cure. It can be started at any point in an illness. In fact, palliative care specialists urge people to consider palliative care at an early stage because the kinds of treatments offered can make it easier to go through the rigor of a chemotherapy regimen, for example.

REMEMBER

Palliative care is covered by most health plans, including Medicare under Part B, Medicaid, and private insurance, on a fee-for-service basis. However, there is no special Medicare benefit for palliative care as there is for hospice. The Medicare hospice benefit is a package of services covered under Part A and doesn't require copays or deductibles. However, the hospice benefit coverage is based on a doctor's determination that the person has six months' or less life expectancy. If, in a hospital setting, you feel that more needs to be done to control pain or discomfort, ask for a consultation with the palliative care team or specialist. This request does not mean changing doctors; it is asking for special expertise to deal with the problems.

For more information about palliative care, go to the Center to Advance Palliative Care at getpalliativecare.org. The website includes a listing of palliative-care resources that you can search by state and city. For a guide comparing hospice and palliative care, see the United Hospital Fund's Next Step in Care website at nextstepincare.org/Caregiver_Home/Hospice.

Hospice

Hospice is a comprehensive service that focuses on controlling pain and symptoms and improving the quality of life for people with a life-threatening illness who have short life expectancies (six months or less). Hospice is a form of palliative care for people who aren't being helped by active treatment or for whom the burdens of treatment outweigh the benefits. People choose hospice when they want to spend their remaining time without aggressive treatments and with care that focuses on comfort and quality of life. Entering hospice requires forgoing treatment intended to cure.

Hospice is a team approach that uses the skills of different medical and nonmedical specialists to create an environment of comfort and emotional and spiritual support for both the patient and the family.

Hospice services may include, in addition to doctors and nurses, physical and occupational therapists, social workers, volunteers, and clergy. Other services are

>> Medications to relieve nausea, pain, shortness of breath, agitation, and other symptoms

>> Medical supplies such as a hospital bed or a wheelchair

>> Support for the family, including counseling and teaching how to do certain healthcare tasks

>> A short hospital stay if the person's symptoms can't be managed at home

>> Short-term respite care — time off for the family

>> Volunteers to provide companionship

>> Bereavement counseling for the family for a year after the person's death

Sometimes doctors recommend hospice, but in other cases a family member has to begin the discussion. If you ask about hospice and are criticized by a doctor or nurse, ask why they are opposed to the idea. If you aren't satisfied, ask for a second opinion.

REMEMBER

Hospice is not right for everyone. Some people want to pursue aggressive treatments to the very end. Home hospice may also require a considerable amount of caregiving by the family. Having new people involved in care may seem overwhelming at a time of great emotional stress. But hospice offers an opportunity for care that sees the whole person and the family as the unit of care and works with them to achieve the best quality of life possible.

Hospice at home or in a facility

In the United States, most hospice services are provided at home, but they can also be provided in nursing homes and assisted-living facilities, which may contract with a local hospice to provide the care. There are, in addition, inpatient hospices in some hospitals and free-standing hospices.

Although a team of professionals, as well as volunteers and aides, provides home hospice services, much of the care is provided by family members. Only in the last few days of life is there likely to be constant care by a member of the hospice team. However, one of the benefits of hospice is that you have a 24-hour number to call if an unexpected problem occurs. A hospice nurse can offer advice and make a home visit if necessary, which can reduce unnecessary and stressful visits to the emergency department.

HOSPICE: FROM VOLUNTEERS TO CORPORATIONS

In London after World War II, Dame Cicely Saunders created St. Christopher's, the first modern hospice, to care for terminally ill people in a holistic, compassionate way. Volunteers provided most of the care. She introduced the concept in the United States during a 1963 visit to Yale University. In 1986, Medicare created a special hospice benefit. Since then the number of people enrolled in hospice has increased. In 2016, an estimated 1.43 million people received hospice services, accounting for about 48 percent of all deaths in the United States. Once in hospice, some people become ineligible because of improvements in their condition, and some choose not to continue. Still, most people are in hospice for a very short time; under a third had three or more days of hospice services. The average length of service was 19 days.

There are now more than 4,300 hospice programs in the United States. They range from small all-volunteer agencies to large, national corporate chains that serve thousands of people daily. More information is available from the National Hospice and Palliative Care Organization at www.nhpco.org/sites/default/files/public/ Statistics_Research/2017_Facts_Figures.pdf.

Hospice benefits under Medicare, Medicaid, and private insurance

Hospice is a benefit under Medicare Part A and is included in Medicare Advantage plans. All other Medicare benefits under Parts A and B continue, including the attending physician's fees. You can continue to get services for conditions that aren't related to the terminal illness. Although it is not one of the mandatory benefits that federal regulations require state Medicaid programs to provide, such as hospital and home healthcare services, most states and the District of Columbia do offer hospice services. The services may vary, so check with your state's Medicaid agency. Most private health insurance plans follow Medicare guidelines on hospice.

To be eligible for the Medicare hospice benefit, a doctor must certify that a person has a six-month or less life expectancy. Some diseases, such as cancer, follow a more or less predictable course. But others, like Alzheimer's disease, do not, and it is much harder to say how much longer a person with Alzheimer's is likely to live. As a result, hospices have been criticized both for taking patients with only a few days to live, when they can't get the full benefit of the services, and taking patients with an unpredictable disease course, which results in higher costs.

Tips for choosing the right hospice

Choosing a hospice, like choosing a home care agency, an assisted-living facility, or a nursing home, requires some research on your part. Here are some questions to ask:

>> Is the hospice certified by Medicare, which means that it meets federal and state guidelines?

>> Is there someone to call 24 hours a day, seven days a week?

>> How does the hospice manage medical emergencies?

>> What kinds of medical equipment will be provided?

>> Although accepting hospice means giving up treatments intended to cure, many medical interventions such as chemotherapy to relieve symptoms and anti-nausea medications are important adjuncts to hospice care. What is the hospice policy on these kinds of treatments?

TIP

You can find out about hospices in your area by asking the doctor, hospital, or state health department or by going to www.medicare.gov/hospicecompare/. This website gives basic information about hospice services in your area, including a checklist of questions to ask when choosing a hospice agency: www.medicare.gov/hospicecompare/scripts/PDF/HospiceChecklist-Final-Clean.pdf.

You can find a list of state hospice associations at hospicefoundation.org/Hospice-Directory. Make sure you check several sources to get a complete list, as some websites list only hospices with which they are affiliated.

Ending hospice care

REMEMBER

A person in hospice care has the right to discontinue the services at any time for any reason. Perhaps your parent is getting better because of the extra attention (some studies show that people in hospice care live longer than those who don't get this care). You can always cease hospice care for a while and start again when necessary. Also, the hospice can discharge the patient. This happens rarely, but usually the reason is that the person wants to pursue treatments intended to cure or no longer meets hospice criteria. The hospice may also say that the home is not safe for its workers or that the family refuses to cooperate with hospice rules. Hospice programs can't discharge people because their care is inconvenient or too expensive.

Some hospices have been forced to close because Medicare auditors determined that they were keeping people for extended periods and their claims were denied. So hospices may be wary of taking persons who have unpredictable courses of illness.

5
Services for Special Groups

Get prepared for the special challenges you may face if you are lesbian, gay, bisexual, or transgender (LGBT). Although social acceptance is growing and the legal context is shifting, there are still areas of concern, such as hospital and nursing-home visitation and discrimination.

Look at a range of long-term care options available only to veterans of military service who are enrolled in Department of Veterans Affairs healthcare (and their caregivers). I guide you through the eligibility requirements for various forms of in-home assistance and care in VA or state-sponsored veterans' homes.

Take advantage of resources to help family caregivers, who provide most long-term care and are an essential element in future care planning.

Chapter **18**

LGBT Older Adults

Lesbian, gay, bisexual, and transgender individuals (LGBT) face all the same problems of planning for future care as their heterosexual and non-transgender counterparts but with additional complicating factors. (Many people now use the expanded term LGBTQ, adding Q for "questioning" or "queer," but in this chapter I use the shorter term.) Although U.S. society has in general become more accepting of LGBT individuals, stigma and discrimination persist in many settings, including healthcare and long-term care. Even when nondiscriminatory laws and policies are in place, institutions and individual staff members may not follow them.

This chapter looks at how to get in place all possible legal protections to help alleviate problems in obtaining services and having them delivered in respectful and sensitive ways. This chapter also helps you find LGBT-friendly service providers and investigate housing options that welcome LGBT residents. It's intended as a supplement to other chapters that deal with specific subjects such as assisted living, nursing homes, home care, and advance directives.

Recognizing LGBT Aging and Health Issues

Older LGBT individuals are at risk for the same kinds of chronic physical and mental health conditions that affect all older adults as well as specific health issues related to sexual orientation and gender identity. Although lesbian, gay, bisexual, and transgender individuals are collectively called LGBT, each group of men and women (and subgroups by age, race and ethnicity, and other characteristics) has distinct features. Still, they share some characteristics that make them particularly vulnerable.

REMEMBER

In addition to dealing with certain increased health risks, which I cover in this section, many LGBT individuals have had difficult experiences with healthcare encounters. In a study called "The Aging and Health Report: Disparities and Resilience among Lesbian, Gay, Bisexual and Transgender Older Adults," a comprehensive report funded by the U.S. National Institute on Aging, 13 percent report being denied healthcare or having received inferior care. More than 20 percent do not disclose their sexual or gender identity to their physicians, which forecloses discussions of related health risks. Although discrimination in healthcare is unacceptable at any point, it is particularly problematic for older adults, who have more contacts with the healthcare system, who may need more assistance from professionals and paraprofessionals, and who may be more vulnerable on all counts. Fear of discrimination, based on personal history, may deter some older LGBT individuals from seeking the help they need and may limit their options for care.

Physical conditions

If you are or have a family member or friend who is LGBT, you know how experiences with discrimination, or perceptions that discrimination will occur, can be a barrier to good medical care. It is important to recognize that LGBT persons are at the same risk — and in some cases even higher risk — than their heterosexual counterparts for chronic illness and disability. You may have to be extra vigilant.

That is the sobering finding of a National Institute on Aging study. The authors reviewed data from the U.S. Centers for Disease Control and Prevention's Behavioral Risk Factor Surveillance System (BRFSS) survey from Washington State, supplemented by a national survey of LGBT adults aged 50 to 95. They found higher rates of disability among lesbian, gay, and bisexual older adults (41 percent) than among heterosexuals of similar ages (35 percent), even when accounting for differences in age, income, and education.

In general the study focused on differences between men and women, and on different subsets of LGBT individuals, not on comparisons with the general population, although these differences are noted and are based on the comparisons with CDC BRFSS data.

LGBT older adults experience higher rates of mental distress and are more likely to smoke and engage in excessive drinking than their heterosexual peers. Lesbians and bisexual older women report higher risk of cardiovascular disease and obesity than heterosexual women, and gay and bisexual older men are more likely to have poor physical health than their heterosexual counterparts. Some of these higher rates of disability may be prevented with good primary care, so it is important to recognize early signs and take preventive action.

Here are some of the key findings of the report:

>> Nearly half (47 percent) of older LGBT individuals had a disability that limited their physical activities or required the use of assistive devices like canes or wheelchairs.

>> A quarter reported visual impairments, even while wearing glasses or contact lenses, and 19 percent experienced acute hearing impairment. Nearly a quarter reported dental problems, which increase the risk of poor nutrition and poor health.

>> Obesity is a serious problem in the LGBT population, as it is in the general population.

>> Other reported health conditions include high blood pressure, high cholesterol, cataracts, asthma, diabetes, hepatitis, and osteoporosis.

>> Approximately 13 percent have some cardiac condition.

>> Nine percent in this survey were living with HIV disease, and among gay and bisexual men, the percentage with HIV disease was 14 percent.

In this survey, compared to men, women reported poorer physical health and higher rates of disability, arthritis, obesity, asthma, and osteoporosis. Men, however, had higher rates of HIV disease, hepatitis, high blood pressure, cardiovascular disease, diabetes, cancer, and hearing impairment.

As may be expected, risks of disability and chronic disease increased with age, and participants with lower incomes and lower educational levels had increased risks of poor physical health. A positive finding, however, was that nearly all (91 percent) engaged in some form of wellness activities. There are also strong indications of resilience as LGBT persons dealt with discrimination.

TIP

If you want to find out more, the complete report is available at www.age-pride. org/wordpress/wp-content/uploads/2011/05/Full-Report-FINAL-11-16-11.pdf.

Mental health risks

Mental health risks are higher among LGBT older adults than among comparable heterosexual age groups. The study from the U.S. National Institute on Aging also reported on mental health issues that affect the LGBT population. Following are some of the findings:

>> Nearly a third (31 percent) of the respondents reported depression, with transgender individuals reporting the highest rates (48 percent).

>> Almost a quarter (24 percent) had been diagnosed with anxiety.

>> Thirty-nine percent had seriously considered suicide at some point in their lives, including 35 percent of lesbians, 40 percent of bisexual women, 37 percent of gay men, 39 percent of bisexual men, and 71 percent of transgender older adults. Among those who considered suicide, 39 percent reported that their suicidal thoughts were related to their sexual orientation or gender identity.

>> Not surprisingly, and like their counterparts in the general population, many LGBT individuals reported stress in their lives, but it is reassuring that a high percentage (69 percent) felt confident that they can handle their personal problems. Again, transgender adults were more likely to report high levels of stress, regardless of age, income, and education.

>> In a related finding, 59 percent of the LGBT older adults reported feeling that they lack companionship, are isolated from others (53 percent), and feel left out (53 percent).

LGBT individuals have the same sorts of workplace, financial, and relationship stresses in their lives as other older adults, but to these are added a history of victimization and discrimination. Eighty-two percent in this survey reported being victimized at least once because of their perceived sexual orientation or gender identity; 64 percent had experienced discrimination three or more times. Many LGBT older adults have experienced discrimination in housing and employment.

Knowing Legal Protections and Their Limits

Legal protections in health and long-term care for older LGBT adults consist of a patchwork of federal and state laws and regulations. Even when they promote equality, federal policies and rulings may not be implemented aggressively by states, much less by individuals working in care settings. Still, three federal actions in the past few years are important steps toward fair and equal treatment for LGBT adults. The opposite trend has been seen in several state legislatures, particularly around transgender rights. You can follow legal developments at the Human Rights Campaign website (www.hrc.org).

The U.S. Supreme Court and same-sex marriage

In June 2013, the U.S. Supreme Court ruled, in the case of *Windsor v. United States*, that Section 3 of the federal ban on recognizing same-sex marriages in the Defense of Marriage Act (DOMA) was unconstitutional. The section that was struck down defined *marriage* as "between one man and one woman as husband and wife," and *spouse* as "person of the opposite sex." In the second ruling in a separate case, the Court let stand a lower court's decision to strike down California's ban on same-sex marriage. These decisions have removed the barriers to many rights that were formerly denied to people in same-sex marriages, but certain gray areas still exist. The Supreme Court ruling should be interpreted and implemented by many federal agencies, and they are doing so at their own pace and with varying degrees of consistency.

The third Supreme Court ruling in June 2015 that expanded rights to same-sex marriages occurred in in the case of *Obergefell v. Hodges*. This ruling expanded to all states the right of same-sex couples to marry. Previously several states had laws limiting marriage to heterosexual couples. This ruling removed the previous barriers in agencies that followed state laws, detailed here.

DOMA had barred same-sex married couples from receiving federal marriage benefits. In healthcare these included

>> **Medicare:** DOMA affected some aspects of Medicare, including eligibility based on a spouse's work record, premium amounts, and delayed enrollment penalties for remaining on a spouse's private health plans. A useful 2016 summary of Medicare and Medicaid and same-sex marriage is at https://lgbtagingcenter.org/resources/pdfs/SAGE%20SHIP%20 Sheet%20Medicare%20Marriage%20FINAL%20Web.pdf

>> **Taxation of health benefits:** Health benefits received through a spouse's employer are not taxable, but because the IRS did not recognize same-sex marriages, gay and lesbian couples had to pay higher tax bills.

>> **Immediate coverage rules:** Federal law lets an employee add new spouses to a health plan without waiting for an enrollment period. This protection did not apply to same-sex married couples.

>> **COBRA coverage:** COBRA is the federal law that requires health plans to continue coverage (at the employee's expense) for an employee and family members for a temporary period if the person loses a job. Under DOMA, plans can provide this coverage to same-sex partners but were not required to.

» **Family and Medical Leave Act:** Under this law, employees in companies with 50 or more employees are entitled to up to 12 weeks of unpaid leave to care for a family member with a serious health condition. Under DOMA employees were not required to provide this time off for married gay and lesbian employees to care for their spouse.

» **Medicaid Managed Long-Term Care Services:** Some states may have protections against spousal impoverishment in these programs. On the other hand, some states prohibit spouses from being paid in Medicaid Consumer-Directed Assistance programs.

» **IRS rules:** In August 2013, the IRS announced that it would recognize as married for tax purposes same-sex couples married in any state that recognizes their union as legal. The further Supreme Court ruling in *Obergefell v. Hodges* means that same-sex marriages are legal in all states. Even so, there are many specific questions that you should ask your accountant or lawyer for advice.

» **Federal employment:** The federal Office of Personnel Management's updated policy is that legally married same-sex spouses of federal employees are eligible for health-insurance coverage. Since the federal government is a major employer, this decision affects many people.

» **Veterans:** The VA has adjusted its policies to recognize same-sex marriages as described at www.va.gov/opa/marriage/. The Department of Defense had earlier announced that same-sex spouses of active duty troops are entitled to equal benefits.

The U.S. Immigration and Citizenship Services, part of the Department of Homeland Security, already uses a *place of celebration* (where the marriage occurred) rather than a place of residence standard for determining the legality of marriages.

TIP

The Social Security Administration has information on "What Same-Sex Couples Need to Know" at www.ssa.gov/pubs/EN-05-10014.pdf. This document describes how SSA administers benefits for married same-sex couples and some categories of nonmarried couples such as domestic partners. It also includes information about children in these families.

REMEMBER

Formal policies may not be followed by everyone at every agency. Be prepared to document your status and the official rules.

Obama presidential memorandum on hospital visitation

The right to choose one's visitors in a hospital or other care facility is particularly important for LGBT older adults, who may not have children or other biological family members to advocate for them. They rely on families of choice or friends to accompany them to the hospital, to ask questions that they may not be able to articulate, and to be their representatives in navigating the complex healthcare and long-term care systems.

One federal ruling has a more direct link to health and long-term care, particularly with regards to visitation. On April 15, 2010, then- President Barack Obama issued a memorandum instructing the Secretary of Health and Human Services to

>> Initiate appropriate rulemaking to ensure that hospitals that participate in Medicare and Medicaid respect the rights of patients to designate visitors, and those hospitals may not deny visitation privileges because of race, color, national origin, religion, sex, sexual orientation, gender identity, or disability.

>> Ensure that all hospitals participating in Medicare and Medicaid are in full compliance with regulations that guarantee that all patients' advance directives, such as durable powers of attorney and healthcare proxies, are respected, and that patients' representatives have the right to make informed decisions regarding patient care.

This ruling recognized the problem encountered by many LGBT spouses and partners, even those with valid advance directives and healthcare proxies, to visit their hospitalized loved ones and to be involved in decision making. The memorandum is available at obamawhitehouse.archives.gov/the-press-office/ presidential-memorandum-hospital-visitation.

New rules for visitation

In May 2011, the Centers for Medicare & Medicaid Services (CMS) issued new rules implementing the memorandum. The rules require hospitals to have written policies detailing visitation rights as well as the circumstances under which the hospital may restrict access based on patient needs. The rules require hospitals to explain to all patients their rights to choose who may visit them, regardless of the relationship, as well as to determine who they do not want as visitors. The rules are available at www.gpo.gov/fdsys/pkg/FR-2010-11-19/pdf/2010-29194.pdf.

In June 2013, CMS issued a reminder to state survey agency directors, who coordinate inspections of skilled nursing facilities, to check with residents and family members to make sure that they have been informed about nondiscriminatory visitation policies. Residents must be notified of their "rights to have visitors on a 24-hour basis that can include but are not limited to spouses (including same-sex spouses), domestic partners (including same-sex domestic partners), other family members, or friends." The Nursing Home Reform Act of 1987 does not mention sexual orientation or gender identity specifically, but its broad descriptions of rights to be treated with dignity and respect prohibit verbal and physical harassments by staff.

In addition to the federal policies, several states have laws requiring hospitals and other healthcare facilities to have nondiscriminatory policies regarding visitation.

Limitations of formal visitation policies

Formal policies can only go so far in ensuring rights, including hospital or nursing-home visitation rights. The legal cases that brought this issue to public and presidential attention, and ultimately to the formal CMS ruling, were not instances in which hospitals had policies of deliberately discriminating against LGBT individuals. They arose because staff members used their own judgments and prejudices to determine who should be allowed to visit a patient. They denied visits to people whose relationships they did not approve of, with tragic results. Some hospitals, especially those involved in lawsuits, have taken steps to improve their care and to prevent outright discrimination. Others may not have given this action a high priority.

A 2013 survey of hospitals in New York State found that many hospitals have improved communications about patients' rights to decide who may be at the bedside. Even so, nearly one in five large New York hospitals had statements on their websites with language directly contrary to the federal regulation and New York State law. In addition, the hospitals had very limited visiting hours and limitations such as "immediate family only."

A follow-up study published in January 2018 found improvements, particularly among hospitals that had provided training, including nine that are part of the public New York Health + Hospitals system. No hospital received a perfect score for its website, and over a third were in the lowest range. Some of the hospitals with low rankings may have formal policies that comply with the federal regulations but have failed to update their websites. In today's world, however, most people go to websites for their initial information and not to formal policies that may or may not be publicly available. (The survey results are available at www.nypirg.org/pubs/201801/NYPIRG_SICK_SCARED_FINAL.pdf.)

TIP

The Human Rights Campaign has a guide to hospital visitation for LGBT families at www.hrc.org/resources/hospital-visitation-guide-for-lgbt-families.

The inconsistency in state laws, erratic compliance with federal regulations, and difficulty in changing long-standing attitudes and behaviors means that you need to be prepared to establish your rights as a patient and to have the people you designate recognized as visitors, healthcare proxies, and, if need be, decision makers.

Keeping Legal Documents at the Ready

Be prepared. You should have legal documents that you update periodically and keep in a safe but easily accessed place. You should give copies to all the people who may be involved in your healthcare, especially your physicians and the person named as a healthcare proxy. Having these documents in the right hands is especially important for an LGBT older adult, whose nonbiological family representatives are more likely to be challenged about their authority to make healthcare decisions on the person's behalf. Despite the troubled family history experienced by many (but certainly not all) LGBT older adults, about a third of the LGBT older adults surveyed in the report cited earlier in this chapter did not have a durable power of attorney for healthcare or a will.

It is a good idea for caregivers of LGBT individuals who are hospitalized to bring copies of all relevant legal documents, including advance directives, the presidential memorandum, and the CMS ruling, to respond to any hospital challenge.

Here is a list of documents that relate to your rights to determine your medical care, especially in advanced illness. You may not need all these documents, but an advance directive and a healthcare proxy are essential.

>> **Advance directive:** *Advance directive* is the generic term for the advance planning documents in which you outline your wishes for treatment or nontreatment and name the individual you want to act as your spokesperson if you're unable to speak for yourself. See Chapter 17 for more information on advance directives.

If you spend time in more than one state, you should have a valid advance directive for each state. AARP has state-specific forms you can download at www.aarp.org/advancedirectives.

>> **Healthcare proxy:** This designation names the individual you want to act as your representative, sometimes called a durable power of attorney for healthcare. Make sure you have discussed this responsibility with this person and that he or she understands your wishes. See Chapter 17 for information on choosing a healthcare proxy.

>> **Living will:** This is a generic name for a document in which you specify the end-of-life treatments you do or do not want to receive.

>> **A list of hospital visitors you approve:** This shouldn't be necessary but can be helpful just in case the hospital tries to restrict who can visit you.

>> **HIPAA release stating the names of people you want to receive your health information:** Some advance directive forms include this listing. Federal law does not require a HIPAA release, but it may be required by hospital policy.

>> **Do not resuscitate order:** If appropriate, a do not resuscitate order (DNR) entered by your doctor in your medical record (see Chapter 17) tells hospital personnel that you do not want to have cardiopulmonary resuscitation (CPR) performed if your heart stops beating. If you're receiving care at home, you may want to talk with your doctor about creating an out-of-hospital DNR order. Without this document available, emergency medical technicians are required to perform CPR.

>> **POLST form:** You may also consider a POLST (Physician Order for Life-Sustaining Treatment) form, which goes by different names in different states. This form is most appropriate for people with advanced illness, especially if they're being transferred from one care or treatment setting to another. The POLST goes into more specific detail on life-sustaining treatments that are or are not to be provided during the end of life. Chapter 17 provides more information on preparing a POLST document.

TIP

In drawing up these or any legal documents, it is advisable to consult an attorney who has expertise in elder or healthcare law and who has worked with LGBT clients before. There are many nuances in state laws that need to be considered. A guide to legal issues, including healthcare documents and questions to ask an attorney, is at www.nclrights.org/wp-content/uploads/2013/04/Resources_Lifelines.pdf.

Finding LGBT-Friendly Providers and Facilities

With something as important and intimate as healthcare, it is essential to have healthcare providers you can talk to and who understand your needs and concerns. In today's rushed and fragmented healthcare world, that's not easy for anyone, especially when we need time to absorb information and to ask questions. It is particularly a challenge for LGBT older adults, who may not have disclosed their sexual identity to a physician or who have experienced discrimination if they did.

Finding healthcare providers

The changing organization of healthcare also means that if you need more than occasional primary care, you will probably see a variety of healthcare providers, most of whom will not know your personal history beforehand. In a hospital, for example, hospitalists (doctors specially trained to provide acute care), not your primary care physician, will take care of you. Some staff will be sensitive to you and your visitors, some may be hostile, and some will not care one way or the other.

Location may play a role. LGBT individuals who live in big cities generally have more choices than those who live in small towns or rural areas. But wherever you live, you should try to find healthcare providers who will be comfortable with you and with whom you will be comfortable.

You can ask LGBT friends or a local community organization that serves LGBT clients for referrals. The Gay and Lesbian Medical Association (GLMA) has an online referral system of providers who have made a commitment to nonjudgmental care of LGBT patients at www.glma.org/index.cfm?fuseaction=Page. viewPage&pageId=939&grandparentID=534&parentID=938&nodeID=1. Another resource is CenterLink, which is the national organization representing all the LGBT community centers in the United States. Go to www.lgbtcenters.org to access their wealth of information.

The Human Rights Campaign has a list of organizations that meet its four criteria of the Healthcare Equity Index. These criteria are patient nondiscrimination, equal visitation, employment nondiscrimination, and training in LGBT patient-centered care. In a 2018 survey, 626 healthcare facilities participated and 418 were designated Leaders in LGBTQ Healthcare Equality. Another 95 facilities met the "Top Peformer" designation. A full description of the survey is available at assets2. hrc.org/files/assets/resources/HEI-2018-FinalReport.pdf?_ga=2. 251582597.2074980739.1522952966-1009849422.1520861382.

REMEMBER

Lists of names and places are only a start. You have to ask questions and visit clinics and doctors' offices yourself to determine the level of care and consideration that is provided.

TIP

LGBT individuals are sometimes both the people in need of care and their caregivers. Because many LGBT individuals are single or childless, they may see themselves or be seen as the best caregiver for an aging relative — despite many instances of estrangement from their families of origin — or an LGBT friend. A United Hospital Fund/SAGE guide to LGBT caregiving is available at www. nextstepincare.org/Caregiver_Home/LGBT_Guide/. The National Center on LGBT Aging has a state-by-state listing of local resources at www.lgbtaging center.org/resources/area.cfm as well as a list of national resources.

Considering independent- or assisted-living facilities and nursing homes

Finding the right independent- or assisted-living facility or nursing home is a challenge for everyone, but again, when the prospective resident is an LGBT older adult, there are additional concerns.

In addition to the many general questions you should ask about the facility, its services, and its management and the observations you make on your visits (see Chapter 8), note whether there are

>> Posted statements about nondiscrimination

>> Indications of an LGBT-friendly environment, such as pictures of same-sex couples, rainbows, or other LGBT symbols on marketing materials, signs, or magazines

DEALING WITH HOSTILITY IN A NURSING HOME

Just as you would if you were investigating assisted living, checking out nursing homes should include observations about the setting and whether there are gay-friendly materials available, questions about whether staff have been trained about LGBT issues, and whether there are any specific LGBT groups or activities. You can glean as much from the style of the responses (staff discomfort, avoidance, vagueness) as from the content.

When an LGBT person lives in a nursing home, hostile and disparaging remarks can come from staff, other residents, residents' families, and other visitors. Some residents have dementia and say things that they would not say in their nondemented state. But understanding the reasons for these remarks does not make them any easier to tolerate.

There are different ways of dealing with hostility. If the offending resident is a roommate, you can ask for a change of rooms or, if possible, a private room. If the hostility is more systematic, which suggests that the administration has not done a good job of training staff and giving them appropriate ways to handle this problem, you can discuss this with the long-term care ombudsman in your area. The ombudsman can work with the administration to alleviate the problem. To find the ombudsman in your area, go to www.ltcombudsman.org/ombudsman. If the problem leads to poor quality of care, such as neglect by staff, you should complain to the regional Beneficiary and Family-Centered Care Quality Improvement Organization (BFCC-QIO), a private agency under contract to CMS. The BFCC-QIOs are listed at www.qioprogram.org/about/what-are-qios. If all else fails, you may have to consider moving to a different nursing home.

You can also ask specifically whether the facility has LGBT residents. If the answer is "No" or "We would never ask that," it is likely that the administration isn't going out of its way to attract LGBT residents. You can also ask whether staff is trained to be sensitive to LGBT issues and whether residents have a safe way to report unwelcome comments.

There is no federal statement of rights for assisted-living residents as there is for nursing homes, but several states have some statement of residents' rights. Check your state's health department or aging agency. Of course, the existence of a state policy on residents' rights is no guarantee that it is honored. Discrimination in nursing homes has been well documented, and it is one reason many LGBT older adults don't want to even consider this option.

TIP

The California Advocates for Nursing Home Reform, an advocacy organization, has prepared a ten-page guide on how to deal with problems when a nursing home restricts visits. Much of the guide, available at www.canhr.org/reports/ VisitationRightsGuide.pdf, is applicable in any state.

Looking at LGBT-specific options

Some LGBT older adults would like to live in a community of their peers. Others want more diversity. For now, the options for special LGBT facilities or communities are limited, but in the past few years, several retirement communities and assisted-living facilities have opened to serve LGBT residents. Some have both LGBT and straight residents. These niche communities are hoping to appeal to a relatively affluent segment of the LGBT community, although a few are geared toward low-income residents. Some new developments encountered financial difficulties in the poor economy. If you're considering one of these facilities, make sure you investigate its funding and business plan.

SAGE, an advocacy organization for LGBT elders, has a state-by-state map of housing alternatives at www.sageusa.org/what-we-do/national-lgbt-housing- initiative/ as well as a series of tip sheets on various aspects of healthcare at www.sageusa.org/issues/health.cfm.

The Assisted Living Directory has lists of gay-friendly facilities at www.assisted- living-directory.com/content/gay-friendly-facilities.cfm. After filling out a questionnaire, the site will direct you to facilities in your area. And as the website notes, some facilities that welcome LGBT residents do not want to be listed for fear that it may deter potential heterosexual customers.

Another good, comprehensive resource is the National Resource Center on LGBT Aging at www.lgbtagingcenter.org/.

Chapter **19**
Services for Veterans

V eterans of U.S. military service have an additional set of options beyond whatever form of healthcare or long-term care insurance other people may have. Many options for both healthcare and long-term services and supports at home or in the community are available to veterans enrolled in the Veterans Health Administration, part of the U.S. Department of Veterans Affairs (VA).

Despite the benefits, navigating the large bureaucracy with its own complex rules, requirements, and delays can be cumbersome. Nevertheless, an extensive 2016 survey of veterans receiving VA services found improvements in health status and satisfaction with many aspects of VA services. Referrals to specialists was noted as a problem. (See www.va.gov/HEALTHPOLICYPLANNING/SoE2016/2016_Survey_of_Veteran_Enrollees_Health_and_Health_Care_rev2.pdf.)

VA benefits are usually more generous than those available through Medicare or private insurance, and less stringent in terms of financial eligibility than Medicaid. This chapter describes the basic way the VA system works and its options for long-term services and supports.

REMEMBER

The VA system is undergoing several changes as part of the VA Mission Act of 2018 in response to investigations about delays in obtaining services and other issues. Veterans and their families should check for current information when considering choices. The biggest change concerns the way in which VA-funded appointments take place in the private sector. The current Veterans Choice program, one of seven different community care programs, will be continued for a year (`www.va.gov/COMMUNITYCARE/programs/veterans/VCP/index.asp`). The goal is to combine all the programs into one funding stream with eligibility criteria for obtaining private services, including distance from a VA center, approval of a VA doctor, and inability of the VA to provide care in a timely way.

Getting into the VA System

The Veterans Health Administration (VHA) is the largest integrated healthcare system in the United States, with more than 170 medical centers, 1,063 outpatient sites of care, community living centers (another name for nursing homes), domiciliaries (mental-health and rehabilitation homes), readjustment counseling centers, and other facilities. About 9 million veterans are enrolled, and more than 6 million use the system each year. Although the VA healthcare network is extensive, it's not distributed equally across the nation, so veterans in some areas, particularly rural areas, may not live close to a VA Medical Center or Community-Based Outpatient Clinic. You can find a list of VA facilities by state at `www.va.gov/directory/guide/allstate.asp?dnum=1`.

REMEMBER

If you're enrolled in the VA system, you can continue to use private or public healthcare insurance and see doctors outside the VA. This arrangement is called Co-Managed Care or Dual Care, and over 70 percent of veterans are enrolled in this program, many of them enrolled in Medicare. However, Medicare won't pay for services from VA providers.

Comparing the VA to other healthcare systems

In many ways, the VA system is unlike other systems with which you are probably more familiar:

>> Unlike Medicare, Medicaid, and private insurance, which only pay for care, the VA provides healthcare as well as pays for it.

>> Unlike Medicare, there is no age, work history, or specific disease requirement for eligibility. Eligibility is based solely on military service, but there are many categories of eligibility and priorities for healthcare services.

>> The VA has no exclusion for preexisting conditions. In fact, veterans with a preexisting condition that is service-related may be given a higher priority to receive services.

>> Like Medicaid, the VA has a means (financial status) test, but unlike Medicaid, it isn't based on poverty guidelines.

>> Under certain circumstances, family members of veterans are eligible for VA health benefits.

TIP

As with most insurance and healthcare programs, you must be enrolled in VA healthcare to be eligible for long-term services and supports. Many older veterans enroll in VA healthcare when they need long-term care. Just being discharged from active service does not enroll you in the VA healthcare system. You must apply. You can do this online, in person at a VA facility, by mail, or by phone (877-222-8387). Go to www.va.gov/HEALTHBENEFITS/apply/index.asp for details on the application process for healthcare benefits. There is an additional step when you apply for long-term care. The VA's Concierge for Care (C4C) program, launched in October 2017, is designed to help service members who are preparing to transition to civilian life. See details at https://www.va.gov/HEALTHBENEFITS/apply/application_process.asp.

TIP

A helpful 2013 report from the Congressional Research Service answers many questions about healthcare for veterans. Go to digitalcommons.ilr.cornell.edu/cgi/viewcontent.cgi?article=2527&context=key_workplace.

Understanding eligibility for VA healthcare

Eligibility for VA healthcare is a tiered system, and you may need some help from the VA to figure out just where you fit. The three basic eligibility considerations for VA healthcare are military service, type of disability, and financial need. The following sections give a brief explanation of each.

Military service

If you served in the active military, including Army, Navy, Marines, Coast Guard, or Air Force, you may qualify for VA healthcare benefits. Reservists and National Guard members may also qualify for the VA healthcare benefits if they were called to active duty (other than for training only) by a federal order and completed the full period for which they were called or ordered to active duty.

REMEMBER

Veterans who were dishonorably discharged are not eligible for VA healthcare, but veterans who had "other than honorable" discharges, often for drug abuse or behavior problems, can still apply. In June 2013, the VA issued a statement that outlined how veterans in these "in-between" categories can apply. Eligibility is determined on a case-by-case basis, but a tentative approval may be granted in emergencies. For an update from May 2017, see www.va.gov/HEALTHBENEFITS/resources/publications/IB10-448_other_than_honorable_discharges5_17.pdf.

Type of disability

You may believe that you must have a service-related injury to be eligible for VA healthcare services. That's not true, although sometimes service-related injuries show up years and years after discharge, as has occurred with some veterans of the Korean and Vietnam conflicts. And you don't have to establish a disability rating (a number that quantifies the extent of your disability from 0 to 100 percent) before you start to get care.

REMEMBER

Being 100 percent disabled is not necessarily a permanent condition. You may recover sufficiently to have your disability rating changed.

The VA has eight priority groups that determine the ranking of eligibility and financial contributions. The key point here is that the most serious disabilities get priority and their financial status is assessed more leniently. As you move down the scale toward less serious conditions, you must show greater financial need.

Group 1 has the highest priority and includes veterans with the most serious service-related disabilities, and Group 2 includes those with less serious service-related disabilities. The priority continues down to groups of veterans who have non-service-related disabilities and can demonstrate financial need. (I discuss the income consideration more in the following section.) For a complete list and description of the priority groups, go to Chapter 2 of the publication at www.va.gov/HEALTHBENEFITS/vhbh/publications/vhbh_sample_handbook_2014.pdf.

TECHNICAL STUFF

In a 2016 survey (www.va.gov/HEALTHPOLICYPLANNING/SoE2016/2016_Survey_of_Veteran_Enrollees_Health_and_Health_Care_rev2.pdf), enrollees classified in Priority Groups 1–3, the most seriously affected, constituted the highest percent (64 percent). The proportion of enrollees in Priority Group 1 increased from 15 percent in 2015 to 24 percent, while enrollees in Priority Groups 7–8 (the least seriously affected) continued a decrease from 28 to 23 percent over the last five years.

Financial considerations

You don't have to be poor to qualify for VA healthcare. If you meet the financial threshold, your care will be free. The income thresholds for 2018 by country and priority area are available at nationalincomelimits.vaftl.us/Legacy GMTThresholds/Index?FiscalYear=2018&PGLevel=8. But even if your income exceeds these limits, and you're eligible based on other criteria, you can get care and pay copays for whatever isn't covered. There are lower financial thresholds for veterans with service-related injuries than for those with non-service-related health problems.

TIP

You can use the VA online Health Benefits Explorer as a first step in determining your eligibility (hbexplorer.vacloud.us). However, eligibility for specific health-care services may depend on several outside factors, including the amount of money Congress appropriates for the VA every year. In some cases, your priority status also affects the services for which you qualify or the level of copays.

In 2012, the VA relaxed some of the requirements for Group 8, the lowest priority, which means that some veterans who previously would have been denied because their incomes were too high may now qualify. To find out about income thresholds in 2018, go to www.va.gov/healthbenefits/cost/income_thresholds.asp. There are also geographical adjustments based on the cost of living in different regions.

TIP

Veterans enrolled in the VA for healthcare coverage have completely satisfied the requirement to have healthcare coverage under the Affordable Care Act. An estimated 1.3 million veterans under the age of 65 are uninsured. States that have opted into the Medicaid expansion part of the Affordable Care Act will provide access to healthcare coverage for low-income veterans, making Medicaid an additional option under the Co-Managed or Dual Care Program. Medicaid would pay, for example, for living in a medical foster home for veterans. Veterans who are eligible for Medicaid don't have to pay VA copays. Even if the state hasn't opted into the Medicaid expansion program, most states opened a Health Insurance Marketplace that has information on Medicaid as well as other options. Check www.healthcare.gov/marketplace-in-your-state/ for more information.

Supporting Veterans and Their Families

The VA's motto is "To care for him who shall have borne the battle, and for his widow, and his orphan." Taken from Abraham Lincoln's stirring second Inaugural Address, delivered one month before his assassination, these words emphasize the VA's moral obligations not only to veterans but also to their families. In today's less stirring but more precise vernacular, the motto may add, "and to his or her caregiver."

Shared decision making

Shared decision making in the VA is an integral part of patient-centered care. It is a process in which the veteran, close family members, the social worker, and the healthcare team collaborate to make healthcare and long-term care decisions. For long-term care, the goal is supporting veterans at the highest level of independence achievable by exploring home- and community-based options that address their health conditions, values, and preferences, as well as family support needs.

Shared Decision Making is introduced, along with videos, at www.va.gov/
GERIATRICS/Guide/LongTermCare/Shared_Decision_Making.asp. The site provides
two decision aids: a worksheet for veterans and a caregiver self-assessment.

>> The shared decision making worksheet guides veterans in thinking through
their needs, resources, and preferences; exploring services and settings; and
involving caregivers, social workers, healthcare providers, and others in the
process of making long-term care choices.

>> The caregiver self-assessment worksheet encourages family members and
others who help the veteran to explore their own needs and resources, in
addition to those of the veteran, and to become informed about long-term
care options so that they can more accurately assess their ability to support
the veteran's needs and choices. It includes sections on the veteran's needs,
who helps now, where the veteran wants to live, and long-term care options
he or she would consider and why they are important. Final sections include
the opinions of people who help the veteran make decisions.

Although the shared decision making process and the accompanying decision
aids are intended for veterans and their caregivers, the basic structure and most
of the questions are useful to anyone investigating long-term care.

Caregiver support

The VA has many programs and policies that support family caregivers, including
some programs that are focused on women's health and family needs. The most
significant advance in this area came through federal legislation, which in 2010
provided a monthly stipend to primary caregivers of veterans injured in military
conflict after September 11, 2001. These caregivers may be spouses but also may be
parents or other relatives. Other benefits include travel expenses to facilities
where the veteran (or before discharge, the soldier or other service member) is
being treated, access to healthcare insurance, mental-health services, and respite
care of 30 days a year.

The VA Mission Act of 2018 expanded the caregiver program to include veterans
injured in active duty prior to May 7, 1995. The program will become eligible to
veterans injured in the years between 1995 and 2001 (the Gulf War years) in about
two years. For the pre-1995 period, there will be a two-year implementation plan
during which the VA must certify that it has an effective staffing plan in place and
that it has upgraded information technology to closely track and administer
benefits.

Many services are available to all VA caregivers. Caregiver support throughout the system is described at www.caregiver.va.gov, or you can call the toll-free hotline at 855-260-3274.

Noting VA Options for Older Veterans

As the veteran population ages along with the rest of the country, the VA system has had to deal with increasing numbers of older veterans who need, in Medicaid terminology, long-term services and supports. Enrolled veterans can obtain all standard benefits and several long-term care benefits. These long-term care services and supports are described in a comprehensive VA guide on geriatrics and extended care available at www.va.gov/geriatrics. Throughout this chapter I refer to specific sections of this guide.

REMEMBER

Included services are:

>> **Geriatric evaluation:** Older veterans can receive a comprehensive assessment of their ability to manage independently, including physical health and social environment. Based on this evaluation, a plan of care can be created that includes treatment, rehabilitation, health promotion, and social services. These evaluations are performed by Inpatient Geriatric Evaluation and Management (GEM) Units at VA hospitals, geriatric primary care clinics, or other outpatient settings.

>> **Adult day healthcare:** This therapeutic daycare program provides medical and rehabilitation services to disabled veterans (www.va.gov/GERIATRICS/Guide/LongTermCare/Adult_Day_Health_Care.asp).

>> **Skilled home healthcare:** Skilled care requires the services of a nurse or other professional and is provided by the VA and contract agencies to veterans who are homebound with chronic diseases. Skilled care includes nursing, physical and occupational therapy, and social services (www.va.gov/GERIATRICS/Guide/LongTermCare/Skilled_Home_Health_Care.asp).

>> **Homemaker and home health aide services:** Trained assistants who can help the veteran with personal care in the home are available to all enrolled veterans with a clinical need. There is no time limit on the services, and the aide is supervised by a nurse (www.va.gov/GERIATRICS/Guide/LongTermCare/Homemaker_and_Home_Health_Aide_Care.asp).

>> **Home Telehealth:** This service can be used to track blood pressure, blood sugar level, weight, blood oxygen level, and heart and lung sounds. Information is transmitted to a care coordinator by landline or cellphone or by video. Equipment is provided by the VA, and the service is available to all enrolled veterans if they meet the criteria for clinical needs. There is no copay for Home Telehealth, although there may be a copay for video visits. (Find out more at www.va.gov/GERIATRICS/Guide/LongTermCare/Telehealth_Care.asp.)

>> **Hospice and palliative care:** These programs provide pain management, symptom control, and other medical services to veterans in the late stages of their diseases. Services include respite care and bereavement counseling to family members. There are no copays for hospice care in any setting (www.va.gov/GERIATRICS/Guide/LongTermCare/Hospice_and_Palliative_Care.asp).

>> **Respite care for family caregivers:** Short-term respite services are provided to give caregivers relief from the physical and emotional demands of caregiving. Respite can be provided at home or in another non-institutional setting (www.va.gov/GERIATRICS/Guide/LongTermCare/Respite_Care.asp).

The following sections describe additional options for older veterans: pensions as well as the Aid and Attendance and Housebound programs.

Receiving pensions

Pensions are funds paid to disabled veterans of wartime service who have low incomes and are no longer able to work. Finding out whether you or your parent is eligible for a VA pension is important because it can provide needed income and is the key to additional benefits for long-term care in the Aid and Attendance and Housebound programs that I discuss in the next section. VA pensions are available to surviving spouses as well as veterans.

Following are the basic requirements for eligibility for a pension:

>> At least 90 days of active duty service, with at least one day during a wartime period. For those who entered active duty after September 7, 1980, the basic requirement is to have served at least 24 months or the full period for which he or she was called, with at least one day during a wartime period.

>> In addition, the veteran must meet **one** of the following requirements:

- 65 years of age or older
- Totally and permanently disabled

- Resident in a nursing home receiving skilled nursing care
- Receiving Social Security Disability Insurance (SSDI)
- Receiving Supplemental Security Income (SSI)
- Annual family income must be less than the amount set by Congress to qualify for the Veterans Pension Benefit

For more information, go to https://benefits.va.gov/pension/. For advice on how to calculate a pension, go to www.benefits.va.gov/PENSION/pencalc.asp. Congress sets the limits for pensions, and the amount a veteran receives is determined by income, assets, and number of dependents.

TIP

Pensions are different from disability compensation, which is a monthly amount awarded to a veteran based on the extent of a service-related disability. Some disabilities and conditions that may arise after service ends but were aggravated by service also count. You can check out https://www.benefits.va.gov/COMPENSATION/ for a schedule of compensation benefits. Note that veterans of the Korean and Vietnam conflicts who were exposed to Agent Orange and other herbicides on land or on ships may be eligible for compensation on that basis. See www.publichealth.va.gov/exposures/agentorange.

Using Aid and Attendance and Housebound programs

Veterans and survivors who are eligible for a pension may also be eligible for additional services at home. Even some who are not eligible for a pension based on income may be eligible for these services. These programs have been available for many years but are not well known.

The Aid and Attendance (A&A) pension provides benefits for veterans and surviving spouses who need the daily assistance of another person to remain at home. A physician must certify that you can't function completely on your own.

Veterans and survivors may be eligible for the A&A pension if they

>> Require the aid of another person to perform activities of daily living (ADLs), to adjust prosthetic devices, or for safety. (Oddly, for an agency dealing with people who have experienced the harsh realities of wartime, the VA primly includes "attending to the wants of nature" as one of the ADLs.)

>> Are bedridden because of disability.

>> Live in a nursing home due to mental or physical incapacity.

>> Are blind or have very low vision.

The Housebound program is similar to Aid and Assistance in that it provides aid and other services in the home, but there is an additional requirement. To be eligible for the Housebound program, you must be substantially confined to home because of permanent disability, which is not a requirement for Aid and Attendance. The Housebound program is an enhanced or special monthly pension benefit paid in addition to a basic pension. A veteran or surviving spouse may not receive Aid and Attendance benefits and Housebound benefits at the same time.

REMEMBER

You can receive an additional pension benefit only for the Aid and Attendance or Housebound program, not both. When applying for either benefit, you should give sufficient detail to make a strong case that you need Aid and Attendance or are housebound. In addition, the financial assessment is rigorous and includes the value of liquid assets like cash, stocks, IRAs, 401(k) plans, other tax-deferred income, bonds, mutual funds, art, coins, stamps, and collectibles. The A&A pension regulations consider whether some or all the veteran's estate should be used to pay for care, including whether the assets can readily be converted into cash, life expectancy, number of dependents, and the potential rate of depletion of the assets, including unusual medical expenses.

TIP

Don't give up if your application for the A&A benefit is turned down on the first try. The VA often has long delays in processing disability claims in general, which it acknowledges. Because the application is complicated, many people make mistakes or leave out important information. Then they have to appeal, maybe more than once. The VA does not allow you to pay someone to help fill out the application from the outset, although it does allow you to pay for a VA-accredited professional to handle an appeal. But not all these people have sufficient training or expertise to handle appeals. VeteranAid, a nonprofit organization, recommends that instead of filing a substantive appeal, as the VA suggests, but which can take up to three years to reach a resolution, you can file a statement in support of claim, including new information or older information presented more clearly. If the claim is still denied, you can file a notice of disagreement and explain the reasons. Then, and only then, will the VA tell you why your application was denied. A full-scale substantive appeal may be the last-ditch attempt, but be prepared to wait. Go to www.VeteranAid.org for more information on the A&A program.

For more information on the A&A and Housebound programs in general, go to www.benefits.va.gov/pension/aid:attendance_housebound.asp.

Finding the Right Residential Setting or Nursing Home for Veterans

The VA has a range of options for long-term care outside the veteran's home. The following sections cover five possibilities.

Veterans' medical foster homes

Medical foster homes are private homes in which a trained caregiver provides long-term services and support to people who need round-the-clock care but don't need to be in a nursing home. The VA inspects and approves all the medical foster homes in its system, and needed medical care is provided by a VA home-based primary care team. This program is quickly expanding across the VA. For more information, see www.va.gov/GERIATRICS/Guide/LongTermCare/Medical_Foster_Homes.asp.

WARNING

The VA doesn't pay for medical foster care homes. The charge is generally about $1,500 to $3,000 a month, based on income and level of care. You'll have to pay out-of-pocket or use other insurance such as Medicaid (see Chapter 11) or long-term care insurance (see Chapter 12).

Community living facilities (nursing homes)

The VA operates 132 community living facilities (which used to be called nursing homes) across the country. Most are on or close to the campus of a VA medical center. Most community living facilities provide 24-hour skilled nursing care, restorative care, access to social-work services, and geriatric evaluation and management. Some also provide mental-health services, special care for veterans with dementia or other cognitive deficits, respite care, and palliative and hospice care. The VA's new name for nursing homes reflects its goal of making these residential settings more home-like and offering veterans more independence and flexibility.

To qualify, veterans must meet specific eligibility requirements, and the VA will pay if you meet certain criteria concerning service-connected status, level of disability, and income. You may still have a copay depending on income. Veterans eligible for Medicaid can apply to that program.

Some veterans can receive nursing-home care in non-VA facilities in the community under contract to the VA if there is a compelling medical or social need. Generally, these are short-term placements — not longer than six months — while longer-term arrangements are made. Of course, veterans with significant assets can pay out-of-pocket to live in a non-VA home.

In general, care in a community living facility is like care in a community nursing home with one exception: Most of the residents in a community nursing home are women, whereas in a VA facility they are men. Some male veterans prefer a VA facility for this reason; it is easier for them to build rapport with other men who have served in the military.

State-operated veteran homes

Every state has at least one nursing home designated for veterans. Many states have more; for example, Oklahoma has seven. Most of these homes offer nursing care, but some may offer assisted living or domiciliary care. These homes started after the Civil War, when many states created them to provide shelter for homeless and disabled veterans. Unlike the community living facilities in the previous section, the VA does not manage state veterans' homes, but it does formally review and certify the facilities each year to make sure they're following VA standards.

Eligibility is based on clinical need and available space. Each state establishes its own eligibility and admission criteria. Some state homes may admit nonveteran spouses and Gold Star parents (who have lost a child in the military). Others admit only veterans.

The cost varies by state, and the veteran is expected to pay a share of the costs. Certified state veteran homes receive some funding from the VA to cover some of the costs for veterans residing in the state home, but it does not pay for care for nonveterans. Space is limited, and an application may not result in an immediate placement. Because of costs and location, as well as a shortage of beds, a Medicaid-certified nursing home may be a better immediate choice. However, qualifying for Medicaid would require the veteran to "spend down" and go through a look-back process to see whether assets were transferred to become eligible. At this time, the VA does not require either as a condition of eligibility.

State veteran homes fall under the category of niche housing described in Chapter 8 in the sense that the residents share a history of military service that may enhance their community living experience. This sense of camaraderie is one reason veterans may prefer to go to a state veterans' home farther from their family than a nearby community nursing home. For a list of state veterans' homes, go to www.va.gov/GERIATRICS/Guide/LongTermCare/State_Veterans_Homes.asp.

The domiciliary program

The domiciliary program is the VA's oldest healthcare program. Established in the late 1860s, the domiciliary program's purpose was to provide a home for disabled volunteer soldiers of the Civil War. The domiciliary has evolved from a soldiers' home to become an active clinical rehabilitation and treatment program for veterans, especially those with mental-health or substance-abuse problems or who are homeless. Domiciliary programs are now integrated into the Mental Health Residential Rehabilitation and Treatment Programs (MH RRTPs).

The program offers both short-term rehabilitation and long-term health maintenance care. It also provides a clinically appropriate level of care for homeless veterans whose healthcare needs don't require more intensive levels of treatment. You can find out more about the care program at www.benefits.gov/benefits/benefit-details/301.

Eligibility requirements for these programs include income, the need for a structured residential environment, and the ability to participate in treatment as well as the ability to independently manage activities of daily living. The goal is to return to the community.

TRICARE For Life

The Department of Defense maintains a system of military hospitals and medical centers in the United States and overseas. TRICARE is the healthcare insurance program that covers healthcare for active-duty personnel, their families, retirees, and members of the National Guard and U.S. Army Reserve. It was formerly called CHAMPUS (Civilian Health and Medical Program of the Uniformed Services).

TRICARE For Life (TFL) offers secondary coverage to Medicare beneficiaries who have both Part A and B coverage (see Chapter 11 for more on Medicare coverage). It is available worldwide. In the United States, Medicare is the primary payer, but overseas, TRICARE is primary. TFL has no enrollment fees, but you must pay Medicare Part B monthly premiums. For services covered by both Medicare and TRICARE, there are no additional out-of-pocket costs. For more information, go to tricare.mil/tfl.

Using Other Resources to Navigate the VA System

Navigating the VA system may take time and persistence, just as it does with health insurance in the private sector or Medicare and Medicaid. In addition to the specific tips throughout this chapter, a good place to get information and assistance is a local Veterans Service Organization (VSO) for VA-specific services and a state or county office for the aging for non-VA services. VSOs are private organizations. Some serve all veterans, such as the American Legion, and some serve specific groups of veterans, such as veterans of the Navy or Air Force or African-American veterans. A VA list of VSOs can be found at www.va.gov/vso/VSO-Directory.pdf. Part I of this listing includes VSOs that have been approved to prepare and present claims to the VA on veterans' behalf.

If you still have unresolved problems, enlist your congressional representative or senator's office. They have staff experienced in assisting veterans and their families.

REMEMBER

Whatever route you take in navigating the system, be prepared with good information, thorough documentation, and patience.

IN THIS CHAPTER

» **Looking at who family caregivers are**

» **Preparing yourself for the responsibilities of the role**

» **Distinguishing different caregiver types**

» **Checking out a caregiver's CareMap**

» **Finding resources for information and support**

Chapter **20**

Family Caregivers

An estimated 80 to 90 percent of future care in the community is provided by unpaid family members. Even when older adults move from their own homes to assisted-living or skilled nursing facilities, family members continue to play an important, albeit different, role. Despite the changes in family structures that exist today and the vastly different healthcare system that makes caregiving different from earlier eras, family ties are still central to most people's lives. And at no time does this become more meaningful than in times of illness or need.

If you are or may become a family caregiver for a parent or other relative, you'll encounter many rewards as well as challenges. And if you're the person needing assistance, you too may face challenges in acknowledging your need for help and adapting to a new relationship.

Each family and each caregiving situation is different. Yet there are some common themes. This chapter stresses both of these ideas. It is intended as a supplement to other chapters that address issues of importance to family caregivers, such as staying in your home (see Chapter 5), Medicare and Medicaid (see Chapter 11), home care (see Chapter 15), and skilled nursing facilities (see Chapter 16).

Defining Family Caregivers

Family caregiver is a relatively new term. It refers to a person who provides unpaid care for a relative, partner, or friend who needs help because of illness, disability, or advanced age. It is a broad term, intended to include people in nontraditional relationships as well as people related by blood or marriage. A caregiver may or may not live with the person needing assistance. Although caregiving traditionally has been considered a woman's role and women still make up the majority of caregivers, men are increasingly taking on this responsibility. Today 40 percent of caregivers are men.

One distinguishing feature is that family caregivers for the most part are unpaid. They take on this role because of love, duty, or religious or cultural traditions. Most have no training for this role, and even many of those who are healthcare or social-service professionals find that their training doesn't prepare them for the emotional impact of caring for a person close to them.

REMEMBER

Some researchers and policymakers call people in this category *informal caregivers* to distinguish them from paid or formal caregivers such as nurses and physical therapists. Other people prefer the term *care partner* or *caretaker*. The term *carer* is used in the United Kingdom and some other countries. In this chapter, I use the term *family caregiver,* recognizing that you may come across other terms.

Family caregivers by the numbers

How many family caregivers are there? Estimates vary, depending on the way the question is asked and the research method used to come up with the answer. The broadest answer is that one in five Americans is caring for an adult over the age of 18.

Despite the challenges, many caregivers feel rewarded by their caregiving, usually because of a deeper relationship with the person needing assistance or because caregiving offers spiritual or emotional growth.

About 42.1 million Americans provide care to an adult with limitations in daily activities at any given time, according to a 2015 AARP Public Policy Institute study, and about 61.6 million adults provided care at some point. The estimated economic value of their unpaid contributions was approximately $470 billion in 2013, a figure that is greater than the total of institutional care and community-based care combined. (If you're interested in finding out the details, you can see the report "Valuing the Invaluable: 2015 Update" at www.aarp.org/content/dam/aarp/ppi/2015/valuing-the-invaluable-2015-update-new.pdf.)

These numbers are so big that they may not seem relevant to you as an individual. To put it into perspective, if you're a family caregiver, you're one of millions of people who are having the same problems and the same experiences. Even though you may feel isolated, you are not alone. And in addition to the assistance you're providing to a family member or more than one person, you're an unpaid part of the elder-care workforce. Family caregivers are often called the foundation or bedrock of long-term care, and these statistics back up that designation.

Although caregivers are found in every age group, including children and teenagers and people in their 70s and 80s, the average age is 49. Recently, greater attention is being devoted to caregivers who are "millennials" age 18 to 34. Among millennial caregivers, more than half are members of minority groups. Almost three in four are employed, but one in three earn less than $30,000 a year. See AARP's report on this group at www.aarp.org/content/dam/aarp/ppi/2018/05/ millennial-family-caregivers.pdf. About one in four family caregivers surveyed in the 2015 report cited earlier is a millennial.

No matter their age, caregivers need to take care of themselves. Unsurprisingly, given the burden the role can place on them, family caregivers may experience serious mental-health consequences. As many as 70 percent may experience depression and anxiety. These strains are most common among women, older caregivers, low-income caregivers, and those with a high level of burden based on hours spent and kinds of tasks. An estimated 17 to 35 percent of family caregivers rate their own health as poor. Studies have shown that family caregivers tend to neglect their own health, not visiting their own doctors or taking their own medications. They are more susceptible than non-caregivers to poor immune-system responses, back and muscle problems, and worsening of chronic conditions.

Taking care of the caregiver is the topic of AARP's *Meditations for Caregivers: Practical, Emotional, and Spiritual Support for You and Your Family.*

ARE WE IN THE GOLDEN AGE OF CAREGIVING?

The AARP Public Policy Institute has warned that the *caregiver support ratio* — the number of potential caregivers for each older adult — is now at a peak level. In 2010, the United States had more than seven potential caregivers age 45 to 64 for every person age 80 and older. By 2030, as the baby boomers age, that number will have dropped to four to one; by 2050, when all baby boomers will be in the high-risk years of later life, it will fall even further to less than three to one. These numbers simply give broad population data indicating the number of *potential* caregivers per care recipient. Yet many caregivers carry the burden alone, and as the care ratio lessens in the future, the chances of being a lone caregiver will be even greater. For the full report, go to www.aarp.org/ home-family/caregiving/info-08-2013/the-aging-of-the-baby-boom- and-the-growing-care-gap-AARP-ppi-ltc.html.

What family caregivers do

REMEMBER

A comprehensive and detailed list of responsibilities for family caregivers would take up the rest of this chapter and more. Basically, family caregivers do whatever needs to be done. For a succinct list, the AARP report "Valuing the Invaluable" outlines what the new normal in caregiving entails:

» Providing companionship and emotional support (often overlooked but an essential element in the relationship)

» Helping with household tasks, such as preparing meals

» Handling bills and dealing with insurance claims

» Carrying out personal care, such as bathing and dressing

» Being responsible for nursing procedures, such as IV infusions and wound care, in the home

» Administering and managing multiple medications, including injections

» Identifying, arranging, and coordinating services and supports

» Hiring and supervising direct-care workers

» Arranging for or providing transportation to medical appointments and community services

» Communicating with health professionals

» Serving as advocate for their loved one during medical appointments or hospitalizations

» Implementing care plans

» Playing a key role of care coordinator during transitions, especially from hospital to home

Not every family caregiver is required to do all these tasks all the time, but family caregiving is a dynamic process. New challenges, requiring new skills, can arise on short notice.

The conventional way of describing caregiver tasks is to divide them into ADLs (activities of daily living) and IADLs (instrumental activities of daily living). ADLs include bathing and dressing, and IADLs include shopping and transportation. While important, these categories don't cover the wide range of medical/nursing tasks that family caregivers are expected to perform at home. An AARP/United Hospital Fund national survey found that nearly half of the caregivers (46 percent) performed one or more tasks like managing complex medications, changing surgical dressings, and operating medical equipment such as feeding tubes. They also helped with ADLs and IADLs.

WHAT FAMILY CAREGIVERS FIND HARD TO DO

In the AARP/United Hospital Fund "Home Alone" survey, caregivers who performed medical/nursing tasks were asked to name two tasks that they found hard to do. The following were the top responses:

- Using incontinence supplies and administering enemas
- Caring for wounds or treating pressure sores or postsurgical wounds
- Managing medications
- Preparing food for special diets
- Operating medical equipment
- Helping with assistive devices for mobility
- Using meters, monitors, test kits, and telehealth equipment
- Operating durable medical equipment

The majority of respondents had no formal training to do these tasks and said they learned at least in part on their own how to do them. As medical care at home becomes more complex, new training and support programs are needed to assist family caregivers with these challenging tasks and others. I refer you to AARP's instructive videos at www.aarp.org/ppi/initiatives/home-alone-alliance.

Being a family caregiver today is more than serving chicken soup and fluffing pillows. You can find a video series that instructs family caregivers on how to perform complex medical and nursing tasks at www.aarp.org/ppi/initiatives/home-alone-alliance. The report, called "Home Alone: Family Caregivers Providing Complex Chronic Care," is available at www.aarp.org/content/dam/aarp/research/public_policy_institute/health/home-alone-family-caregivers-providing-complex-chronic-care-rev-AARP-ppi-health.pdf. (An update is expected in 2019.)

Family caregivers' rights and obligations

Although some family caregiver advocates have developed lists of caregiver rights, these are mostly statements about how caregivers should be treated and what they should expect from others. They are aspirations rather than actual rights that can be enforced. The following sections go into more detail about caregivers' rights and obligations.

Rights

Regrettably, the list of legal family caregiver rights is quite small. Even so, caregivers may have significant legal rights related to some aspects of their responsibilities. For example, if you have been named the attorney in fact (or agent), you have the right to manage the financial matters specified in the document. Or if you have been named your parent's healthcare proxy, you have the right to make healthcare decisions if he or she is unable to do so.

REMEMBER

One important right comes from the Health Insurance Accountability and Portability Act (HIPAA), a 1996 federal law that protects the privacy of a patient's medical information. According to the law, unless the patient objects, healthcare professionals can share relevant information with a family member or other person directly involved in the patient's care or paying for care. This is especially important in hospitals and other facilities where staff may be reluctant to share information, even with the patient. For more information about HIPAA, see the United Hospital Fund's guide at www.nextstepincare.org/Caregiver_Home/HIPAA.

The findings of the "Home Alone" survey led AARP to consider what legislative steps can help caregivers when family members were hospitalized and planning to return home. The result was the Caregiver Advise, Record, Enable (CARE) Act, which is now law in 42 states and territories. Although the language of the law differs from state to state, these are the key elements:

>> As soon as possible on admission to a hospital, a patient is asked if he or she wishes to identify a person (a caregiver) who will be able to help at home.

>> If the patient names a caregiver, the caregiver's contact information is entered in the electronic health record.

>> With the patient's permission (in some states, it must be in writing), healthcare providers can share relevant medical information with the caregiver.

>> The caregiver should be notified when a discharge date is determined.

>> The caregiver should be given instruction in the tasks he or she will be providing at home.

TIP

There is a map of states with CARE Act legislation at www.aarp.org/politics-society/advocacy/caregiving-advocacy/info-2014/aarp-creates-model-state-bill.html and a report for the AARP Public Policy Institute on the implementation of the legislation at blog.aarp.org/2017/08/29/154354/.

Obligations

The other side of rights is, of course, obligations. A caregiver's primary obligation is to advocate for family members and ensure that they receive adequate, appropriate, and good-quality care, including protection from abuse. If you have a power of attorney for financial affairs, you have a legal duty to act in the best interests of your family member and to avoid conflicts of interest. That means, for one thing, that you can't use the money for your own expenses, even if you fully intend to pay it back, unless there is an explicit agreement that allows you to do this.

Unless adult children have been legally designated a parent's guardian, they do not generally have financial obligations to their parents. However, 20 states and Puerto Rico have so-called *filial responsibility* laws, mostly dating from the 1800s, that establish this responsibility, except in extreme cases of hardship or prior abuse. Although these laws are rarely enforced, they do exist and you should be aware of them.

PROTECTING YOUR FAMILY MEMBER FROM ABUSE AND NEGLECT

Abuse may be physical, verbal, financial, or sexual. These problems can arise at home as well as in nursing homes and assisted-living facilities, so it is particularly important to be aware of the potential for abuse when hiring workers to help you. Background checks and references are helpful but only a start. Frequent monitoring is essential.

Sometimes family caregivers are unaware of neglect by home care or nursing-home workers because they see only their family member's clean face and combed hair and not the underlying problems of bedsores or other warning signs. Although you may feel intrusive and uncomfortable, it is important to check for these problems. If left untreated, bedsores can lead to serious infections and hospitalizations.

Neglect is in some ways harder to deal with than outright abuse. Most cases of neglect among older adults are self-neglect when the person fails to bathe, change clothes, eat regular meals, and keep the kitchen and bathroom clean. He or she generally falls into a pattern of being disheveled and dirty and living with hoards of papers and junk. Often when someone gets to this state of inability to care for herself, there is some underlying dementia or mental illness. If not addressed (and it is not easy), these problems can lead to removal from the home. If you live with the person, you may be considered abusive because you did not take preventive action. Neighbors may complain and call the police or Adult Protective Services. To avoid these drastic and upsetting actions, it is important to involve outside assistance, such as a social worker or psychologist, early on.

Lawsuits are most likely to be initiated by nursing homes when the resident has not applied for Medicaid or has been turned down. In a 2012 Pennsylvania case, a son was held liable for more than $92,000 in nursing-home costs incurred by his mother while she was waiting for Medicaid approval, which was eventually denied. The judgment was upheld on appeal. On the other hand, a Montana court ruled in favor of a son who was being sued for $15,000 for his mother's nursing-home costs. Legislators in some states, including Pennsylvania, are trying to repeal their filial responsibility laws. New Hampshire, for example, repealed its law in 2013.

Spouses are legally responsible for each other's bills and other obligations. Medicaid statutes vary, but most allow spouses of Medicaid recipients to retain some funds for their own use.

Becoming a Family Caregiver

Taking on the role of family caregiver is a big and even life-changing event. You may even be performing many of the duties without even recognizing that you're acting as a caregiver. This section helps you identify the role of caregiver and discusses the importance of negotiation skills in this role.

TIP

If you have no family to rely on, you can turn to friends and people from community groups, such as faith-based organizations, disease organizations, and social-service agencies. Many caregivers find that support groups are helpful ways to meet people who understand their circumstances and can provide emotional as well as practical support.

Identifying yourself as a family caregiver

Family caregivers themselves often do not recognize that they are doing anything beyond what a daughter, son, spouse, partner, or friend should do for someone who is ill or needs assistance. In the jargon of caregiving, they do not *self-identify.*

REMEMBER

Even when they do recognize themselves in the description of what family caregivers do, they may worry that identifying themselves as family caregivers means in some way giving up the primary relationship. My response to this concern is that *family* is who you are in relation to the person needing assistance, and that doesn't change; *caregiver* is your role, and that does change over time and as the person improves or becomes sicker.

Here is a quick family caregiver identification test: Do you regularly or occasionally

>> Take care of someone who has a chronic illness, disability, or disease?

>> Manage medications?

>> Talk to doctors or nurses on someone's behalf?

>> Help bathe or dress someone who is frail, is disabled, or needs assistance?

>> Take care of household chores, meals, or bills for someone who can't do these things alone?

>> Accompany someone who is ill or frail to a doctor's appointment?

>> Provide emotional support to someone who is ill or frail?

If you answered yes to any of these questions, you are a family caregiver. Chances are that if you're reading this book because of your concern for another person, you are or will become a family caregiver. And looking ahead, perhaps one day, you may need a family caregiver.

Readying yourself for negotiation

In addition to the managerial, technical, and organizational skills it takes to be a family caregiver, add negotiating skills. As a family caregiver, you must navigate the tricky shoals of a changed and sometimes rocky relationship with your family member. That person may be resistant to help, uncooperative, and even aggressive or hostile. Perhaps this behavior is an exaggeration of qualities that existed before the illness or disability; perhaps it stems from depression or dementia. Whatever the cause, it takes extreme patience and new ways of communicating to work out caregiving routines that are less stressful for both of you.

REMEMBER

Another form of negotiation is required when dealing with healthcare professionals on whom you and your family member depend for treatment, advice, and support. They may or may not recognize your deep knowledge about the person in front of them, and they may not include you in decision making, even though the decision affects you as well as the patient. Being an advocate for your family member at times means being an advocate for yourself. This is particularly important when caregiving requires understanding complex medication regimens, performing procedures, and other technical tasks. Sometimes professionals describe something as *simple*, which it may be for them, but not for you.

Managing the financial aspects of care, including dealing with insurance companies, banks, transportation services, and government agencies, can also require persistence and negotiating skills.

REMEMBER

Finally, if you have other family members, whether they are involved in caregiving or not, you need negotiating skills to deal with them. In several earlier chapters, I stress the importance of transparency in money matters, living arrangements, and all the details that go into chronic care. Some families are brought closer by an illness and share the responsibilities equitably, which means that each person does the best that he or she can, given their financial, familial, and employment circumstances. Sometimes, however, illness tears families apart. The situation may eventually turn into a crisis, usually over money or end-of-life decisions. The situation can be even more difficult for estranged family members. If reasonable efforts to share information and responsibilities are not working out, then an objective family or eldercare mediator may be needed.

TIP

For guidance in managing conflict, see AARP's *Common Caregiving Conflicts* care guide, free at www.aarp.org/careguides.

Checking Out Different Types of Family Caregivers

Family caregivers come in all ages, and from different backgrounds and cultures. Some may be otherwise employed and perform caregiver duties in addition to their daily job; others may have cultural differences that make caring for an older or ill person even more challenging. The next few sections help you navigate the trials that many caregivers face.

Family caregivers who are employed

The 2015 National Alliance for Caregiving/AARP survey of family caregivers found that more than half (59 percent) of all family caregivers are employed full- or part-time in a position in addition to their caregiver responsibilities. In addition to their full- or part-time job, they spent on average 20 hours a week caring for a family member. In addition to the conventional measures of caregiving — doing ADLs and IADLs — a separate analysis of the "Home Alone" survey respondents described earlier in this chapter found that employed caregivers are also performing the same range of medical/nursing tasks as their non-employed counterparts.

Employed family caregivers who managed medications considered it one of their two hardest tasks because it took so much time, was inconvenient, or both. Employed family caregivers who performed medical/nursing tasks were more likely than non-employed caregivers to report that juggling the demands of caregiving with their other responsibilities caused them stress (61 percent versus 49 percent). The number of tasks they performed also increased the levels of stress. The report is available at www.aarp.org/home-family/caregiving/info-11-2013/employed-family-caregivers-providing-complex-chronic-care-AARP-ppi-health.html.

Beyond the stresses of daily life, employed caregivers may give up opportunities for travel or advancement, and they may fear disclosing their caregiving role to employers.

TIP

Keeping caregiving a secret is hard to do in a busy workplace. If you're constantly distracted and not paying attention to your job, people will notice, and it will likely be attributed to poor work habits or a bad attitude. It is better, if possible, to discuss your caregiving situation frankly with your employer and your coworkers and try to reach reasonable accommodations. Your caregiving affects them as well. This is easier in some jobs than in others. Try to keep any caregiving responsibilities you need to do during your working hours to a minimum, and do everything you can to keep your family member's home situation as stable as possible.

WARNING

Well-meaning friends and other family members may urge you to quit your job, or even expect that you will. Think very hard before you make this move. Although it may seem the only way to manage, it is a big step. Family caregivers who leave their jobs or go to part-time status make a financial sacrifice, not only in terms of lost income at the time but also in future benefits such as Social Security or contributions to retirement plans. Many caregivers find that their caregiving tenure lasts a lot longer than they anticipated and that it is very hard to return to the workplace at the same level at which they left, if they can find employment at all. And many caregivers gain much more than money from their jobs; it is a meaningful and necessary part of their lives.

When the Families and Work Institute asked employed family caregivers for their top wishes for the way in which workplaces can better support them, their responses were

>> Greater flexibility

>> More options for managing time

>> Time off for elder care, especially time off without having to use up vacation time

>> More understanding of their situation from management

For now, these wishes are only partially fulfilled and only for some employed caregivers.

TIP

AARP's *Juggling Life, Work, and Caregiving* by Amy Goyer, at www.aarp.org/caregivingbooks, is a poignant and comprehensive resource for caregivers who work. You can also find information on how to balance work and caregiving at www.aarp.org/caregiving/life-balance/info-2017/work-benefits-rights.html.

The following sections describe a few programs designed to help employed family caregivers.

The Family and Medical Leave Act

The Family and Medical Leave Act (FMLA), a federal law enacted in 1993, guarantees up to 12 weeks a year of unpaid leave for workers to take care of their own health needs or to take care of family members. The leave doesn't have to be taken all at one time. This is an important right, but it applies only to people working in businesses with more than 50 employees, and it limits the family members needing care to spouses, children, or parents. Grandparents and siblings, for example, are not covered. FMLA has most often been used when a period of leave time can be planned — for example, by new parents. Family caregiving for an older adult is more episodic, and it is more difficult to arrange short times away from work. And of course, FMLA is unpaid leave, which makes it hard for even those who are eligible to take advantage of the law. For more information, go to the U.S. Department of Labor at www.dol.gov/whd/fmla.

TIP

Some employers have leave policies even if not required by law. Check with your manager or HR representative to find out your company's policies. Employed caregivers should always find out what FMLA policies are, regardless of the size of the company.

Paid family leave insurance

In January 2018, New York became the fourth state in the nation to offer paid family leave insurance to eligible working caregivers. Rhode Island, California, and New Jersey already had this policy, which offers full or partial income replacement while a worker is at home taking care of a personal health condition, adjusting to a new child, or taking care of a family member with serious health needs. In Hawaii, the Kuhuna (grandparent) law gives employed caregivers a daily allowance that they can use to access services for their relatives.

ReACT

ReACT (Respect a Caregiver's Time), begun in 2010, is a coalition of corporations and organizations dedicated to addressing the challenges faced by employed caregivers. AARP and the National Alliance for Caregiving created a tool kit and resource guide for employers that describes how many companies have created more caregiver-friendly workplaces. Although intended for employers, the tool kit is helpful for caregivers to assess their own workplace and suggest better policies. Go to https://respectcaregivers.org/.

PROTECTING FAMILY CAREGIVERS FROM WORKPLACE DISCRIMINATION

Family caregivers may experience discrimination (real or perceived) in the workplace because of their need to take time off to attend to their family member. A patchwork of federal, state, and local laws attempts to address this problem, but policies and enforcement are inconsistent. The U.S. Equal Employment Opportunity Commission (EEOC) in 2007 issued guidance to employers intended to prevent discrimination because of pregnancy, parenting, and caring for aging parents or ill or disabled spouses or family members.

The most common forms of employment protection today for employed family caregivers caring for older adults are local laws. According to the University of California's Center for WorkLife Law, at least 67 localities in 22 different states have laws that prohibit discrimination against employees with certain family responsibilities. For a list, see www.aarp.org/content/dam/aarp/research/public_policy_institute/health/protecting-caregivers-employment-discrimination-insight-AARP-ppi-ltc.pdf. Of these, more than half cover only childcare. Only seven laws explicitly recognize employed caregivers with elder-care responsibilities. In 2013, Vermont and San Francisco passed laws that create a formal mechanism for workers to inquire about altering their work schedules. While neither law requires employers to agree to the request, they both protect caregivers from retaliation or discrimination.

Long-distance family caregivers

The U.S. National Institute on Aging defines long-distance caregivers as those who live an hour or more away from the person and estimates that as many as 7 million people may fall into that category. Family caregivers who live with the person needing assistance are constantly on the job, but family caregivers who live at a distance from the person needing assistance face a different source of stress: relying on episodic visits to evaluate the situation and on reports from the person or others about what is needed. They also face the additional costs of travel and phone calls, and perhaps the need for paid help for their parent or other relative or to care for pets. A long-distance caregiver who is also employed and has children to take care of has a triple dose of stress.

Some long-distance caregivers react to the constant stress by thinking that the only solution is to move the parent or other relative into their own home, or even to pull up stakes and move to the parent's location. Yet this may not be the best solution, either for the older adult or for the caregiver and his or her family. See Chapter 6 on multigenerational households for more information and advice if this is something you are considering.

TIP

AARP has a helpful list of tips to manage long-distance caregiving at `www.aarp.org/relationships/caregiving-resource-center/info-09-2010/pc_tips_for_long_distance_caregiver.html` and a more comprehensive care guide at `www.aarp.org/careguides`. Tips include the following:

>> Create a contact list of addresses and phone numbers of all the people who are in regular contact with your parent or other relative, and include at least one person who can (and is willing to) check in daily.

>> Collect important information before a crisis, including medication lists, names and numbers of regularly seen doctors, health-insurance information, utility information (including cable, phone, and Internet), and relevant financial and legal details.

>> Make your visits productive by planning ahead to take care of priority items like visiting doctors, shopping for essentials, and checking for safety hazards.

>> Gather information on community services that can help with transportation, adult daycare, home-delivered meals, counseling, and other services.

At some point, you may decide you need a geriatric care manager or social worker to help coordinate care, especially if your parent needs in-home help.

TIP

The U.S. National Institute on Aging's report, "Long-Distance Caregiving: Twenty Questions and Answers," has extensive lists of resources and stories about people in similar situations. It is available at `https://order.nia.nih.gov/sites/default/files/2017-07/L-D-Caregiving_508.pdf`.

Multicultural caregivers

Family caregivers from ethnic, cultural, and religious minorities may face special challenges as they try to integrate their family traditions and beliefs into a health-care system that is not well suited to recognizing and adapting to these differences.

In some families, perhaps in yours, English is not the primary language, even for the family caregiver. Getting accurate information from professionals is difficult, even when a professional interpreter is available. In extended immigrant families, there may also be differences in the degree to which some members have adapted to U.S. society. Sometimes these relate to gender roles. Other differences include willingness to accept help from people outside the family or community.

If you're a family caregiver from a multicultural family, you can do a few things to help your parent or other relative and yourself, in addition to following general advice given to all caregivers about reducing stress and asking for help. Start close to home. Try to find a local community group with staff that speaks your language and is familiar with your traditions. Some religious groups have outreach programs for older adults that can act as a bridge to healthcare professionals.

In your dealings with healthcare and social-service staff on behalf of your family member, explain how culture affects your relative's understanding of illness, including

>> What are his concepts of personal space and contact — how close is too close? Is physical contact, such as a handshake or an embrace, taboo?

>> What is the appropriate way to address the person?

>> Who counts as family? Are there specific decision makers (who may or may not be the people who carry out the daily tasks of caregiving)?

>> What are customs and taboos around food?

>> What is understood as the cause of this disease? What treatments are acceptable? What kinds of alternative treatments are being used?

TIP

Dementia has different meanings in different cultures. Ethnic Elders Care, a network devoted to information and resources about dementia in multicultural older adults, has tips for caregivers at ethnicelderscare.net/.

As a family caregiver in these situations, you have the additional responsibility of making it easier for your family member to accept the help that is needed and to advise staff on how to provide respectful and appropriate care.

Looking at Your Caregiving Experience through a CareMap

The CareMap (introduced in Chapter 2) is a new tool that is available online at atlasofcaregiving.com/caremap to help you determine the people in your circle who help you and those who you help. It was created by Atlas of Caregiving as part of a research project to understand what caregivers really do all day long. You can draw your CareMap by hand, as the earliest users did, using a sheet of paper and a pencil and adding simple icons to represent people and services. There is also a digital version online for people who are comfortable with computers. You may ask someone to help you as you become more confident. A video tutorial provides step-by-step guidance.

Here are the basics of creating a CareMap: Starting with you at the center, you draw your home, adding people who help you daily, weekly, or periodically, and people you help. You can add pets who both provide emotional support and need care. You can add people who live close by, at a middle distance, and farther away. Needed services like doctors, transportation, and food delivery can also be added. At the end you have a picture that shows what exists in your life and, equally important, what's missing.

The CareMap in Figure 20-1 looks complicated. That's because Christi and Mike, the couple at the center of the CareMap, care for several people in different locations and with different intensity. But it's no more complicated — and probably even less so — than other real-life caregiving situations.

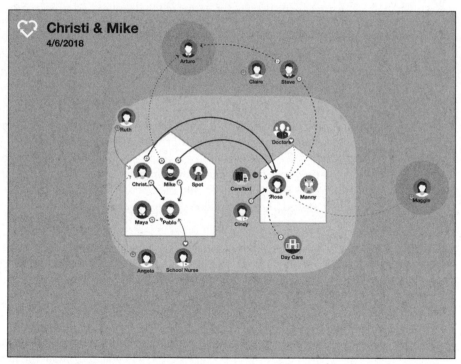

Illustration courtesy of Atlas of Caregiving

FIGURE 20-1: Christi and Mike's CareMap describes their caregiving responsibilities.

Note: You can compare Lucy's CareMap in Chapter 2 with this one. That CareMap was intended to show how CareMaps can be used to help people think about their future by drawing the people and services that are most important to them.

In this example, Christi and Mike have two children at home: Maya and Pablo. Pablo has diabetes and asthma and is monitored by a school nurse. They also have a dog named Spot, who is a great source of emotional support to Pablo. Maya is a good big sister to Pablo; she helps him with his homework and makes sure he takes his medications if Christi is not around. Christi's good friends Ruth and Angela are her main outside sources of support.

Mike's mother, Rosa, lives next door and requires a lot of assistance because she is frail and has increasing signs of dementia. The heavier lines linking Christi and Mike with Rosa indicate frequent visits. Manny, Rosa's cat, is also in the picture. A home care aide, Cindy, spends a few hours most weekdays. Rosa attends an adult daycare center with transportation by a taxi. Because of her health condition, she sees several doctors regularly.

Mike is also involved in the care of his father, Arturo, but Arturo lives far away in another state (indicated by the darker background) so he can provide only limited personal help. Another brother, Steve, and his wife, Claire, also care for Arturo, visit Rosa occasionally, and pay for some of Rosa's household expenses. Maggie, Rosa's only daughter, is less involved.

Looking at their CareMap, Christi and Mike realize that this situation is fragile and that they will soon need to find other sources of support for Rosa, possibly live-in help or a move to a facility that can provide more intensive kinds of assistance.

Looking for Help

Family caregiving shouldn't be a solo performance. But where do you find the supporting players? For some caregivers, asking for help isn't easy, and the help that is available may not be what is needed. The following sections can help you in your search.

Family and friends

This may seem obvious, but it isn't always easy to ask for and get help from those who are the closest to you. Sometimes caregivers are asked why they don't get their family to help more, but this deceptively simple question steps on a huge emotional land mine. Some families cooperate without any hesitation or difficulty; in others, sharing responsibility is fraught with emotional traps. Some caregivers choose, for their own reasons, not to rely on other family members; others would like the help but either don't get it or find it comes with too many conditions.

TIP

A trained professional (such as a family or eldercare mediator or perhaps a geriatric care manager or social worker) can mediate and perhaps work out an acceptable division of labor. You can find a certified geriatric care manager in your area by going to the Aging Life Care Association website (formerly the National Association of Professional Geriatric Care Managers) at www.caremanager.org/. Some health systems have social workers on staff, and you can find the local chapter of the National Association of Social Workers at www.socialworkers.org/About/Chapters/Find-a-Chapter. That office may be able to refer you to social workers who specialize in geriatrics. I also refer you to AARP's *Common Caregiving Conflicts* care guide, free at www.aarp.org/careguides.

On major issues like housing, finances, and medical decisions, early, ongoing, and honest discussions with close family members can reduce the likelihood of tension and perhaps result in more equitable caregiving arrangements. But there is no guarantee.

When some family members aren't closely involved in care, they may say things like, "I don't see what you're complaining about. Dad seems fine to me." Elderly dads and moms have an uncanny ability to marshal their resources for the occasional visit of the out-of-town or uninvolved child, making the caregiving child's accounts of their behavior seem unreasonable. This statement has many variations: "Dad has always gotten lost and driven too fast"; "Mom never can balance a checkbook"; "I forget things too." Less-involved siblings should make a point of dropping in unannounced and staying for a long enough time to see how Mom or Dad acts under everyday circumstances.

Sometimes friends will say, "Just call me if you need some help" or "I want there were something I can do to help." Most caregivers have learned that imprecise, indefinite, offhand offers of help are expressions of goodwill but that it may be up to the caregivers to nail down an offer. Many people may want to help but don't know exactly what is needed, so it's up to caregivers to think about specific ways others can help.

Friends or other family members who really want to help should make specific offers such as "I'm going to the farmer's market; can I bring you some vegetables?"; "How about if I stay with Mom on Saturday so you can do some shopping or go to a movie?"; or "I know it's hard for you to get out for dinner, so I'd like to bring dinner to you one night this week." These acts of assistance are small things; the list can get progressively more complex and demanding. But whatever the offer, it should be firm.

Federal programs

Two federal programs provide help to family caregivers. The first, the National Family Caregiver Support Program (NFCSP), established in 2000, provides grants to states and territories, based on their share of the population age 70 and over, to fund a range of supports that assist family caregivers to care for their relatives at home for as long as possible.

The NFCSP offers

>> Information to caregivers about available services

>> Assistance to caregivers in gaining access to the services

>> Individual counseling, organization of support groups, and caregiver training

>> Respite care (time off from caregiving)

>> Supplemental services, such as home modification, on a limited basis

The following people are eligible for NFCSP services:

>> Adult family members or other informal caregivers age 18 and older providing care to individuals 60 years of age and older

>> Adult family members or other informal caregivers age 18 and older providing care to individuals of any age with Alzheimer's disease and related disorders

>> Grandparents and other relatives (not parents) 55 years of age and older providing care to children under the age of 18

>> Grandparents and other relatives (not parents) 55 years of age and older providing care to adults age 18 to 59 with disabilities

The NFCSP is implemented at a local level through Area Agencies on Aging. To find your local AAA, call Eldercare Locator at 1-800-677-1116 or go to https:// eldercare.acl.gov/Public/Index.aspx.

TECHNICAL STUFF

The NFCSP's assistance is limited by a lack of funding, which has been stuck at around $153 million since 2008. The 2018 bipartisan budget bill increased this amount by $300 million.

The second federal program, the Lifespan Respite Care Act of 2006, provides ways for caregivers to have some time off, whether that is a few hours, a day, or longer. The program provides for

>> Lifespan respite programs at the state and local levels

>> Planned and emergency respite for family caregivers

>> Training/recruitment of respite workers and volunteers

>> Provision of information to caregivers about respite/support services

>> Assistance for caregivers in gaining access to these services

>> Establishment of a National Resource Center on Lifespan Respite Care and the ARCH (Access to Respite Care and Help) National Respite Network and Resource Center

The program is administered through state coalitions. To find respite services in your area, go to https://archrespite.org/us-map for an interactive map.

TIP

Respite is probably the most often requested service by family caregivers, and yet one of the least used. Many caregivers are reluctant to leave a family member with strangers, and many ill family members resist the idea of someone else taking over, even for a short time. If you use a respite service, ask about the background and training of the workers, how they handle emergencies, and how they match workers with clients. Sometimes other family members can take over while the caregiver takes a break. Unless these family members are well acquainted with the routines and enjoy a good relationship with the person being cared for, it may not be a good experience for all.

State programs

Most states have their own programs of caregiver support and services. Some of them are under the broad heading of *home and community-based services,* in which caregiver services are an adjunct to the primary purpose of assisting an older person or someone with a disability, who generally must be eligible for Medicaid. Some states have respite programs for caregivers whose family member is enrolled in the basic Home and Community-Based Services program.

Some states have *cash and counseling programs* that allow a person on Medicaid and eligible for home care to hire and pay family members to provide the care. Many states won't pay spouses under these programs. If this is an option you want to explore, check with your local Medicaid office.

Community-based organizations

Organizations in your community are an important source of assistance. Although the services are directed toward the person needing assistance, they also benefit the family caregiver. These organizations may be religious groups, senior centers, veterans' groups, or disease-specific organizations or be organized around some other characteristic. They typically offer services like transportation, friendly visiting, minor home repairs, snow removal, yardwork, and similar chores. Home-delivered meals and homemaker services may also be available. Many enlist volunteers from the community.

Senior centers often have caregiver events and informational sessions. They may have exercise and fitness programs, nutrition advice, counseling on legal and financial matters, and other useful programs. Adult daycare programs are also valuable resources for people who can attend.

Usually the most comprehensive and up-to-date source for your community is the Area Agency on Aging (AAA), which you can find via https://eldercare. acl.gov/Public/Index.aspx.

Internet resources

Search for the phrase "family caregiver" on the Internet, and you can spend hours going through the options. Many websites are valuable sources of information, and many are marketing tools (which can be valuable if you're in the market for one of their products). You'll find a lot of repetition, which can be reassuring or annoying. You'll also find a heavy dose of cheerleading, which you may appreciate or dislike. After several forays into this world, you will figure out which sites are useful to you and which you can skip.

With apologies to all the excellent online resources I am not listing, I recommend that you start with these four:

>> **AARP Caregiving Resource Center** (www.aarp.org/caregiving in English, www.aarp.org/cuidar in Spanish): This site has a wealth of topics, blogs, advice, and a call-in number (1-877-333-5885 in English, 1-888-971-2013 in Spanish) with extended hours (7 a.m. to 11 p.m. Eastern time, Monday to Friday). AARP also has an online community devoted to caregiving at www.aarp.org/caregivingcommunity.

>> **The Alzheimer's Association** (www.alz.org): This site has information for caregivers in many different categories and an interactive map of chapters at www.alz.org/apps/findus.asp. Local chapters of the organization have their own websites.

» **Family Caregiver Alliance** (www.caregiver.org/caregiver/jsp/home.jsp): This San Francisco–based organization has guides and fact sheets on many topics related to family caregiving in English, Spanish, and Chinese. The FCA Family Care Navigator has a map of resources by state available at www.caregiver.org/caregiver/jsp/fcn_content_node.jsp?nodeid=2083.

» **Next Step in Care** (www.nextstepincare.org): This website, created by the United Hospital Fund, has free guides in four languages (English, Spanish, Chinese, and Russian) for family caregivers on navigating the healthcare system, especially during transitions, and a Links and Resources section with categories for national organizations, government agencies, and disease-specific organizations.

REMEMBER

No single resource can answer all your questions. But after you understand the territory and know where to go for answers, you will be on a better path as a caregiver.

6

The Part of Tens

Discard ten myths that pervade discussions about navigating your later years. Some relate to aging itself, and others relate to financing and changing expectations.

Refer to a handy list of websites and resources that provide state-by-state information on Medicare, community services, and other troves of information about navigating your later years.

Chapter **21**

Ten Myths about Aging and Future Care

There are two kinds of myths. One is a legend or folktale passed down from one generation to the next to explain a natural occurrence like an eclipse or the creation of a culture. Many people recognize that these types of myths aren't literally true. The second kind of myth is a widely held but largely false belief that people cling to, even in the face of evidence, because it confirms a broader view of the world.

The ten myths in this chapter belong to the second group. They don't involve supernatural beings or explain the phases of the moon. They are widespread beliefs about aging and long-term care, some based on a kernel of truth, that are deeply entrenched in American society. Some are relatively harmless, but others can lead to serious misunderstandings.

Serious Memory Lapses Are Normal in Older Adults

The myth that memory loss is naturally associated with aging is deeply engrained in societal attitudes toward older adults. Sometimes the link is made in a condescending way, and sometimes even as a joke at the older person's expense.

But these so-called *senior moments* are also experienced by younger people. Who hasn't been challenged from time to time to recall the name of a movie or book or person? In an era of information overload, some facts or figures go astray. In these instances, the lost information comes back without too much delay.

Although some physiological changes explain the tendency of older people to experience temporary and occasional memory lapses, serious memory lapses are *not* normal. Some of the joking about memory loss may be displacement of anxiety about dementia. Alzheimer's disease is one of the most feared diseases of our era, arguably more dreaded than cancer.

Forgetfulness can be distinguished from early signs of Alzheimer's disease or other forms of dementia. The Alzheimer's Association says that a typical age-related change involves sometimes forgetting names or appointments but remembering them later. On the other hand, a common sign of Alzheimer's is memory loss that disrupts your daily life, especially recently learned information. Examples include forgetting important dates or events, asking for the same information over and over, and needing to rely on notes or other memory aids for things you used to handle on your own.

Similarly, many people (of all ages) make occasional errors when balancing a checkbook, but a more worrisome problem is a change in the ability to follow a familiar recipe or keep track of monthly bills.

Some problems typically associated with dementia may not be dementia but may be due to other causes. For example, difficulty reading, judging distance, and determining color may be due to cataracts or other vision problems, not a sign of Alzheimer's. Medications can cause delirium, which is a temporary condition that may be confused with dementia.

REMEMBER

Bottom line: Not everyone who grows older loses his memory, and not every incident of memory loss is a sign of dementia. However, regular and problematic memory loss is not normal and should prompt a checkup with a doctor.

Older People Fall: Not Much You Can Do about It

Falls are the primary cause of injury among older adults and often lead to serious consequences, including death. Despite the dire statistics, the belief is prevalent even among older people themselves that falls are bound to happen and are not all that big a deal. Many think it won't happen to them even though one in three older adults — about 12 million people — fall each year in the United States.

Some people believe that if they limit their activity or stay at home, they won't fall. In fact, the reverse is true. Doing strength and balance exercises to build flexibility and ordinary walking are important in preventing falls. And over half of all falls take place at home, including falls that involve head injury and hospitalizations.

Reasonably simple home modifications (removing throw rugs, installing grab bars, improving lighting) can prevent falls (see Chapter 5 for more about modifying a home). Other measures include asking a physician about side effects of medications, having vision checks, and using mobility aids like canes or walkers after being trained by a physical therapist on how best to use them.

REMEMBER

Falls are a serious risk to health and function, not a normal part of aging.

Antibiotics Are the Best Drugs for Older Adults with Coughs and Colds

Antibiotics were the first "miracle" drugs; when they were introduced in the 1940s, they saved the lives of many people with serious infections. But over time they have become prescribed so freely by doctors (often at the request of patients) that they are no longer miracles. In fact, they have created a new set of medical problems.

Antibiotics and similar drugs, together called *antimicrobial agents,* have been used so widely and for so long that the infectious organisms the antibiotics are designed to kill have adapted to them, making the drugs less effective.

How serious is this problem? Each year in the United States, at least 2 million people become infected with bacteria that are resistant to antibiotics, and at least 23,000 people die each year as a direct result of these infections. That's why doctors are now urging caution to limit the use of antibiotics.

The Centers for Disease Control and Prevention (CDC) reports that about 44 percent of antibiotics prescribed in outpatient settings such as doctors' offices go to patients with respiratory conditions such as sore throats, colds, coughs, and flu. An estimated half of these prescriptions are unnecessary. These illnesses are usually caused by a virus. Antibiotics work when the illness is caused by bacteria; they don't work against viral illnesses.

The result has been a global problem of antibiotic resistance. This affects not only individuals who become antibiotic-resistant, but it can also affect whole populations. And there is no endless line of new antibiotics coming along that will take the place of standard drugs.

TIP

What can you do? For upper respiratory infections, such as sore throats, ear infections, sinus infections, colds, and bronchitis, the CDC recommends trying to

>> Get plenty of rest

>> Drink plenty of fluids

>> Use a clean humidifier or cool mist vaporizer

>> Avoid smoking, secondhand smoke, and other pollutants (airborne chemicals or irritants)

>> Take acetaminophen, ibuprofen, or naproxen to relieve pain or fever

>> Use saline nasal spray or drops

REMEMBER

Of course, check with your doctor, who may give you specific advice about relieving symptoms. Be sure to report any serious symptoms such as fever, chills, pain, or breathing difficulties. Chances are you'll recover without an antibiotic, but if you do need one, you want it to work.

Americans Dump Their Older Relatives in Nursing Homes

The use of the word "dump" in the formulation of this myth suggests that Americans get rid of their older relatives like so much garbage by leaving them at the nursing-home door and ignoring them from then on. Often there is a comparison to other countries and cultures, where older people are presumed to live at home and are treated with great deference and respect.

TECHNICAL STUFF

This belief about other cultures also has mythic aspects. As more traditional cultures experience demographic changes that include aging and fewer children, more participation of women in the labor force, and urbanization, older patterns of caregiving are also giving way. In 2013, for example, the Chinese government felt it necessary to make visiting an older parent at least twice a year a legal requirement, not just a cultural tradition.

These are the facts: About 1.5 million people, or 4.5 percent of the U.S. population over 65, are residents in one of the nation's 15,000 nursing homes. Nursing homes are not overflowing: They operate at about 85 percent capacity, and very few (if any) new ones are being built. The percentage of older adults in nursing homes has been steadily declining even as the older population increases; in 1990 it was 5.1 percent. This decline may be related to an increase in home- and community-based services, consumer demand for in-home care, or nursing homes' focus on enrolling short-term rehab patients (paid for by Medicare and private insurance) as opposed to long-stay residents (paid for largely by Medicaid at lower rates. Even adding in the million or so people in assisted-living facilities (which do not provide nursing-home-level care), this is hardly a picture that supports the myth of abandonment.

Rather than ignoring their relatives, many family members play an important role in residents' lives, and most nursing homes have both resident and family councils. Why then does this myth persist? All it takes is one news story or anecdote about an older person being placed in a nursing home against his or her will or being ignored by family to strengthen the belief that this occurrence is common.

Many people look back to the "good old days" through a fog of nostalgia, often for a past that never really existed. Believing that Americans abandon their older relatives fits into a worldview that fears changing social structures and family relationships. That may be understandable, but this myth demeans nursing-home residents by portraying them as unloved and unwanted and their family members by suggesting they're selfish and uncaring.

Medicare Pays for All Long-Term Care

Unlike the myth about abandonment of older people, the myth that Medicare pays for all the living and care expenses you may incur as you age is more of a want than a criticism. Everyone wants it to be true; therefore, it must be. Confusion about what is and is not covered may also be a cause of this false belief. People who need assistance with personal care and other nonmedical care — the conventional view of long-term care — also need doctor and hospital and other services, especially because many of them have multiple chronic conditions as well as difficulties functioning independently. These medical services *are* covered under Medicare; the nonmedical aspects are mostly not, even when they are as essential to the person's survival as drugs and doctor visits. Change may be coming, albeit slowly, as evidence mounts that clinical outcomes are influenced by social factors as well as clinical care.

When people hear that someone has gone to a nursing home and Medicare paid the bill, the belief is reinforced. The difference is that the person was in the rehab unit of the facility for a short-term stay, not a resident in a long-stay unit.

Many chapters in this book (like Chapter 11) and other resources explain in detail just what Medicare pays and doesn't pay for, but it appears nothing brings this home as much as actually taking the first steps to create a long-term care plan. This myth is also quickly dispelled when home care agencies, assisted-living facilities, or other providers refuse to provide services not covered by Medicare unless the person or family pays. However, this is a rude awakening. Better know from the outset that — dare I say it again? — Medicare does not cover long-term care, and the failure of many Americans to take long-term care seriously and make other financial arrangements is a serious problem for many families.

Hospice Is Just a Place Where People Go to Die

Most people say that they want to die at home without "all those tubes and monitors," yet end-of-life care continues to be dominated by aggressive interventions and high costs. Medicare costs for people in the last month of life are heavily weighted toward hospital inpatient stays, including intensive care units (ICUs).

Many policy experts say the reason is Medicare's fee-for-service structure, which incentivizes technological interventions and expensive tests. But another reason relates to the myth that *hospice* is a place where people go to die. This remains a barrier for physician referrals and patients' acceptance of hospice as an alternative approach to a hospital. Hospice is often seen as giving up and abandonment. The modest proposal in health reform legislation that would have encouraged physicians to engage in voluntary end-of-life discussions with their patients (so that individuals' wishes can be known and respected), which would have included discussions of hospice and palliative care, went down in flames under the politically charged label of *death panels.*

In fact, most hospice care is given in the place the person calls home, whether that is a residence, an assisted-living facility, or a nursing home. There are some inpatient hospices as well. And hospice is a philosophy of care, not a specific course of treatment, that emphasizes the whole person, quality of life, and relief of symptoms. Hospice is a team approach, with many different professionals providing services and a strong volunteer component as well. Much hospice care is provided by families.

Although the numbers of people opting for hospice services has increased steadily (approximately 1.43 million people received hospice services in 2017), it is still often very late in the course of their disease. According to the National Hospice and Palliative Care Organization, in 2017 the median length of service was 24 days, an increase from 19.1 days in 2011. This means that half of hospice patients and their families received services for about three weeks, while half received services for more than three weeks. Very short stays do not permit the patient and family to receive the full benefits of hospice care, such as understanding the dying process, controlling pains and symptoms, and receiving counseling. Under the Medicare hospice benefit, individuals can receive care for up to six months, and sometimes even longer. Studies have shown that people enrolled in hospice live longer with a better quality of life than those who choose more aggressive options.

While hospice started as a volunteer, nonprofit system of care, it is now dominated by for-profit organizations. In 2017 67 percent of active Medicare Provider Numbers were assigned to hospice providers with for-profit tax status and 29 percent were assigned to those with not-for-profit status. Only 3.9 percent of hospices were run by the government.

Other myths around hospice include the idea that your regular physician can't be involved (not true) and that active treatments must be discontinued (true only of treatments intended to cure, not those intended to treat symptoms). Hospice focuses on the immediate needs of the person and the family by addressing all their spiritual, emotional, and physical needs.

TIP

For more information, see AARP's "Facts about Hospice" at www.aarp.org/relationships/caregiving-resource-center/info-08-2010/elc_facts_about_hospice.html.

Millionaires Take Advantage of Medicaid

You've heard this myth many times: A millionaire or zillionaire — a film star, a CEO of a Fortune 500 company, or a highly paid athlete — can legally transfer all his or her assets and after a five-year look-back period become eligible for Medicaid nursing-home care at taxpayer expense. Lots of people believe that the ranks of Medicaid recipients are full of rich people who have done just that.

This myth is bolstered by the occasional news story about a person who defrauded Medicaid by concealing assets. Sometimes people assume estate planning is Medicaid planning. There is no shame in estate planning, and rich people do it all the time but without ever intending to become eligible for Medicaid. The rules for transferring assets are rigorously applied in Medicaid applications, and most people who eventually become eligible for Medicaid have exhausted all their resources.

There is little evidence that people with substantial incomes or assets are improperly transferring them to become eligible for Medicaid. An Urban Institute study showed that people with disabilities who need Medicaid assistance not only had lower incomes and assets when they needed assistance but also were at a disadvantage during their peak earning years. Half of those who received Medicaid assistance for nursing-home care had less than $10,000 in nonhousing assets ten years or more before entering the nursing home. The report concluded, "Among people who spend down, few are asset rich and income poor." (For more detail, see the AARP blog at blog.aarp.org/2013/08/15/do-the-rich-benefit-from-medicaid/.)

Who among the 1 percent — our nation's richest and most privileged — would really want to go through the legal process of losing control of their assets to be eligible for Medicaid? In addition, Medicaid does not provide the kind of special treatment and considerations that the rich and famous expect. Nursing homes do not have suites and special restaurant food and other luxuries for the formerly rich. In Medicaid, formerly rich does not get you anything better than always poor.

REMEMBER

Most people look on Medicaid as a last resort. It is a safety net and not a velvet cushion.

If I Need Care, I'll Wind Up in a Nursing Home

Surveys consistently show that only a third of American adults think that they will need long-term care, when actually about 70 percent of people over age 65 will need at least some form of long-term care during their lifetimes. Part of the reason for this discrepancy is that many people link long-term care to nursing-home care, and they say firmly, "I don't want to go there."

In fact, as noted in earlier chapters, nursing homes are now the last resort, not the first option, in long-term care. Many more options exist to remain at home, with assistance and perhaps home modifications (see Chapter 5). Long-term services and supports — the new terminology for community care — are alternatives to nursing homes. So are assisted-living facilities (see Chapter 8), although they do not provide the level of nursing care that may be required for someone who is very ill or has dementia.

Still the myth persists. Because of its staying power, some people are reluctant to engage in long-term care planning because they find the prospect of being in a nursing home not only distasteful but also hugely expensive.

What will they do if they become ill or disabled? Here the answers get a little murky. Some say, "My family will take care of me." Others say, "I won't stay around long enough to find out," suggesting that they will die by suicide at the first sign of debility. This is largely bravado, but it does suggest the depth of anxiety about dependence and illness.

More exposure to alternatives to nursing-home care may help dispel this myth, as would information about changes in nursing homes that create a more inviting environment.

Assisted-Living Facilities Are Regulated Like Nursing Homes

Nursing homes are highly regulated by both federal and state governments. It would seem obvious that assisted-living facilities, promoted as an alternative to nursing homes, would also be regulated in similar ways, but this is not the case.

There are no federal regulations for assisted-living facilities, which vary widely in the population they serve, services, management, and location. In January 2014, however, the Centers for Medicare & Medicaid Services (CMS) issued a rule allowing states to include assisted-living facilities in their home- and community-based waiver programs. Check with your state Medicaid agency to see whether this rule applies to your state. States do regulate assisted-living facilities but license them under different categories and call them by different names.

Generally, state regulations are concerned with assisted-living facilities as congregate housing sites. Fire safety, evacuation procedures, and structural soundness are examples of common standards. They may or may not set requirements for a minimum level of staff training. There may or may not be a nurse on-site at all times. They may or may not require CPR training. State surveyors may visit just once a year or even less often.

REMEMBER

More regulation does not necessarily mean better care, but regulations set a baseline. Anyone considering a move to an assisted-living facility should find out what the state regulates and what it doesn't. It won't answer all your questions, but at least it's a start.

Long-Term Care Insurance Covers All Your Needs

The myth that all your long-term needs will be covered by insurance comes with some qualifications. If you have a very comprehensive long-term care insurance policy with a highly reliable company, the policy has built-in options for all the possible variations on what kinds of long-term care you may need, and it has protections for inflation, then it is possible that all your long-term care needs will be covered. But that kind of policy is costly, and the amount you have contributed over many years may not justify the benefits you'll receive. It is more realistic to expect that a long-term care insurance policy will cover about 60 to 70 percent of expenses.

Long-term care policies are priced by the age of the applicant, the benefit period (the length of time you expect to need long-term care), the setting of care (nursing home, assisted living, home), and other factors. Long-term care insurance can be a valuable asset but has limitations. Newer variations on traditional policies are now available that may provide the level of benefits you need at a more affordable cost. See Chapter 12 for details.

Chapter **22**

Ten Resources with State-by-State Information

ouldn't it be nice if there were just one place where you can get all the information you need about planning for navigating your later years? Unfortunately, it's not so easy. This chapter has some guidance to help you find what you need.

In the U.S. federal system, much of the responsibility for healthcare, nonmedical services such as personal care and homemaker services, and social services falls within the jurisdiction of the states, even though there is federal oversight and funding. And states have different ways of dealing with these issues. To make the process of getting the information you need a little easier, several websites offer state-by-state information, either through an interactive map in which you click on your state or an alphabetical listing where you enter the location by state, city, or zip code.

This chapter offers a selection of ten of these topics with some background about why they may be useful. The ten topics are organized very loosely into two main categories: resources for housing and community services (assisted living, Area Agencies on Aging, Eldercare Locator, home modification, and family caregiver support) and special topics related to medical care and quality-of-care issues (Medicaid, cost of care, advance directives, long-term care ombudsmen, and Beneficiary and Family-Centered Care Quality Improvement Organizations).

TIP

One way to use this information is to go to the website, find your state, and write down the name of the agency, email address, phone number, and any other relevant data. Keep the notes in a file so you can refer to the resources whenever needed. You can also bookmark the relevant pages on your computer. You may have noted some of these resources in earlier chapters on specific topics; if so, consider this information a refresher.

Identifying Local Services through Area Agencies on Aging

A major source of local information is your Area Agency on Aging (AAA). (These are often called triple As, but don't confuse them with the automobile club!). AAAs were established under the federal Older Americans Act in 1973 to respond to the needs of Americans age 60 and over in every local community. By providing a range of options that allow older adults to choose the home- and community-based services and living arrangements that suit them best, AAAs make it possible for many older adults to remain in their homes and communities as long as possible.

In 1978, under amendments to the Older Americans Act, Indian tribal organizations that received grants under Title VI of the Act were designated AAAs. These Native American aging programs provide nutritional and supportive services to older American Indians, Alaskan Natives, and Native Hawaiians and provide services to their elders comparable to services offered to other older adults by AAAs.

AAAs also administer the federal National Family Caregiver Support Program, which offers caregiver counseling, support groups, and other services.

The National Association of Area Agencies on Aging (n4a) supports the national network of 622 Area Agencies on Aging and 246 Title VI Native American aging programs. To find the nearest AAA, the website at www.n4a.org/about-n4a/?fa=aaa-title-VI has a two-step process: First, search by your city and state or zip code, and then scroll through the state's listings to find your city, town, or county.

Assessing Assisted-Living and Rehabilitation Facilities

Unlike nursing homes, which are governed by federal as well as state regulations, assisted-living facilities (covered in Chapter 8) are subject only to state regulation, and not every state has regulations in place. There is no handy website to compare all assisted-living facilities and no all-inclusive listing. So you're largely on your own in searching for information about assisted-living facilities. However, some websites do have limited state-by-state information:

>> **Argentum (formerly the Assisted Living Federation of America)** (www.argentum.org/about-argentum/state-partners/): This website has a list of its member organizations in several categories: assisted-living facilities, independent-living communities, nursing homes, continuing-care communities, and Alzheimer's care communities. You can find member organizations in your community by clicking on your state in the map or by scrolling through the alphabetical list below the map.

>> **The Commission on Accreditation of Rehabilitation Facilities** (www.carf.org/providerSearch.aspx): This is an independent nonprofit accrediting agency of health and human services in aging services, medical rehabilitation, durable medical equipment, and other areas. It lists accredited providers, including continuing-care retirement communities, by zip code, city, state, name, program type, or keyword. It has special lists for brain injury, stroke, and spinal cord injury.

>> **Leading Age** (www.leadingage.org/find-member): Leading Age, a membership organization of nonprofit organizations and businesses, can guide you to its members who run assisted-living facilities as well as continuing-care communities, home- and community-based services, nursing facilities, and senior housing.

>> **The National Center for Assisted Living** (www.ahcancal.org/ncal/about/Pages/StateAffiliates.aspx): This affiliate of the American Health Care Association, which is an association of long-term and post-acute care providers, has a list of state-by-state affiliates.

Finding Services and Housing Options through Eldercare Locator

REMEMBER

Nearly every chapter in this book refers to Eldercare Locator, because this website is a basic resource. Funded by the federal Administration on Aging and administered by the National Association of Area Agencies on Aging (n4a), Eldercare Locator has information on many community services and housing options. The most common inquiries it receives are on general aging resources, financial assistance, transportation, housing options, and in-home services. Go to `eldercare.acl.gov/Public/Index.aspx` for a list of the types of services that you can access through Eldercare Locator.

You can search the Eldercare Locator site by city, state, or zip code, or you can call 800-677-1116. An information specialist is available Monday through Friday, 9 a.m. to 8 p.m. Eastern time. You can also start an online chat with a representative by clicking on the link on the home page. Spanish-speaking information specialists are available.

Eldercare Locator information specialists connect older adults and caregivers directly to local Area Agencies on Aging, Title VI Native American aging programs, Aging and Disability Resources Centers, and other pertinent aging resources nationwide.

Getting Support for Family Caregivers

Among its many caregiver resources, AARP has a list of local caregiving resources at `www.aarp.org/caregiving/local/info-2017/resource-guides.html`. The guides are listed by state and where appropriate by city.

The Family Caregiver Alliance, a San Francisco–based nonprofit dedicated to assisting family caregivers of all kinds, has a Family Care Navigator with an interactive map that lists many resources by state. Some are for support services for caregivers, and others are for the family member who needs assistance with housing, legal assistance, and disease-specific support. The site also has a list of common questions, such as "Can I get paid to care for a family member?" Clicking on the question takes you to an answer with further information and other resources. Where available, these resources are listed by state as well. Go to `https://www.caregiver.org/family-care-navigator`.

Modifying Your Home with Rebuilding Together

Aging in place often requires home modifications (see Chapter 5). Rebuilding Together is a national network of local Rebuilding Together affiliates, corporate and individual donors, skilled tradesmen and associations, and almost 200,000 citizen volunteers. Rebuilding Together provides critical repairs, accessibility modifications, and energy-efficient upgrades to low-income homes and community centers at no cost to the service recipient.

To find an affiliate in your area, go to an interactive map at rebuildingtogether. org/affiliates. Click on the PDF for lists in your state, or contact the national office at communications@rebuildingtogether.org.

Getting Information on Medicaid in Your State

REMEMBER

Medicaid, the federal-state program for low-income people, is the primary payer for long-term care services in the community and in nursing homes. The federal rules require some services to be provided (hospital care, for example), but states can choose what additional services they want to offer. The federal website has an interactive map that takes you to your state's Medicaid program and gives information about changes to the Medicaid program under the Affordable Care Act (ACA). Go to www.healthcare.gov/do-i-qualify-for-medicaid.

Calculating Costs

You need accurate information about the costs of various options. You can find basic information about places you can receive care, what to expect, and how to find local providers at the Centers for Medicare & Medicaid Services (CMS) website at longtermcare.acl.gov/the-basics/. The same link takes you to an LTC Pathfinder with information based on your age.

Another source is the Genworth Financial annual survey of costs of long-term care. The 2017 survey is at www.genworth.com/corporate/about-genworth/ industry-expertise/cost-of-care.html. It has an interactive map of states, including 437 regions, and additional information about how the survey is conducted. You can also download the data with an app, which may be handy if you are visiting several facilities and want to compare costs. AARP also has a Long-Term Care Calculator at `www.aarp.org/relationships/caregiving-resource-center/LTCC`.

Finding Your State's Advance Directives

Advance directives is the generic term for documents that set out the types of medical treatment a person wants or doesn't want if he cannot speak for himself. Advance directives also name the person who is authorized to make healthcare decisions in that situation. Each state has its own legal form for this purpose. In addition, some people want to add documents such as Five Wishes that outline in more detail their preferences. But only the state's official advance directive document has legal weight.

Caring Connections, a program of the National Hospice and Palliative Care Organization (NHPCO), is a national consumer and community engagement initiative to improve care at the end of life. It provides free advance directives and instructions for each state that can be opened as a PDF file: `www.caringinfo.org/i4a/pages/index.cfm?pageid=3289`. These documents are also available on the AARP website at `www.aarp.org/advancedirectives`.

TIP

If you have any legal questions regarding these documents, contact your state attorney general's office or an attorney.

TIP

Caring Connections warns that due to formatting and printing requirements, for some states a blank page appears in the Acrobat Reader as the first page. This does not mean the document has not loaded correctly. Use the navigation toolbar to go to the next page. If you have any questions, you can call Caring Connection's help line at 800-658-8898 or send an email to caringinfo@nhpco.org.

REMEMBER

If you spend time in more than one state, you should have advance directives that are legally recognized in all these states.

Solving Problems through an Ombudsman

Long-term care ombudsmen are advocates for residents of nursing homes, board and care homes, and assisted-living facilities. Ombudsmen provide information about how to find a facility and what to do to get quality care. They are trained to resolve problems. If you choose, the ombudsman can assist you with complaints. But unless you give the ombudsman permission to share your concerns, these matters are kept confidential. Under the federal Older Americans Act, every state is required to have an ombudsman program that addresses complaints and advocates for improvements in the long-term care system.

The ombudsman program is administered by the Administration on Aging. The network has 8,813 volunteers certified to handle complaints and 1,167 paid staff. Most state ombudsman programs are housed in their State Unit on Aging.

A long-term care ombudsman performs the following tasks:

>> Resolves complaints made by or for residents of long-term care facilities

>> Educates consumers and long-term care providers about residents' rights and good care practices

>> Promotes community involvement through volunteer opportunities

>> Provides information to the public on nursing homes and other long-term care facilities and services, residents' rights, and legislative and policy issues

>> Advocates for residents' rights and quality care in nursing homes, personal care, residential care, and other long-term care facilities

>> Promotes the development of citizen organizations, family councils, and resident councils

You can find the ombudsmen in your state through an interactive state map at www.ltcombudsman.org/ombudsman.

Resolving Complaints through BFCC-QIOs

REMEMBER

If you have a complaint or a problem with medical care — for example, you're a Medicare beneficiary and you want to appeal a hospital discharge that you think is premature — you may turn to a Beneficiary and Family-Centered Care Quality Improvement Organization (BFCC-QIO) for help. BFCC-QIOs are private, mostly not-for-profit organizations, which are staffed by professionals, mostly doctors and other healthcare professionals, who are trained to review medical care and help beneficiaries with complaints about the quality of care and to implement improvements in the quality of care available throughout the spectrum of care. The Centers for Medicare & Medicaid Services (CMS) contracts with two organizations (Livanta and Kepro) that cover different states, as well as the District of Columbia, Puerto Rico, and the U.S. Virgin Islands, to serve as that state/jurisdiction's BFCC-QIO contractor.

By law, the mission of the BFCC–QIO program is to improve the effectiveness, efficiency, economy, and quality of services delivered to Medicare beneficiaries. The core functions of the program are

» Improving quality of care for beneficiaries

» Protecting the integrity of the Medicare Trust Fund by ensuring that Medicare pays only for services and goods that are reasonable and necessary and that are provided in the most appropriate setting

» Protecting beneficiaries by expeditiously addressing individual complaints, such as beneficiary complaints, provider-based notice appeals, violations of the Emergency Medical Treatment and Labor Act (EMTALA), and other related responsibilities as articulated in BFCC-QIO-related law

You can find the BFCC–QIO for your state at www.qualitynet.org/dcs/ContentServer?pagename=QnetPublic%2FPage%2FQnetTier2&cid=1144767874793.

7

Appendixes

Appendix A

Glossary

Accessibility: The characteristics of a home or community environment that make it easy for people, especially those with limited mobility, to navigate and manage independently. Examples include wider doorways, lower countertops and sinks, grab bars in tubs and showers, and light switches and electrical outlets at waist height.

Activities of daily living (ADLs): Personal care activities and tasks that people typically do on their own, like dressing, bathing, going to the bathroom, moving from bed to chair, and feeding themselves.

Acute Care for Elders (ACE) units: Hospital units staffed by a specially trained interdisciplinary team, which can include geriatricians, advanced practice nurses, social workers, pharmacists, and physical therapists.

Adaptability: Changes that can be made to a home or other building without requiring a complete redesign or the use of different materials for essential features.

Adult day healthcare: A therapeutic daycare program that provides medical and rehabilitation services.

Adult day programs: Social programs that offer activities and meals in a community setting.

Advance directives: The generic term for legal documents that tell family and healthcare professionals what kinds of treatments a person wants or does not want in end-of-life scenarios. Examples include tube feedings, dialysis, pain medication, mechanical ventilation, and other options.

Affinity or niche communities: Housing arrangements designed for people with a common background, usually because of prior employment or other shared interests.

Affordable Care Act (ACA): Often referred to as *Obamacare,* the Patient Protection and Affordable Care Act (P.L. 111-148) and the Health Care and Education Reconciliation Act of 2010 (P.L. 111-152), which aim to provide Americans with better health security by putting in place comprehensive health insurance reforms that expand coverage, hold insurance companies accountable, lower healthcare costs, offer more choice, and enhance the quality of care. While some aspects of the Affordable Care Act have been altered, the basic law remains intact.

Age-friendly communities: Places where services, settings, and structures support and enable people to age actively. These communities recognize a wide range of ability, capacity, and resources for older people, anticipate and respond flexibly to aging-related needs of inhabitants, respect the decisions and lifestyle choices of the aging, protect those who are most vulnerable, and promote their inclusion and contribution to community life.

Agent/attorney-in-fact: A person designated to act on behalf of an individual to manage financial matters.

Aging in place: The ability to live in one's own home and community safely, independently, and comfortably, regardless of age or ability level.

Aid and Attendance (A&A pension): In-home support services for veterans who require the aid of another person to perform activities of daily living, adjust prosthetic devices, or be safe.

Americans with Disabilities Act (ADA): Signed into law in 1990, the ADA prohibits discrimination based on ability and ensures equal opportunity for persons with disabilities in employment, state and local government services, public accommodations, commercial facilities, and transportation.

Annuity: A contract between an individual and an insurance company providing that, in return for a lump-sum payment or series of payments, the company will offer tax-deferred growth and make periodic payments beginning immediately or at some future date. The three general types of annuities are fixed, indexed, and variable.

Assisted-living facility (ALF): A general term referring to a type of congregate living where people share meals and other activities and where individuals can receive personal assistance to maintain their independence.

Assistive technology: Devices and adaptations that are designed to help people who are aging or have disabilities to function independently.

Capacity: A legal finding that a person can understand choices, appreciate the consequences, and act to make certain kinds of decisions such as healthcare decisions; lack of capacity can be the trigger for appointing or empowering a surrogate or alternate decision maker.

Cardiopulmonary resuscitation (CPR): An emergency procedure performed when someone has stopped breathing or has no heartbeat.

Caregiver Advise, Record, Enable (CARE) Act: Laws in 42 states and territories that require hospitals to ask a patient upon admission if he or she wants to identify a caregiver. If so, the caregiver's contact information is entered in the medical record; the caregiver is informed about the date of discharge and is given instruction in post-discharge tasks.

Caregiver contract: An agreement between a person needing assistance and (usually) a family member that sets out terms for payment for caregiving and defines responsibilities.

Caregiver self-assessment: The process by which a family caregiver reviews personal strengths, limitations, and worries concerning his or her ability to provide care for another person, to more accurately assess the ability to support the family member's needs and choices.

CareMap: A visual representation of a person's support system and needed services. The map can be used to identify gaps and to enlist family or community support.

Cash and counseling programs: Medicaid programs allowing a person on Medicaid and eligible for home care to hire and pay attendants, including certain groups of family members. One example is included later in this appendix: Consumer-Directed Personal Assistance Program.

Certified nursing assistant (CNA): Aides in a nursing home who must meet certain standards and undergo training.

Chronic condition: Persistent or long-lasting illness or disease that may be controlled but not cured.

COBRA (Consolidated Omnibus Budget Reconciliation Act): A federal law passed in 1985 that provides the opportunity for workers who have lost their jobs and health insurance to continue to receive insurance benefits under a group plan; the workers may be required to pay the entire premium.

Cohousing: An agreement among friends or neighbors who live in separate houses and manage their own finances to work together to manage their own community. Some cohousing projects are started by housing developers. There are entry fees and monthly charges.

Coinsurance: An individual's share of the costs of a healthcare service covered by insurance, calculated as a percentage (for example, 20 percent of the allowed amount for the service).

Community property: Property acquired during a marriage that is shared equally by both spouses, regardless of who earned the money. States have different laws regarding distribution of community property following death or divorce.

Community-based agencies: Organizations and agencies, separate from a medical facility or organization, that provide support services in the community. Examples include social-service agencies, neighborhood houses, and senior centers, which typically offer services like adult daycare, transportation, friendly visiting, minor home repairs, snow removal, yardwork, and similar chores.

Complex chronic conditions: Conditions involving multiple long-term illnesses or diseases that exist at the same time and require the attention of different healthcare providers.

Comprehensive driving evaluation: Identifies the physical, visual, and cognitive challenges of driving. It is often conducted by an occupational therapist but may also be arranged through some state departments of motor vehicles.

Consumer-Directed Personal Assistance Program (CDPAP): A Medicaid program that provides services to chronically ill or disabled individuals with a medical need for help with ADLs or a need for skilled nursing services. Recipients can hire their own caregivers. This program varies by state.

Continuing-care retirement community (CCRC): A tiered approach to long-term care services that includes on the same site independent living, assisted living, and nursing-home-level care.

Copayment: A predetermined amount for a covered healthcare service usually paid at the time of receiving the service.

Custodial care: Help with personal care such as bathing, dressing, and eating.

Deductible: The amount owed for healthcare services covered by health insurance before the insurance starts to pay.

Delirium: A sudden, acute, often unrecognized but treatable onset of confusion.

Dementia: A general term to describe symptoms such as memory loss, poor judgment, inhibition, and deteriorating language and motor skills. The most common diseases to display dementia symptoms are Alzheimer's and Parkinson's diseases.

Direct-care workers: Paid home care aides, personal attendants, certified nursing assistants, and others who provide hands-on care to a person.

Disability insurance: Insurance that pays for a portion of lost income if a person becomes disabled and unable to work because of an accident or illness.

Discharge planner: A hospital or nursing-home staff member, typically a social worker or nurse, who organizes the transition from facility to home or to another facility.

Do not resuscitate (DNR) order: A physician's order that states that a person should not be given CPR if he or she stops breathing or has no heartbeat. A DNR order does not limit the provision of pain medicine or comfort care.

Domiciliary program: An active clinical rehabilitation and treatment program for veterans, especially those with mental-health or substance-abuse problems or who are homeless. Domiciliary programs are now integrated into the VA's Mental Health Residential Rehabilitation and Treatment Programs (MH RRTPs).

Duals (dually eligible): People who are eligible for both Medicare and Medicaid. Medicare is the first payer.

Durable medical equipment (DME): Devices such as canes, walkers, wheelchairs, hospital beds, commodes, and other aids that someone needs because of a medical condition.

Durable power of attorney: A legal document that assigns the authority to make financial decisions to another individual even after the person who appointed the agent is incapacitated.

Durable power of attorney for healthcare decisions: See **healthcare proxy.**

Emergency department (ED) or emergency room (ER): The hospital area that provides acute care on a walk-in basis to individuals with sudden serious illness or trauma.

Employment or registry agencies for home care: Agencies that provide names of nurses and aides available to provide home care. The workers are contacted and paid directly. Some states maintain a registry through the Department of Health.

Entry fee: The upfront cost of admission to, for instance, an assisted-living facility.

Equal visitation rights: Rules enacted by the Centers for Medicare & Medicaid that protect patients' rights to choose their visitors, including same-sex domestic partners, during a hospital stay.

Estate: All the property and assets a person owns — for example, real estate, life insurance, jewelry, art, and antiques.

Estate recovery laws: State laws that recover the costs a state has expended in Medicaid services for a deceased person by laying claim to the person's property and estate.

Estate taxes: Federal and state taxes levied on the estate of a person before distribution of the estate to the heirs/beneficiaries.

Executor: The person legally responsible for making sure that the instructions in a will are followed.

Extensive- or life-care contract: A type of contract for continuing-care retirement communities that provides housing, services, and amenities, including unlimited use of healthcare services at little or no increase in monthly fees as a resident moves from independent living to assisted living to nursing-home care. This type of contract is the costliest but carries the least risk.

Fair Housing Act: Passed in 1968 and administered by the U.S. Department of Housing and Urban Development (HUD), the FHA is designed to prevent discrimination in housing based on race, color, gender, and handicap (disability), among other characteristics.

Family and Medical Leave Act (FMLA): The 1993 federal law that guarantees up to 12 weeks of unpaid leave for eligible workers to take care of their own health needs or to take care of family members.

Family caregiver: A person who provides or manages assistance for a relative, domestic partner, or friend who needs help because of illness, disability, or advanced age. Sometimes called *informal caregiver, caretaker, care partner,* or *carer.*

Federal Commission on Long-Term Care: A commission created to propose financing strategies and changes in delivery services for long-term services and supports; issued report in 2013.

Federal poverty guidelines: The minimum amount of income that a family needs for food, clothing, transportation, shelter, and other necessities. The guidelines are updated each year and vary by state.

Fiduciary duty: The obligation of a person placed in a position of trust to act only for that person's benefit, and to act with good faith in furthering his or her interests in the handling of that person's money or property.

Filial-responsibility laws: Old laws that establish an obligation of an adult child to support his or her parents.

Financial power of attorney: A document signed by one person giving another person permission to take care of different kinds of financial affairs, like signing checks, agreeing to pay a contractor for home repairs, handling bank accounts, and taking care of other tasks. It does not extend to making healthcare decisions.

Fixed assets: Long-term kinds of property that are used to generate income but are not easily or quickly converted into cash, such as real estate or bonds.

Formal home care services: Nursing or aide services provided through an agency and paid for by insurance or privately.

Geriatric evaluation: A comprehensive assessment of a person's ability to manage independently, including physical health and social environment.

Geriatricians: Physicians, primarily internal medicine doctors, who have taken additional training that focuses on the diseases of aging and their treatments. They have been certified by the American Board of Internal Medicine to practice geriatric medicine.

Gerontologists: Scholars who study the mental, physical, environmental, and social aspects of aging. They do research, teach aging in universities, and contribute to the broad knowledge about the impact of aging on individuals and society.

Granny-pod: A self-contained structure on the same property but not attached to a main house that has water, electricity, and plumbing, and may incorporate assistive technology like monitoring vital signs, filtering air contaminants, and many other services.

Group homes: Houses in residential neighborhoods that accommodate a small number of people for a fee. The owner provides meals and assists with some ADLs.

Guardianship/conservatorship: A court process in which a judge appoints someone to make decisions about a person's care and finances after that person is unable to act on his or her own.

Guardianship of the estate: The authority to manage money and other assets; called a *conservatorship* in some states.

Guardianship of the person: The responsibility to make healthcare and other decisions that affect the well-being of a person.

Health Insurance Marketplace/Exchange: Under the Affordable Care Act, a website that offers information on and enrollment in a range of selected private health plans as well as Medicaid.

Healthcare proxy: A person appointed to make healthcare decisions if the person is unable to make decisions on his or her own; may be called *surrogate decision maker* or *healthcare agent*.

HIPAA (Health Insurance Portability and Accountability Act): A federal law protecting the privacy of a patient's medical information. According to the law, with the patient's consent, healthcare professionals can share relevant information with a family member or other person directly involved in the patient's care or paying for care.

Hoarding: A compulsion to collect and inability to part with things and animals regardless of their value, utility, or safety risk. Hoarding interferes with everyday life by making it impossible to use space in the home as intended and impedes access in an emergency.

Home- and community-based services (HCBS): An umbrella term for services including case management, home care aide services, personal care, adult daycare, and respite care, as well as other services, such as home modification assistance. HCBS are intended to keep people at home for as long as possible.

Home care: Various in-home services provided to a chronically or seriously ill person. Services are usually provided by a nurse or aide but can also be provided by a physician, physical or occupational therapist, social worker, home health aide, home health attendant, or medical equipment services.

Home health advance beneficiary notice (HHABN): A written notice that explains the reason for a reduction or termination of home health services.

Home telehealth: A service used by healthcare providers to remotely monitor a patient's condition and track blood pressure, blood sugar level, weight, blood oxygen level, and heart and lung sounds. Information is transmitted to a care coordinator by landline or cellphone or by video.

Hospice: A comprehensive, team-based philosophy that focuses on controlling pain and symptoms and improving the quality of life for people with a short life expectancy; it is covered by Medicare and often by private health insurance. States may choose to cover hospice under their Medicaid program, but it is not mandatory.

Hospital discharge plan: The plan for a patient transition to home or to another healthcare facility after the hospital stay is completed.

Hospitalists: Doctors trained in critical-care medicine and skilled at handling medical crises that happen to seriously ill patients; they work in hospitals but do not generally see patients in the community.

Hybrid policies: Insurance policies that combine a life-insurance policy or annuity with long-term care insurance benefits.

Improvement standard: The notion that to continue to receive therapeutic services under Medicare, a patient had to show continuous improvement or the services would not be covered; federal court decision ruled that it violated Medicare regulations.

Independent living: Any housing arrangement for people age 55 and over; may be apartment-style living or freestanding homes, subsidized low-income senior housing, or high-end retirement communities.

Informal home care services: Unpaid care provided by family members or friends.

In-home DNR order: A physician's order that tells emergency workers called to the home that they should not perform CPR on this person.

Instrumental activities of daily living (IADLs): Tasks that most people manage for themselves, such as making phone calls, managing money, managing medications, shopping, and cooking.

Intestate: The term applied to a person who dies without a will. Probate court may be needed to determine how property from the estate will be divided.

LGBT or LGBTQ: Lesbian, gay, bisexual, transgender, or questioning/queer individuals.

Licensed home care agency: A home care agency that is licensed by the state to provide nursing services and aides who do personal care. Some are contracted through Medicaid to provide long-term personal care.

Life settlement/viatical settlement: A life-insurance policy that is sold to a third party at an amount that is less than the policy's death benefit. The settlement is termed a *viatical settlement* when the seller is terminally or chronically ill and has a short (less than two years) life expectancy.

Liquid assets: Things of value that can quickly be turned into cash, such as bank accounts (checking and savings), certificates of deposit, and money market funds.

Livable communities: Places with affordable, appropriate housing; adequate transportation; and supportive community features and services, where inhabitants can age in place and engage in the community's civic, economic, and social life.

Living trust: A written agreement laying out wishes concerning finances. A person both owns and controls as both the trustee and the beneficiary while alive and not disabled. The trustee also names the successor trustee who will manage the trust after disability or death and successor beneficiaries who will get the assets in the trust after the trustee's death.

Living will: A form of advance directive that outlines medical treatment wishes.

Long-term care: The spectrum of medical and nonmedical services needed over a long time by a person who is ill or disabled.

Long-term care insurance: A policy purchased to help provide financial support when assistance is needed. Policies vary in coverage, benefit period, and other aspects. Some policies are linked to life insurance or annuities or are short duration policies.

Long-term care ombudsman: An official responsible for investigating complaints in nursing homes and assisted-care facilities in a state.

Long-term services and supports (LTSS): An umbrella term covering the nonmedical services that are intended to meet the needs of an individual living in the community.

Look-back: The period during which transfer of assets for less than market value counts against Medicaid eligibility.

Medicaid: A joint federal and state program that helps with medical costs and long-term care in homes, communities, and nursing homes for some people with limited income and resources.

Medicaid managed long-term care: Plans run by private insurance companies under contract to the state to coordinate services and supports for people eligible for Medicaid.

Medicaid waiver: An agreement between the federal government and a state allowing the state to use some of its Medicaid funding for specific services to keep people in the community.

Medical day programs: Unlike adult social day programs, these programs help with healthcare needs as well as social activities.

Medical foster homes: Private homes in which a trained caregiver provides long-term services and supports to people who need round-the-clock care but do not need to be in a nursing home.

Medically Needy Program: A Medicaid program that assists people who have high medical expenses but whose income exceeds the maximum threshold for Medicaid eligibility.

Medicare: The federal health-insurance program for people who are 65 or older, certain younger people with disabilities, and people with end-stage renal disease. In Original Medicare, Part A covers hospital insurance, Part B pays for doctor bills and outpatient services, Part C is a Medicare Advantage plan, and Part D is prescription drug coverage.

Medicare Advantage Plan or MA (Medicare Part C): A Medicare plan administered by a health insurance organization or plan. The plan covers all Part A and B benefits; most Advantage plans also cover prescription drug benefits.

Medicare Part D doughnut hole: A gap in coverage that begins when the beneficiary and drug plan have spent a certain amount for covered drugs. Scheduled to be eliminated by 2019.

Medicare-Certified Home Health Agencies (HHAs): Agencies approved by the Center for Medicare & Medicaid Services (CMS) and licensed by the state to provide skilled services, primarily nurse visits, but also physical therapy or social-work visits, among others.

Medication administration: The preparing and giving of medications.

Medigap: A general term for supplemental insurance coverage used to pay for additional expenses not covered by Medicare.

Multigenerational living: A living arrangement in which multiple generations of the same family live together. Multigenerational households may include two or more consecutive generations or include skipped generations, such as grandparents caring for grandchildren whose parents are unable to care for them.

Multiparty account without a right of survivorship/convenience account: A type of joint bank account where the agent has the authority to make deposits and withdrawals; if the primary person dies, the remainder of the account goes into the estate and does not pass to the cosignator.

Naturally occurring retirement communities (NORCs): Residences or communities in which many people are aging in place and live near others in the same stage of life. They are places that were not specifically built for seniors but now have a significant proportion of older residents. Neighborhood/open/horizontal NORCs are arranged across a number of one- and two-family homes in age-integrated neighborhoods; housing-based/classic/closed/vertical NORCs are located in single-age integrated buildings or across a housing complex with the same management.

Nonmedical or companion agency: Agencies that provide companion services, which include reading and conversation, assisting with clothing selection, organizing the mail, and picking up prescriptions from the pharmacy. They are not usually licensed by the state.

NORC programs: Programs that coordinate a broad range of social and medical services to support the residents in a NORC designated area.

Notice of Medicare provider noncoverage: A notice that tells the date covered services will end.

NSAIDS: Nonsteroidal anti-inflammatory drugs.

Observation status/observation service: Hospital services given to a person while the doctor decides whether the patient needs to be admitted as an inpatient or can be discharged. In the context of a hospital stay, being on observation may affect the amount an individual on Medicare has to pay for services and eligibility for rehabilitation services in a skilled nursing facility.

Original Medicare: The traditional, fee-for-service plan of Medicare, in which healthcare providers are paid directly by the government for the services the patient receives.

OTC drugs: Over-the-counter drugs.

PACE (Program of All-Inclusive Care for the Elderly): Programs open to people who are eligible for Medicare, Medicaid, or both, and who have been deemed to need nursing-home-level care. The programs provide care primarily in an adult daycare center. Comprehensive services include primary care, hospital care, medical specialty services, prescription drugs, home care, physical and occupational therapy, recreation therapy, nutritional counseling, transportation, and social-work counseling.

Paid family leave insurance: Insurance available to eligible working caregivers, which offers full or partial income replacement while a worker is at home taking care of a personal health condition, adjusting to a new child, or taking care of a family member with serious health needs.

Palliative care: A medical specialty and a range of services that improve how a person with a serious illness functions, even as she or he undergoes active treatment. Care focuses on pain relief, symptom control, and quality of life. Palliative care can be time-limited or ongoing. The ill person and family members are considered part of the care team.

Paratransit: Public transportation service provided for people with disabilities.

Payable on death certificates of deposit: Bank accounts that are payable upon death to a beneficiary designated by the account holder. Sometimes called *testamentary accounts*.

Personal emergency-response system (PERS): A device, such as a necklace or bracelet, used to call for help in an emergency. It connects the victim with an emergency response center, which then dispatches help.

Physician order for life-sustaining treatment (POLST): A physician's order that lists medical treatments that should or should not be provided when a person with advanced illness is transferred from one setting to another; called different names in different states.

Polypharmacy: Multiple drugs used by a single individual to treat medical conditions.

Power of attorney (POA): Written authorization to act on someone else's behalf. This authorization ends when a person becomes legally incompetent unless the person has signed a **durable power of attorney.**

Principal: The person signing a power-of-attorney document to assign someone else to act on his or her behalf.

Probate: The process of settling an estate. *Small estate probate* is the simplest form of probate that can be used for estates ranging in value from $1,000 to $10,000 depending on state law; *unsupervised* or *independent probate* is used when the estate has more than the value of a small estate but doesn't require a lot of court supervision; *supervised probate* applies to large estates and wills with complicated provisions where the court plays a major role in approving every action.

Respite: A short period of rest from caregiving duties.

Reverse mortgage: A financial product that gives a homeowner a line of credit, a lump sum, or monthly payments, which are not repaid until the owner sells the home, moves permanently into a nursing home, or dies.

Shared decision making: The process in which the patient, close family members, social worker, and healthcare team collaborate to make healthcare and long-term care decisions; a formal process in the VA.

Single-purpose mortgage: A federally insured mortgage for which the proceeds can be used only for a specified purpose, such as property maintenance or repairs.

Skilled care: Care provided by a nurse or a physical therapist or other professional. Some examples of skilled nursing care are IV injections, tube feedings, and wound care.

Skilled nursing facility (SNF): A facility licensed to provide short-term rehabilitation services as well as long-stay care by professionals.

Special-needs trust: A legal instrument that allows a parent or other person to set aside money for special types of care and support for a person with disabilities without jeopardizing the person's Medicaid status.

Spend-down: The process of using up one's income and assets to meet Medicaid eligibility requirements.

Springing durable power of attorney: A document that sets conditions under which the durable power of attorney goes ("springs") into effect; for example, when a doctor certifies that the person has become incapacitated.

State Health Insurance Assistance Program (SHIP): Programs that provide one-on-one, personal counseling to guide individuals through their insurance choices.

State Pharmacy Assistance Programs (SPAPs): State programs that help some people pay for prescription drugs based on financial need, age, or medical conditions.

Stranger-originated life insurance (STOLIs): Transactions that usually involve an older person being approached by a licensed life-insurance agent or another party to obtain new life insurance, with the policy being controlled from the start and paid for by a third party. These products carry considerable risk.

Supplemental Security Income: The federal program that pays benefits to disabled adults and children who have limited income and resources, and older adults who are not disabled but who meet the financial limits.

Supplemental transportation programs (STPs): Nontraditional transportation services for older adults who don't drive and others who need assistance. Most STPs provide door-to-door rides, and some arrange for a driver to stay with passengers until they are ready to go home.

Testamentary trust: A trust created with the assets from a decedent's estate or through a will that places conditions on their use.

TRICARE: TRICARE is the healthcare insurance program that covers healthcare for active-duty personnel, their families, retirees, members of the National Guard, and U.S. Army Reserve.

TRICARE For Life (TFL): Part of TRICARE that offers secondary coverage to Medicare beneficiaries who have both Part A and Part B coverage. It is available worldwide.

Trust: A legal arrangement in which one person gives the rights to another to hold title to property and/or assets for the benefit of a third party.

Universal design: Designs for homes, commercial buildings, and public spaces that are easy for all people to use, sturdy, and reliable. Universal design features include no-step entries, no-slip flooring, and grab bars.

Urgent care centers: Medical facilities that operate as walk-in clinics for people with non-life-threatening illnesses or injuries, such as sprains, cuts, infection, and flu. Waiting time is usually shorter than in an emergency department, and the urgent care center can call an ambulance to take you to an emergency department if warranted.

VA: U.S. Department of Veterans Affairs.

VA health benefits priority groups: The method by which the VA prioritizes the enrollment of veterans for health benefits. There are eight priority groups with various eligibility requirements, and eligibility must be verified by the VA before a priority group is assigned.

Veteran's pension: Funds paid to veterans or disabled veterans of wartime service who have low incomes and are no longer able to work.

Villages: Housing arrangements for independent nonprofit organizations with membership dues where members pool resources to leverage buying power and obtain services more cheaply. Services may include home maintenance and repair, home health and personal care, housekeeping, legal, and financial assistance.

Waiting period: In insurance policies, the time that must pass before coverage can become effective or benefits begin. Also called a *qualifying* or *elimination period*.

Will: A legal declaration of how an individual wants his or her assets distributed after death. A *simple will* is a document used for the outright distribution of assets; a *pour-over will* assigns some assets to a trust that has already been established; a *holographic will* is handwritten but not witnessed; and an *oral will* is spoken but not written down.

Appendix B

Resources

Every chapter includes resources for further investigation. This appendix brings together some of the major resources in one convenient location and adds a few that aren't mentioned elsewhere.

AARP

AARP is the nation's largest nonprofit, nonpartisan organization dedicated to empowering people 50 and older to choose how they live as they age. With a nationwide presence and nearly 38 million members, AARP strengthens communities and advocates for what matters most to families: health security, financial stability, and personal fulfillment.

AARP offers consumer-oriented information about long-term care, family caregiving, Medicare, and other programs. You'll also find information on housing, downsizing, and moving.

The best place to start is the AARP website, www.aarp.org. For specific topics, see the following area-specific web pages:

>> **AARP Caregiving Resource Center** (www.aarp.org/caregiving): This site has a wealth of articles, tools, blogs, and advice. You can also call the Caregiving Resource Center at 877-333-5885, or 888-971-2013 for Spanish speakers, weekdays 7 a.m. to 11 p.m. Eastern time.

>> **AARP Driver Safety** (www.aarp.org/driversafety): This site has links to register for online or classroom driver safety courses, vision tips for older drivers, and other information.

>> **AARP Livable Communities** (www.aarp.org/livablecommunities): Here you'll find information on local communities, including a tool to help you assess the resources of your community or an area you're considering moving to.

- » **AARP Money** (www.aarp.org/money): The "Money" section has news and advice about a range of financial matters from choosing the best cellphone provider to investments and annuities. It has tools that help you calculate a mortgage or credit card payoff.

- » **AARP Public Policy Institute** (www.aarp.org/ppi): AARP's Public Policy Institute offers information about federal and state policies regarding long-term care, workforce issues, and many other topics.

Centers for Medicare & Medicaid Services (CMS)

CMS is the federal agency that oversees Medicare and Medicaid. Here are some of the most commonly used resources:

- » **Medicaid** (www.medicaid.gov): This site has information about federal policies and state developments; for individual state programs, see the state Department of Health website or Medicaid office.

- » **Medicare** (www.medicare.gov): You can also call 800-633-4227. This site has material on various aspects of Medicare such as the rules regarding home healthcare eligibility, durable medical equipment, and the ins and outs of Part D for prescription drugs. Two important links are Nursing Home Compare and Home Health Compare, described in this list.

- » **Nursing Home Compare** (www.medicare.gov/nursinghomecompare/search.html): This site allows you to search for nursing homes by location or facility name. It provides information on staffing, training, prevention of abuse and neglect, reporting incidents of poor quality, and other standards.

- » **Home Health Compare** (www.medicare.gov/homehealthcompare/search.html): Home Health Compare is a CMS website that gives you information on specific agencies and how they are doing with meeting federal standards.

- » **Hospice Compare** (www.medicare.gov/hospicecompare): A companion to Nursing Home Compare and Home Health Compare that provides quality information on hospices and a guide to locating hospice services in your area.

- » **Beneficiary and Family-Centered Care Quality Improvement Organizations (BFCC-QIOs):** Part of the CMS structure, each state has a designated BFCC-QIO that is responsible for ensuring and improving quality of care and for reviewing complaints. If, for example, you feel that you're being discharged from a hospital too quickly, you can appeal the decision to the local BFCC-QIO. There are two organizations — Livanta and Kepro — that cover different regions. Most people don't know about these organizations, but they can be very helpful in resolving problems. This website will tell you which organization covers your state: www.qualitynet.org/dcs/ContentServer?cid=1228774346765&pagename=QnetPublic%2FPage%2FQnetTier4&c=Page.

Administration for Community Living

The Administration for Community Living (ACL) is the federal agency responsible for increasing access to community supports for older Americans and people with disabilities of any age. Its general website is www.acl.gov, and the following departments within the ACL provide more specific information.

>> **Administration on Aging** (www.acl.gov/): The Administration on Aging (AoA) has been incorporated into the ACL. It supports what is often called the "Aging Network" of agencies and professionals. AoA was created in 1965 with the passage of the Older Americans Act and provides support services, nutrition services, preventive health services, the National Family Caregiver Support Program, elder-rights services, and services to Native Alaskans, Native Hawaiians, and Native Americans.

>> **Area Agencies on Aging (AAAs)** (www.n4a.org/about-n4a/?fa=aaa-title-VI): Part of the AoA's Aging Network, more than 600 Area Agencies on Aging provide information and referrals to services such as adult daycare and senior-center programs in their region. Some state associations also have maps of their locations within the state to help you find services.

>> **Aging and Disability Resource Centers (ADRCs)** (eldercare.acl.gov/Public/About/Aging_Network/ADRC.aspx): A collaborative effort of the Administration for Community Living, Centers for Medicare & Medicaid Services, and now the Veterans Health Administration (VHA), ADRCs serve as single entry points into the long-term supports and services system for older adults and people with disabilities.

>> **Eldercare Locator** (eldercare.acl.gov/Public/Index.aspx): The Eldercare Locator, a free service of AoA, is a basic go-to site for locating resources in your community. You can also call 800-677-1116 for information.

>> **The National Center on Elder Abuse** (https://ncea.acl.gov/): This website offers information on the types of elder abuse and national and state resources on elder abuse.

>> **National Family Caregiver Support Program** (www.acl.gov/programs/ support-caregivers/national-family-caregiver-support-program): This program, administered through your local Area Agency on Aging, offers information and support to family caregivers, including support groups, and (where available) legal and financial advice and respite. Each program has its own set of services, depending on resources.

>> **Long-Term Care Ombudsmen** (www.acl.gov/programs/protecting- rights-and-preventing-abuse/long-term-care-ombudsman-program): Ombudsmen investigate complaints and negotiate solutions to problems in nursing homes and assisted-living facilities.

Other Resources

Following are an assortment of links to other agencies and organizations that may be able to assist you in planning for long-term care:

>> **AbleData** (www.abledata.com): A project of the National Institute for Disability and Rehabilitation Research, AbleData has information about assistive devices and resources.

>> **Aging Life Care Association** (formerly National Association of Professional Geriatric Care Managers; www.aginglifecare.org): This organization of trained geriatric professionals assists individuals and families in finding appropriate housing, home care services, medical management, social activities, and legal and financial advice. The website has a database of its members, searchable by zip code.

>> **Aging with Dignity** (www.agingwithdignity.org): This national nonprofit organization has the mission of affirming and safeguarding the human dignity of individuals as they age and of promoting better care for those near the end of life. Its "Five Wishes" form gives you the opportunity to convey your personal, emotional, and spiritual needs as well as your medical wishes. In 42 states and the District of Columbia, it substantially meets the legal require- ments for an advance directive.

>> **Alzheimer's Association** (www.alz.org): At this website you can find links to local chapters, which offer educational sessions, support groups, and other services. The main site has information, including research and treatment, about Alzheimer's disease and other dementias.

>> **American Bar Association's Commission on Law and Aging** (www. americanbar.org/groups/law_aging.html): This commission and its website examine a wide range of legal issues affecting older persons.

» **American Diabetes Association** (www.diabetes.org): This website has links to local chapters and information on prevention, treatment, and services.

» **American Heart Association** (www.heart.org/HEARTORG): The AHA has information about heart disease and stroke and their treatments and prevention.

» **CancerCare** (www.cancercare.org): CancerCare's website provides free, professional support services to anyone affected by cancer. The organization has educational programs for patients and caregivers, counseling services, and limited financial assistance. Services are available online and by phone.

» **Caring and Aging with Pride** (age-pride.org): This is the first national project to study health and wellness among lesbian, gay, bisexual, and transgender older adults and their caregivers.

» **Center to Advance Palliative Care** (www.getpalliativecare.org): This website offers information about what palliative care is and resources for locating palliative-care providers.

» **Center for Medicare Advocacy** (www.medicareadvocacy.org): This nonprofit organization is focused on education, advocacy, and legal assistance for older adults and people who are disabled.

» **CenterLink** (www.lgbtcenters.org): This national organization represents all the LGBT community centers in the United States.

» **Eden Alternative** (www.edenalt.org): The Eden Alternative is a specific model of nursing-home care focusing on small-group residences, control by residents, and inclusion of plants and animals. Its principles can be found at www.edenalt.org/journey-through-the-ten-principles, and state-by-state resources about Eden can be found at www.edenalt.org/resources/find-a-registry-member/registry-member-map.

» **Family Caregiver Alliance** (www.caregiver.org/caregiver/jsp/home.jsp): This organization has guides and fact sheets on many topics related to family caregiving in English, Spanish, and Chinese. Its Family Care Navigator has a map of resources by state available at www.caregiver.org/caregiver/jsp/fcn_content_node.jsp?nodeid=2083.

» **Green House Project** (thegreenhouseproject.org): The Green House Project is a model for building or converting residential homes into settings that can provide high levels of care for people as they age. The site features an interactive map that shows homes operating and in development by state.

» **Human Rights Campaign** (www.hrc.org): This organization works for equal rights for LGBTQ individuals. Its site has a state-by-state map of hospital visitation laws, and its Healthcare Equity Index helps determine whether a healthcare organization is designated as a leader in LGBTQ healthcare equality.

>> **Medicare Rights Center** (www.medicarerights.org): This advocacy group has online guidance as well as trained volunteers available at 800-333-4114.

>> **National Association of Social Workers (NASW)** (www.socialworkers.org): NASW works to enhance the professional growth and development of its members, to create and maintain professional standards, and to advance sound social policies. You can also find lists of licensed social workers and therapists, mostly NASW members, at www.helpstartshere.org/helpstartshere/?page_id=3677.

>> **National Association of State Veterans Homes** (www.nasvh.org): This website has a list of veterans' community living facilities by state.

>> **The National Consumer Voice for Quality Long-Term Care** (www.theconsumervoice.org): This consumer advocacy group provides support and training for long-term care consumers and their caregivers. They offer information for residents, including a complete list of residents' rights guaranteed by the 1987 Nursing Home Reform Law.

>> **National Council on Aging** (www.ncoa.org): Through its BenefitsCheckUp tool, NCOA has information for older adults on accessing benefits such as help paying for medications or food. The tool is organized by state or zip code.

>> **National Hospice and Palliative Care Organization** (www.nhpco.org): This website has information about end-of-life concerns and links to help you find providers of both types of services. The resource directory at www.nhpco.org/find-hospice helps you locate a hospice and palliative care providers. Its Caring Connections program has a list of state-by-state forms for advance directives available at www.caringinfo.org/i4a/pages/index.cfm?pageid=3289.

>> **National Resource Center on Lifespan Respite Care — the ARCH (Access to Respite Care and Help)** (https://archrespite.org/respitelocator): This site has information on finding respite services in your area.

>> **Next Step in Care** (www.nextstepincare.org): Created by the United Hospital Fund, NSIC has free guides in four languages (English, Spanish, Chinese, and Russian) for family caregivers on navigating the healthcare system, especially during transitions, and links to national organizations, government agencies, and disease-specific organizations.

>> **Pet Partners** (www.petpartners.org): This nonprofit organization provides information about service animals for people with disabilities, animal programs in assisted-living facilities and nursing homes, and research about the human-animal bond.

>> **SAGE (Services and Advocacy for Gay, Lesbian, Bisexual, and Transgender Elders)** (www.sageusa.org): This group provides services and support, including the National Center on LGBT Aging and the National LGBT Aging Roundtable; SAGECAP (Caring and Preparing) offers counseling and information for people caring for an LGBT individual.

>> **Social Security Administration (SSA)** (www.ssa.gov): The Social Security Administration administers Social Security benefits, which may be an important part of the financial side of your long-term care plan. The agency's website lets you check or estimate your retirement benefits online and get other information.

>> **U.S. Department of Veterans Affairs** (va.gov): The VA has information for veterans and their families on adult day healthcare, caregiver assessment, geriatrics and extended care, home telehealth, homemaker and home health aide services, hospice and palliative care, respite for family caregivers, shared decision making, and other topics.

Index

prescription drug coverage, 144, 147, 148–150, 155, 163

principal, defined, 337

private health insurance, 66, 160, 251

private transit, 133, 135–137

probate, 186–187, 337

professional advice/help, 19–20, 24–25, 93

Program of All-Inclusive Care for the Elderly (PACE) programs, 159, 336

proprietary reverse mortgages, 176

Prosch, Tim (author)

The Other Talk: A Guide to Talking with Your Adult Children About the Result of Your Life, 242

Protection and Advocacy (P&A) agency, 36, 221

Prudential, 168

public transit, 133, 134

Q

Quartet (movie), 110

R

raised toilet seats, 67

ramp, 60, 61, 63, 118, 147

ReACT (Respect a Caregiver's Time), 294

Rebuilding Together, Inc., 64, 321

record-keeping, 48–49

Red Cross, 68, 69, 70, 92

registry agencies, 215

Rehabilitation Engineering and Assistive Technology Society of North America (RESNA), 60

remodeling. See home modification/renovation

residential care facilities for the elderly (California), 97

residential facilities for groups (Nevada), 97

residential-care homes, 112

resources, 339–345

respite, 337

respite services, 302

retirement accounts, 183, 186

reverse mortgages, 162, 174–176, 337

rightsizing, 87

Robert Wood Johnson Foundation, 238

Robot & Frank (movie), 67

roll-in bathtub/shower, 63, 64

Rutgers School of Social Work, 124

S

SAGE (Services and Advocacy for Gay, Lesbian, Bisexual, and Transgender Elders), 265, 267, 345

same-sex couples/marriage, 144, 259

San Francisco, On Lok program, 159

Saunders, Dame Cicely (founder of St. Christopher's), 251

scams, 35, 63, 83, 176, 279

SCAN Foundation, 165

security deposit, 102

sedative-hypnotics, 210

senior centers, 67, 302, 303

senior moments, 308

"Seniors Beware: What You Should Know About Life Settlements" (Financial Industry Regulatory Authority), 173

services. See also community-based organizations/agencies/services; home care agencies/services; home healthcare services; home-based services/programs; respite services; smartphone app car services

in community-based organizations, 38–39

federal government programs, 34–36

finding community services, 119–121

for housing, 40–42

organizing your research about care options, 33–34

seeking help at home, 65–68

state and local programs, 36–37

for veterans, 269–282

where to turn to for help, 31–42

Share the Care, 50

shared decision making, 273–274, 337

About the Author

Carol Levine has taken the "road less traveled" on her career path. As an undergraduate at Cornell University, she studied Russian history, literature, and language, and continued her studies at Columbia University, where she received a master's degree in public law and government. The link to her current position as director of the United Hospital Fund's Families and Health Care Project is not immediately apparent, but she says each step along the way involved honing her skills as a researcher, analyst, and writer.

She was introduced to the world of medical ethics through her tenure at The Hastings Center, where she edited the *Hastings Center Report* and is now a Hastings Center Fellow. Much of her work in the 1980s and early 1990s concerned HIV/AIDS and ethics, and in 1993 she was awarded a MacArthur Foundation Fellowship for that work.

She joined the United Hospital Fund in 1996 to work on issues related to family caregiving, a professional interest that grew out of her personal experience as a caregiver to her late husband, who was disabled as the result of an automobile accident. That work has been recognized by her designation as a WebMD Health Hero in 2007 and a Civic Ventures Purpose Prize Fellow in 2009. She was named one of *Next Avenue*'s 2016 Influencers in Aging. She serves on many advisory boards related to family caregiving and long-term care. Her current work resonates with her HIV/AIDS work as she is co-director of a UHF project on the impact of the opioid epidemic on children, adolescents, and families.

In addition to publishing many professional and consumer articles, she edited *Always On Call: When Illness Turns Families into Caregivers* (2nd ed., Vanderbilt University Press, 2004), and, with Thomas H. Murray, co-edited *The Cultures of Caregiving: Conflict and Common Ground among Families, Health Professionals, and Policy Makers* (Johns Hopkins University Press, 2004). To bring her interest in literature full circle, she edited an anthology, *Living in the Land of Limbo: Fiction and Poetry about Family Caregiving*, published in 2014 by Vanderbilt University Press.

Carol lives in New York City, surrounded by books and needlepoint and, as often as possible, by children and grandchildren.

Dedication

To my mother, Betty Solomon, *alav ha-shalom* (of blessed memory). She navigated her later years with grace and determination.

Author's Acknowledgments

In keeping with this book's broad perspective, a great many people contributed to the various iterations of the text. Each brought special expertise and a collaborative spirit that helped shape the book and make it not only more precise and up-to-date but also more relevant to readers.

Numerous AARP staff members, including Danielle Arigoni, David John, Jen Martin, Lori Trawinski, and Kathleen Ujvari, reviewed and commented on various sections of the manuscript, as did Sally Hurme. A special thank you to Jodi Lipson, Director of AARP's Book Division.

My colleagues at the United Hospital Fund answered many questions, and I especially want to thank Nathan Meyers, Chad Shearer, and Peter Newell for their advice. More generally I have benefited over the years from the thoughtful discussions of health policy and family caregiving that have been at the heart of UHF's mission. Madeleine Tuten assisted with Internet research. Rajiv Mehta of the Atlas of Caregiving contributed the CareMaps in the book.

Such a diverse group of experts was bound to bring a variety of opinions and interpretations to their review. While I valued all these comments and incorporated many of them, the opinions and advice expressed in the book represent my views and should be read in that light. They are not formal policy statements from either AARP or UHF.

Sincere thanks to my agent, John Thornton, and to the talented and supportive editorial staff at Wiley: Tracy Boggier, Senior Acquisitions Editor; Michelle Hacker, Project Manager; Georgette Beatty, Development Editor; Christine Pingleton, Copy Editor; and Mark Friedlich, Technical Editor.

Publisher's Acknowledgments

Senior Acquisitions Editor: Tracy Boggier

Project Manager: Michelle Hacker

Development Editor: Georgette Beatty

Copy Editor: Christine Pingleton

Technical Editor: Mark Friedlich

Production Editor: Mohammed Zafar Ali

Cover Photos: –VICTOR– / iStockphoto; ganolmc / iStockphoto; lushik / iStockphoto